DEATH BY HOSTILITY

A SAMANTHA HARRIS NOVEL

DEATH BY HOSTILITY

DANI CLIFTON

Dark Rose Press

Death by Hostility
Dark Rose Press

© 2022 by Dani Clifton

Line editing, proofreading, cover design, interior book design, and ebook conversion provided by Indigo: Editing, Design, and More:

- Line editor: Kristen Hall-Geisler
- Proofreaders: Ali Shaw and Sarah Currin
- Cover designer: Olivia Hammerman
- Interior book designer and ebook conversion: Vinnie Kinsella

www.indigoediting.com

ISBN: 978-1-7343796-2-4
eISBN: 978-1-7343796-3-1

Dedicated to the memory of Helen Lansdale
and
The Ginger Jesus

CHAPTER ONE

THE BLUE PLASTIC MUFFS ON MY EARS MUTED THE ROOM. THE FIRING range was like a large gymnasium built of masonry blocks. It had an open floor plan beyond the short wall at the firing point where I stood. I looked down the barrel of my Heckler & Koch 9mm.

The air around me was cool. Too cool. A chill could throw off the shot's entire trajectory. Like a car, a bullet will go where the eyes go. Keeping both of mine open, I focused on the paper target a hundred meters downrange. I planned on putting a tight cluster of bullets in the center of that outlined torso. The gun was perfectly balanced in my hands. It fit my grasp like I was born with it there. My next exhale rode slowly out through my nose, completely emptying my lungs. Only then did I squeeze the trigger. The bullet shredded through the target and deflected off the backstop, the casing tinkling down into the collection bin. I kept squeezing until hot metal stopped coming out of the barrel. Never be stingy with your bullets.

The center of the target had been obliterated. Satisfied, I slapped the red button on the side of my firing line control booth, and the demolished target fluttered toward me along the ceiling baffle.

"Nice shooting, Harris," called out a familiar voice when I dropped the muffs down around my neck. "Tight grouping, empty clip. Looks like you're ready to ruin someone's day."

I wheeled and found homicide detective Julio "Stan" Wickowski standing behind me. We hadn't seen or spoken to each other in weeks. There wasn't any real reason for our being incommunicado. Just life, I guess. He and I weren't just professional acquaintances; we were the closest thing we each had to a best friend. I say the closest thing because people like Wick and I didn't trust easily and we weren't that social. Neither of us was a people collector. I knew little more about Wickowski other than what I needed to: he was a damn good cop and a decent human being. Any other information about the guy was superfluous. We each carried tremendous mutual respect and trusted the other with our lives.

I turned to hang the next target then zipped it out 100 meters. A new magazine slipped; another bullet chambered.

"Burnell know you're down here?" he asked, referring to homicide division's captain—who had never been my greatest fan.

"Probably not," I answered nonchalantly, "unless someone alerts him. The mayor gave me all sorts of privileges since I helped the city avoid a lawsuit." I threw a thumb over my shoulder. "Free parking pass for my rig to boot. He mentioned a key to the city, but I declined. You know how I like to stay humble."

Wickowski was always the tallest guy in the room despite being half Latino (from his mother's side). He'd inherited her dark features and, when he was pissed off, her fiery personality. His gray suit was the same one I'd last seen him in, which, like I said, was ages ago. His wardrobe was limited. I knew him to have the one he was wearing, plus two more identical to it, but in tan and dark blue. His button-downs were white and professionally laundered and pressed. He owned three ties: one maroon, one navy, and one black. He was wearing the black. There was a worn patch in the middle where he'd scrubbed at a stain too vigorously, too many times. There were fresh coffee stains that added to the overall condition of the neck accessory. Wickowski proved you didn't have to have fashion sense to be one of the good guys.

"You look good," he said. "Like the shirt."

I looked down at myself. I was wearing a white t-shirt that had Underestimate Me. That'll Be Fun splashed across the chest.

My jeans were new. They'd come with the knees stylishly ripped out. My pixie-short, choppy dark hair was finger-combed back away from my face. I didn't wear makeup on the daily, and that day wasn't any different.

Wickowski ran a hand through his regulation-cut dark hair as he explained his presence. "I'm heading out to a scene. Body in the Willamette, just west of the St. Johns Bridge. That's all I know so far. Want to tag along?"

"Wouldn't that be the sheriff department's jurisdiction?" I knew Wick's authority ended at the city limits.

"It is," he said simply. "Their gesture's purely out of professional courtesy."

"Who's taking lead?"

Wickowski shrugged. "The county has their own investigators."

"Yeah, and the Pope has an entire guard in drag, but I don't take them seriously either." I pulled the muffs back up over my ears and emptied another clip. One more tattered hole inside the kill zone. I kept the last round for a groin shot. Wickowski's physical wince made me chuckle inside. Nothing personal. I ejected the magazine and cleared the chamber before dropping the muffs one last time.

"Burnell know you're soliciting my perspective?" I pried.

Wickowski raised his brows. "Is that what I'm doing?"

"Why else would you ask me to tag along?" I had a point, and we both knew it.

"I didn't ask the captain, and I don't care." He turned back for the door. "Now, can we get going?"

I bundled the HK into its case and followed Wickowski out of the building. I hiked a hip up onto the passenger seat of the SUV from motor pool.

"What's with the big rig today?" I asked innocently. Only then did I notice the tall, steaming to-go cup of coffee in my side's cupholder. I recognized leverage when I saw it. He'd planned on plying me with caffeine should my first answer have been no.

"It's muddy as hell down there." He turned the key, and the rig's diesel engine roared to life. "Hence the four-by-four."

That made sense. I had both hands wrapped appreciatively around the paper coffee cup. The lifted utility vehicle had substantial ground clearance and its wide, knobby tires were perfect for off-road recoveries.

"For a moment there, I was concerned for your penis." Wickowski shot me a questioning look. "It's a terribly enhanced truck," I explained. He gave me a sideways smirk. We both knew I was referring to Lieutenant Joe Weber, self-proclaimed ladies' man, and owner of a jacked-up four-by-four that had never seen anything other than asphalt.

I sipped my coffee and listened to the diesel's turbo as it spooled up. Wickowski usually drove his own car to crime scenes. Three years ago, the entire Multnomah County motor pool replaced all seventy of the Portland Police Bureau's Crown Victoria sedans with the utility version of the Ford Interceptor. The swap was to more comfortably accommodate the size of officers, along with their gear. It cost the city $2.3 million and came out of the fleet vehicle budget. I think it would have been more cost effective to install a fitness regimen and take the vending machines out of the break room, but nobody asked my opinion on these sorts of things.

We followed Highway 30 west out of town. The sky was obscured by fog that grew thicker the closer we got to the river. We pulled off the highway just past the Sauvie Island exit, roughly sixteen miles out, onto a narrow two-track that crossed a marshy stretch of field to the river's edge. Mounds of large-caned blackberry bushes the size of school buses had claimed much of the landscape. First responder trucks were already on-site and had laid a path to the riverbank. The medical examiner's van had pulled off the highway but couldn't manage the terrain to the river. An empty gurney stood in the mushy grass. The driver and his assistant were working out between themselves how to best proceed.

Wickowski put his rig into four and made easy work of the muddy topography. We parked beside a black Chevy Tahoe with the gold insignia of the Multnomah County Sheriff's department on the doors. The sheriff's department covered over 280 square miles of unincorporated Multnomah County and assisted the Portland PB when needed. Or vice versa, as in this case. A green-canopied aluminum boat belonging to the sheriff's department was anchored offshore, and a dive flag bobbed in the water twenty feet from the hull. The sheriff's department had a recovery team underwater. Better them than me—that water had to be frigid.

Thankful I'd worn my black combat boots that morning in lieu of my sporty white Converse, I stepped out onto the mushy ground. The thick leather uppers and insoles of the boots were impervious to grease, oil, and mud. The dense rubber soles had deep waffle tread. A steel shank covered the toecap. They weren't boots made for walking or fashion but for their attitude. Heavy stomping boots. Kicking-in-teeth boots. Footwear preferred by rioters and thugs. And the occasional former FBI agent with a bad attitude.

Two sheriff deputies stepped forward to shake hands with Wickowski and introduce themselves as Quinn and McBride. Quinn stood comfortably around the six-foot-one, one-eighty mark. Lean and fit, he had an impressive shoulder span. He wore a tactical vest that had SHERIFF emblazoned in yellow front and back. He made the city boys in blue look soft. Quinn's stylishly cropped mousey-brown hair was made to look windblown. The noon-the-next-day outgrowth that stubbled his chin and jaw were authentic. McBride was softer and balding, with beautiful almond-shaped blue eyes that would make drag queens and soccer moms jealous. He wore the same tactical vest as Quinn but filled it out quite differently. They flanked Wickowski. Both were crisp in their pressed khaki-green uniforms. Wickowski's attire was...worn. He wasn't a stickler for dress codes.

The crackle of a transistor had everyone with a sheriff's department logo reaching for their radios. Wickowski and I were out of earshot, but we followed everyone's gaze when they turned toward the water. The deputies aboard the recovery boat used a small mechanical winch to lift a netted stretcher onboard. The blue, bloated remains of someone's loved one cleared the river's surface. Water strained from the stretcher as it was winched over the lip of the recovery boat's hull. One deputy, a woman with a tidily banded ponytail down her back, guided the stretcher down onto the boat's deck. It landed with a heavy thud. A cinder block was chained to the victim's bound ankles. This was clearly no accident.

The wet-suited deputy still in the water moved his respirator aside to speak to Ponytail, who relayed through the radio that another body had been discovered below the first.

"Double homicide." I whistled low under my breath. "Think the county boys are up to the task?" Wickowski nodded solemnly but added nothing to my commentary.

The crew on the boat zipped the first body into a black vinyl bag meant for such things then lowered the stretcher back down to the water. The whole scene played out again with the second body: the winching, the straining, the bagging. Once the rescue boat had zipped the two bodies ashore, the dive team went back under to see what else they might discover related to the victims.

Quinn met the boat when it reached shore. I didn't ask for permission to join him. The ground was squelchy and made soft suction noises each time I took a step. The air was noticeably cooler beside the river. Quinn glanced in my direction when I reached his elbow, but he didn't shoo me away either. McBride and Wickowski soon joined us.

"Male," Ponytail began, "no immediate COD." Cause of death. "With the watery grave and the bound limbs, I think we can safely assume COD was drowning."

"I think it's too early to be making assumptions," Quinn reprimanded Ponytail.

"I find it best to *never* make them," I countered. "An assumption can take an investigation in the entirely wrong direction. Besides"—I shrugged—"you know, it makes an *ass* out of *u* and, well, anyone else who listens to that kind of irresponsible bullshit. No offense," I added in an attempt to soften the response. Quinn didn't laugh. But he didn't scowl either. McBride suppressed an anxious guffaw, like he was used to playing second to Quinn's lead. Their version of the age-old good-cop, bad-cop tactic. What neither of these guys understood was that I spoke both languages. Fluently.

McBride intervened to keep the peace. "We'll get a better idea of what happened once we get the body to the ME's office." Interagency cooperation aside, the sheriff's department used the Portland PB's forensics department and medical examiner because the city had a larger budget and was better equipped than the county.

Another Multnomah County Sheriff's Office rig arrived towing a flatbed trailer that carried a forest-green Yamaha Grizzly ATV. The boys from the ME's office watched as a deputy unloaded the four-wheeled all-terrain machine they'd be using to transport the bodies across the muck. A stretcher with a folded black body bag was balanced on the rack in front of the handlebars. One deputy walked beside the Grizzly with a balancing hand on the stretcher, while another deputy slowly motored his way across the mud. The ME and his assistant followed on foot, gingerly picking their footing through the mire. Once they reached the river's edge, three deputies transferred the male body onto the medical examiner's waiting stretcher. Once the transfer was done, the boat retreated back into the deeper channel of the river where the dive flag bobbed in the water to wait for the dive team to resurface.

Quinn was engrossed in conversation with one of the deputies from the rescue boat. His back was to me when I leaned over the body bag. He seemed to have cooled his temper, because when I asked for a pair of fresh gloves, he passed them to me, no questions asked. Whether he liked it or not, Quinn had accepted I was part of the investigative party. At least he understood he could glean some insight from my experience.

I unzipped the bag. The victim had been in the water for at least two days. White bone and teeth showed where the river's aquatic life had eaten away at the lips and soft tissue around the victim's mouth. Angry discoloration at his wrists showed the victim had been tightly bound. The victim's face was distended and mottled, unrecognizable to anyone who'd known him. With gloved fingers I lifted the victim's hand. "What did they do to you, man?" I asked out loud to nobody in general. The dead guy certainly wasn't going to answer.

With a sharp inhale and a lift of his chin, Quinn suddenly pivoted and squatted on the balls of his feet beside me. "What's your story?"

"What do you mean?" I asked, still bent over the body.

"You show up here, all attitude and aggression—" He had me guffawing at aggression. He'd not yet seen my aggressive side. "—you glove up and step into my investigation like someone invited you."

"Someone did invite me." I hooked a thumb toward Wickowski.

"Neither of you are part of my jurisdiction," Quinn said matter-of-factly.

I stood up and peeled the latex gloves off, wrapping one inside the other then depositing them both into the front pocket of my jeans. "No," I agreed, "but we're all on the same team." We both knew I wasn't a part of the investigation but I soon would be. And Quinn was going to be doing the inviting.

"I'm not sure if I like you or not, Ms. Harris," Quinn said.

"No worries, Quinn. I'm not everyone's cup of tea."

"No, she's more like a slug of your crazy uncle's moonshine." Wickowski said as he joined us by the river.

Ignoring the two of them, I unzipped the second body bag. By the cascade of auburn hair and long manicured nails painted a bright red, it seemed the second victim was female. Neither victim had any identification on them. No tattoos. No jewelry. All exposed tissue had been eaten by aquatic life, including the soft pads of both victim's fingers. Dental records were going to be needed to make identifications.

The boys from the ME's office stepped in to take the first body away with their ATV; then they returned for the second. Wickowski and I slogged through the mud with them back to his rig. Deputy Quinn eyed me the entire time like he wanted to say something but couldn't find the balls to do so. That was all right. When he found them, I was sure he'd let me know.

CHAPTER TWO

WICKOWSKI AND I RETURNED TO THE PRECINCT JUST PAST THE NOON lunch hour. We grabbed some coffee from the breakroom, and I asked his opinion of Quinn. He seemed to think the deputy was a solid guy. Burnell glared at me from across the hall when I followed Wickowski back to his desk, where I lingered longer than I needed to because I knew it irked Burnell. I chatted with Wickowski until he made it clear he had cop stuff to do. I gave Burnell my usual four-finger wave as I passed his office window before driving home.

Home was a loft in a refurbished textile mill in the gentrified district of Northwest Portland known as the Pearl. I parked in my space in the lot beneath the building and took the stairs up, two at a time. By the rumble and boom coming from down the hall, I could tell my neighbor, Mole, was doing epic battle in whatever video game he was engrossed in that week. I didn't bother stopping by. My stomach growled. Wickowski and I should have grabbed lunch, not burned coffee from the break room. A slight headache had begun to build behind my right eye. I keyed my way into my loft and went straight for the kitchen, where I found some leftover pizza in the fridge. I didn't even bother reheating the cold pepperoni slice; I just folded it in half and ate it over the sink.

A series of rapid-fire knocks against my front door interrupted my casual feast. *Knock-knockity-knock.* That particular pattern had become Mole's signature of late, like a ringtone. I hollered that the door wasn't locked, and he let himself in. His unruly black curls were overdue for a trim. Nothing new. His black *Cyberpunk* video game t-shirt was either freshly laundered or brand-new by the lack of its usual...fragrance, a mix between the need for a shower and, lately, curry.

"Afternoon, Sammy!" He was especially exuberant. Uncharacteristically so.

"What's got you so chipper?" I asked around a mouthful of cold pizza.

Mole beamed and adjusted his black-framed forties-military-style glasses. "Guess who just hacked his way into the president's personal computer."

I plugged my fingers into my ears. "Plausible deniability!" I reminded him. I neither needed nor wanted to know what he was up to in his personal time. Where Wickowski was the closest thing I had to a BFF, Mole was the closest thing I'd say I had to family, outside of my actual family, who lived on the East Coast. Mole and I clicked because we had the same mindset: rules and laws were more suggestions than absolutes.

"I'm going to crash his State of the Union Address." Mole just couldn't contain his glee. "When that windbag gets up to the teleprompter, he's going to read a very different version of his speech than his team anticipates."

Mole possessed the skills to pin down legitimate work, but he opted for the easy way—as one does when they're a world-class computer hacker. He used his talents to dominate and control. In short, he stole from the crooked for his own gain, making a buttload of enemies in the process. I know what you're thinking: How do a former FBI agent and a cybercriminal get on?

"And what's my usual answer when you tell me things like this?" I asked, somewhat irritated. Mole liked to play it fast and loose with his taunting of the opposition, in this case, the American government, which he believed worked too hard at keeping its unfair advantage when it came to information. Mole's take on the subject was pretty cut and dried: information and intel that affected life as we collectively knew it belonged to the public. A broad definition of "by the people, for the people." I was wholeheartedly down to screw the guys on the hill, but I liked not having to look over my shoulder in the first place a whole lot better.

Other than spending my morning at the range, I didn't have any real plans for my day. Of course, I could always get a head start on my next job. I'd been hired to investigate the security of two companies wanting to merge. As sole proprietor of Harris Securities, I analyzed corporate security. High-tech, high-profile companies around the globe hired me to find their security weaknesses, whether that vulnerability be digital or in-house. The digital aspect was contracted out to Mole. I managed the deep background checks, personal profiles, and individual interviews where I asked fierce questions of employees and board members and judged responses against many factors: body language, micro-expressions, and congruent inconsistencies. Overconfidence was suspect. It really breaks down to rudimentary psychology and observation. Basically, I interrogated each of them. My company's services didn't come cheap, and I'd be lying if I claimed not to have made a few...*adversaries* in the process. It turns out, when you deconstruct someone's lies, they don't take it well. Personally, I had no skin in the game past exposing liabilities. Business decisions after that had nothing to do with me.

Since moving my office to my loft and no longer having to pay a commercial lease, I'd gotten pretty lax about the whole nine-to-five. All client meetups were online, over an app. I rarely even put pants on until well past noon, even if I had a digital meeting scheduled. That afternoon I put in a couple of billable hours then called it a day. I settled on the couch to peruse the net on my phone for something to do around town on a Thursday evening. Nothing caught my attention. It was just as well. I ran a hot bath and put on a podcast Mole had recommended by comedian and commentator Joe Rogan, whose guest was a former FBI special agent who claimed to have once been a part of a secret mission to an unknown planet. I told myself I'd give the first five minutes of the podcast a listen so I could appease Mole. Three hours and four hot water fills later, the show ended. No, I hadn't bought into any of it, but I was entertained nonetheless, so it'd been time well spent.

Toweled and dressed in a clean pair of sweats, I checked in on Mole, who was still busy gaming and wasn't interested in hanging out. I didn't take it personally. I threw myself on the couch and dozed on and off through a vintage James Bond film circa 1979, the one where 007 must prevent the plot to murder the entire human race and restart humanity from outer space. In the age of computer-generated graphics, the analog simplicity of dated special effects seemed cheesy. Sometime in the night I pulled the blanket down off the back of the couch and called it bed.

That's where I was when Wickowski came around late the next morning. I made sure I was clothed before letting him in. He was beaming, holding a hot coffee that I knew was meant for me. And positive IDs on the two bodies pulled from the river.

"That was quick," I said, taking a sip and shutting the door behind him.

"Mr. and Mrs. Lannister," he announced as he unbuttoned his suit jacket, the tan one, scooted my blanket aside, and took a seat on the couch. "Anthony and Lana were reported missing almost a week ago. She never showed up to her yoga studio, and several of her students phoned in their concern to their local station. Anthony, a software developer, hadn't been able to be reached by his business partner in as many days. We sent a car around to their Linnton home, just west of here. Both of the Lannisters' cars were parked in the driveway. Our guys knocked on the doors, rang the doorbell. Did a walk-around, looked in windows. They saw no signs of a struggle, nor was anybody home. Quinn was able to get ahold of their dental records and the ME made a positive match. The bodies pulled from the river were Anthony and Lana Lannister."

"So my work here is done," I said facetiously and dusted my hands together. I wasn't part of any of this.

"Yeah, well sit down. The plot thickens." Wickowski pulled a folded paper from the inside pocket of his jacket and handed it to me. It was a police report filed by Anthony Lannister dated sixteen days prior.

Wickowski continued, "It turns out Anthony Lannister came into the precinct a couple of weeks ago with a complaint he wasn't fully able to verbalize. He said he felt...watched, and he felt threatened by it. The officer on duty who took the report questioned him, but Lannister was vague. Skittish. All the officer was able to get out of him was that he felt someone had broken into their home, but there were no signs of forced entry and nothing was stolen. He'd added that he'd received correspondence several months prior from a private antiquities collector wanting to know if Lannister had any notebooks belonging to his late grandfather."

"Says here 'journals,'" I pointed out on the report. I looked up at Wickowski. "What kind of journals?"

"Lannister wasn't willing to clarify. He was very elusive around the question. Seemed almost spooked by it. The books—or *journals*"—he gestured toward the report in my hand—"must have been important to someone."

I held up my free hand. "Wait a minute. So Lannister walks himself into the precinct to file a report, but he's not willing to share any pertinent details regarding the situation?"

Wickowski shook his head, at a loss for an explanation. "He either didn't trust the system, or he was afraid to talk in general. Maybe he was afraid of retaliation."

"If that was the case, why walk into the precinct? Why not by-pass the local cops and drive straight to the FBI's Portland field office?" Not that the local field office could do anything more than the local precinct without anything to go on, but the FBI seemed to give civilians a warm, fuzzy, safe feeling.

Wickowski scratched his head. "Perhaps he just wanted whoever he felt was stalking him to see him go inside the police station. Maybe he was just trying to scare them off." I could tell by the way Wickowski's nose crinkled in distaste that he didn't like that scenario. "The victim didn't give the officer much to go on. She couldn't help him, other than suggest he get a security system."

"That alludes to something dark going on in those journals," I posited and returned my attention to the report. "It doesn't mention on here who 'Grandfather' was."

Wickowski grinned. "Like I said, he wasn't willing to divulge. I figured you and your research prowess might give that one a shot?"

"Are you asking on the city's behalf?"

Wickowski didn't answer right away. I could see his mentals working, balancing the decision to step on the county's toes by turning me loose on Lannister's life history or playing it by the red tape that defined interagency guidelines. Basically, how pissed off was my presence going to make someone, and how much would it splash back on him? "See what you can find, and we'll talk after that. It's really Quinn's place to invite you in."

That made me do a mental eyeroll. Quinn didn't strike me as the kind of guy who liked to share—neither investigations nor accolades. Formal invitations notwithstanding, we both knew I was going to do what I was about to do.

CHAPTER THREE

"I'VE GOT SOMETHING I COULD USE YOUR HELP ON," I SAID WHEN I pushed through Mole's front door.

"Tell me what's shakin', bacon," he said jovially, then gave his words a second thought. "Ex-bacon," he corrected, even though he knew I was an agent, not a cop.

I gave Mole the ninety-second synopsis of the previous day's river excursion, the identification, and the conversation between Wickowski and me about Lannister's journals. "I need you to dig into Lannister's life. Specifically, who his grandfather was and what he might have left Lannister in his will. Is that something you'd possibly be interested in?"

Mole was seated at his computer and swiveled in his chair. "This a paying gig?"

"Sure," I said, "but the guy we're investigating won't be compensating me, so we'll have to work something out between us."

"Wait. Back up." Mole scratched at his goatee. "Why isn't this guy paying you?" he asked suspiciously.

"Because dead men tend to...stiff you." Ha-ha.

Mole's eyes grew wide. I'd seen this reaction a few times when it came to my requests. "Why is this guy dead, Sammy?" He plugged his fingers into his ears. "You know, on second thought, I don't want to know the truth." Mole scared easily. He could rarely handle the truth.

"I didn't shoot him, if that's what you're asking. Do what you do best. Background, contacts, dump their phones, security cameras, personal emails—and everything. I'm looking specifically for information around those journals. What are they, who might want them, and why? I'm extremely interested in the grandfather who passed them down."

Mole stared at me and blinked. Repeatedly. "Is that all? You just fired off quite a list of bullet points. It might take me a minute."

"Oh, and dig into Lannister himself. Something isn't adding up for me. I want to know who he really was."

"Are you sure that's everything?" His question was attitude-laden.

I knew what his hesitation was about. It wasn't unwillingness or inability to do the task; it was Mole's way of asking what kind of payday he could expect, all things considered. I didn't need to dicker—I needed intel, so I cut to the chase. "I can promise you at least a six-pack of your choosing, dinner on me, and..." I couldn't come up with anything else that might satiate Mole. No way was I hiring him an escort. I was saved from making Mole any further promises when my cell vibrated in my back pocket. It was Wickowski again. He'd barely left.

"The county made a request to pull surveillance videos, including doorbell cams, if there were any. Linnton's a small community with the houses spread out. It might take a few days to compile it all, but when it comes together, want to review it over a pie from Bonatelli's?"

I couldn't share with Wickowski that I'd have all the footage from those exact places, including the hours preceding and following, and that it would probably be done in an hour—two at the most. It would raise too many questions, and most of them would have a legal bent. The words *warrant* and *lawsuit* would be tossed around. Those words were synonymous with "legal restrictions," which was tantamount to stalling out an investigation. I know—legalities, blah, blah, blah.

"And beers?" I said.

Wickowski guffawed. "Of course!"

"Yeah, but shouldn't Quinn be doing the honors?" I asked.

"I told him I'd do him a solid with the footage," he pointed out. "He gave me the go-ahead."

"So he has you doing his grunt work. No, Wick, that's not how this works. Make Quinn do his own menial tasks."

Wickowski grumbled something in Spanish I didn't quite catch before he hung up. I'm sure it wasn't pleasant.

All that talk of pizza from Bonatelli's had me craving it. It was just past lunchtime. I used an app on my phone and had a Spicy Manifesto—four different kinds of spicy meats, fresh basil, and Romano on a garlic-oil base—delivered. I may have been overestimating his abilities, but I had a feeling Mole would have something to share with me by the time the driver rang the bell downstairs.

I wasn't wrong in my faith regarding Mole's tenacity and speed. He enthusiastically waved me down when I stepped off the elevator.

"Is that a Spicy Manifesto?" he asked, sniffing the air. He waited until I was opening my door before he plucked the box from my grasp. "The perfect payment for services rendered," he said over his shoulder as he retreated to his lair.

Okay, that was fair, but not before I could satisfy my craving! I followed, hot on his heels. No way was I missing out on at least a slice. I waited patiently until he held the open box toward me. I slid a slice onto a paper plate from a stack Mole kept near his workstation, adding two packets of the red pepper flakes that came with the order to the sausage, chorizo, pepperoni, and salami landscape. It was going to burn so good.

Mole settled into his computer chair. I hovered over his shoulder. We both ate as he pecked one-handedly at the keyboard. He'd strung together all the pertinent video footage from the various sources—doorbells, traffic cams, building-mounted surveillance cameras—onto one feed. He brought up the scene of a dark street shot from the vantage point of Lannister's across-the-street neighbor. Their doorbell's camera wasn't at a direct angle but offset in a way that it only captured the left edge of the Lannisters' driveway. By nature, doorbell cameras only record when they sense movement. Mole had edited out passing deer and raccoon photobombs.

The comings and goings of neighbors from their own drive-ways, visitors, and delivery drivers who parked at the curb or behind the homeowners in the drive were all captured in silent footage. A neighbor's gray sedan came and went multiple times throughout the day. The Lannisters arriving home within thirty minutes of each other. A delivery van, this one with a global courier's logo on the side, backed up the Lannisters' driveway then disappeared from line of sight the closer to the garage it got. The next time the doorbell's camera was triggered, the same delivery van was leaving, pulling out of the Lannisters' driveway.

"Want to bet, dead or alive, the Lannisters were in the back of that van when it left?" Mole said with a low whistle.

It was possible, but there was no way of knowing. Even if Mole were able to ascertain the height of the van's deck, the body weight of two people, even adults, wouldn't make a difference to the vehicle's suspension.

My phone rang. It was Quinn. "My tech guy was able to get a copy of both the Lannisters' phone records. We've got one of our techs poring over them. They'll have a report sometime tomorrow."

I wanted to tell him not to bother because Mole was on it, but I wasn't ready to admit Mole's existence to anyone. Especially someone inside the law. I also wanted to suggest he have his guy pull records all the way back to when the grandfather kicked it—that'd give him a broader idea of who they were in contact with in a timeline. But I didn't. No, not because I was being catty (okay, maybe just a little), but mostly because Quinn needed to do his own footwork. Yeah, yeah, I know—wasn't I guilty of that which I was accusing Quinn of doing by having Mole work his magic? No. It was different. I'm changing the subject now.

Mole and I continued watching security video, "I've already reviewed this footage, but I want to show you this specifically." Mole fast-forwarded to a timestamped marker then slowed the video to play. It was taken from the Lannisters' doorbell just before dusk. "Watch right...here." Mole hit pause and froze the video. A dark SUV entered the edge of the screen. Mole inched the video forward frame by frame. The further the vehicle entered into view, the more detail the camera picked up. The SUV was black with tinted windows. It didn't slow as it rolled past. The driver showed no sign of interest in the Lannisters' house, but it did circle back an hour later when the sun had fully set and the street was plunged into darkness. That time the SUV slowed to a creep but never fully stopped.

"Pause there," I told Mole. Something had caught my eye on the screen. He obliged by rewinding back several seconds then hit play again, "There!" I said enthusiastically and pointed at the screen. Mole zoomed in to get a better look at what had me excited.

"That looks like a barcode from a rental agency." I pointed at the SUV's rear window. The departure angle was wrong, making the barcode difficult to make out.

"I see that, and I'll get on it in a minute, see if I can't clean the image up." He motioned back to the screen. "Keep watching."

Playing again in real time, the SUV passed from the frame, and nothing else moved. The feed went dark. Then it triggered again, this time by two shadows whose movements were barely discernible at the far edge of the screen. They must have rolled from the SUV when it slowed to a creep. The porch was fully illuminated by the light beside the door. Two men in ski masks approached the front door. They hugged the side of the house, keeping to the shadows, but their movement was enough to trigger the doorbell cam, capturing their obscured features. Broad chested and beefy. The kind of guys someone sends around to do their dirty work. One of them picked their way through the front door. Both disappeared inside. Exactly forty-five minutes later, the camera caught them exiting. Both of them, from what I could tell from the video, empty-handed.

I ran both of my hands through my hair. "What do you have on the Lannisters?"

"So far all I have is normal," he said, eyes never lifting from the screen. "Normal as boring white bread gets. He worked for a small software development company in Old Town; she volunteered at a community garden and taught yoga at the rec center there in Linnton. They were season ticket holders for the Portland Timbers—"

"Soccer fans, huh? Is there anything less threatening than a soccer fan?"

"Have you ever watched a championship match from Europe?" Mole scoffed. "Those fans can be brutal!"

Point taken.

"Anyway, neither of them has...had...a record of any kind. No moving violations, no speeding tickets. Mrs. Lannister got off of a parking ticket three years ago, but other than that, they read as annoyingly squeaky. Give me a minute to look into their social media pages..." He went off on a keyboard-tapping excursion and came up with two sets of Instagram pages, both full of classmates and hobbies. He was into fly-fishing and woodworking; she, gardening and wine. Social media told the world more than a person making the posts realized. I perused both pages. Neither of them had children, together nor from previous relationships. They were both social and liked to go out to eat (as childless couples can do) and weren't by any stretch teetotalers. Nothing in their histories screamed target.

I dropped down onto Mole's couch to think. Nobody was that innocuous. Nobody. Not even the Pope. The longer Mole dug, the more chance he had of uncovering something unsavory. Unsavory things tend to become leads. Or at least directional signposts. People who wished to appear squeaky went to great lengths to protect that image. And if Mole had taught me anything, it was that the harder someone tried to hide something, the easier it was for him to find it. It's like a sort of twisted karma.

"You know what this reeks of, don't you, Sammy?" Mole kept attacking the keyboard.

I did. "Like WITSEC." I calmly stated.

"Exactly," Mole agreed, "but I've not found a single indication of federal witness protection anywhere. Both of the Lannisters were born and raised in Oregon." Mole scratched at his goatee again. "They sound like a boring, normal couple who didn't get caught up in anything as much as they *found* themselves there."

I had to admit, before Wickowski had stopped by the shooting range yesterday, I'd been bored and had, deep down, hoped something exciting might happen in the city. Or at least something mildly interesting might land itself in my lap. But I was thinking more along the lines of a complex securities job or Wickowski needing my help on a cold murder case.

"I dumped both their phones, and every call in and out was verifiable, save for a couple of calls that came in last month to his phone. Both those calls were from burners."

I shook my head in disappointment. Disposable phones were a criminal's best friend. "No way to track those. Dammit. Anything else?"

"I'm working on locating the family cloud. I'm trying to get access to his workstation."

"Where's that?"

"Lannister was a software designer at a digital marketing agency over on Glisan."

"And you can access their company system from here?"

Mole shot me an incredulous look. "Have we met?" he asked facetiously. He had a point. He *had* hacked into the White House earlier, after all.

Screw plausible deniability. I stood back up to peer over his shoulder. "Sorry." If Mole couldn't hack into a facility, it probably couldn't be done. Out of fascination I watched his fingers fly over the keyboard as he tapped into the system. He brought up the company's internal login screen, which he bypassed with a cloned password. I had no idea how any of it worked.

"Okay, here are Lannister's work emails." The printer beneath Mole's workstation hummed to life and began spitting out copies of all his correspondence. There were dozens of pages.

"Grab everything he's ever received," I instructed, "every email he's ever sent, and every one he's ever been copied to. Filter out anything unrelated and throw them on a thumb drive. I'll go over them later."

"Will do." Mole was already making my request happen. "Anything else?"

I thought on that for a moment. I needed a direction to pursue. "It might be a long shot, but extend the search and grab traffic cam footage within five miles of the Lannister house, including back streets to get a better idea who travelled that stretch in the days leading up to their disappearance." That was potentially going to be a lot of cars to scrutinize, but I had to start somewhere.

"What are you going to be doing in the meantime?" Mole asked.

I turned at the door. "I'm going to go cross a police line." I could wait for Mole, but I didn't do stagnant well. There may not have been any leads, but that didn't mean I couldn't go out and find some.

CHAPTER FOUR

IT WASN'T QUITE A STRAIGHT SHOT FROM MY DOORSTEP TO THE Lannisters'. I took Highway 30 due west, headed toward the coast. The stretch of highway between downtown Portland and the Lannisters' Linnton neighborhood had been a swampy wetland back in Portland's early days. In the 1880s, the Northern Pacific Railway built the railyard and laid down tracks, and helped bring industry to the region. Now the area was one of the few remaining large urban heavy industrial districts that hadn't been gentrified. Distribution warehouses, grain elevators, and refineries dotted the river's shore and added to the overall industrial, diesel smell of the air.

The Lannisters' neighborhood was nestled between Forest Park and Highway 30, a small grouping of cozy postwar houses hidden from the highway by a grove of evergreens. The Lannisters' lot was at the end of the block. I parked on the cement apron of their driveway. I stepped down from my rig and turned in a full circle to take in my surroundings.

The community wasn't set in the normal block pattern of an inner-city neighborhood, with straight streets, ninety-degree corners, and driveways set directly across from one another. The streets here meandered and wove through the trees. Houses were positioned on either side of the street but offset from one another and separated by large yards, some an acre or more. A wide grassy patch separated the Lannisters from their only next-door neighbor.

The opportunity for witnesses was slim at best. There were two, maybe three, if I counted next door—as long as the neighbor had been outside, on the edge of his front lawn, peering west. Only two houses had any possible line of sight: the one directly across the street whose doorbell camera had captured the courier van, and the other that sat catty-corner and up a short, inclined driveway. As I was mentally working through the possibilities, the blinds of the house across the street moved aside, paused, then fell back into place. Neighborhood watch? A concerned citizen? There was only one way to find out. Nosy neighbors might be annoying if you live among them, but they can be an investigator's best friend when it comes to witnesses.

The home's well-groomed lawn was lined on three sides with edged flowerbeds. Each bed was a mass planting of colorful perennial blooms. Whoever lived here was a meticulous gardener. A weed wouldn't stand a chance. A plaque above the garage door announced that Jesus was the head of the house. An American flag hung limp from a flagpole cemented into the corner of the walk near the garage door. Blue clay pots filled with ferns welcomed visitors to the porch. The sun glinted off a small chrome No Soliciting sign mounted above the doorbell. I wasn't soliciting anything other than answers.

I fingered the doorbell and could make out a version of Beethoven's Ninth chiming from within. Seconds later the door pulled open to a kindly woman who brought Santa's better half to mind. Her white hair was pulled into a loose bun at the back of her head. Stray hairs spilled out in various directions. She wore thin denim pants with an elastic waistband and no pockets. A short-sleeved floral blouse hung loosely from her stooped shoulders. Her build was thin but not frail. I was sure it was her back that had labored all those flowers into their beds. Seasons toiling under the sun shone on the topography of her face.

"Can I help you?" she softly asked. The room behind her was dated with low-shag mauve carpeting and furniture draped with plastic dustcovers. And crochet—there were a lot of crocheted covers over inanimate objects like tabletops, tissue boxes, an upright vacuum, and the backs of chairs.

"Good afternoon, ma'am," I said in my sincerest voice. "My name is Samantha Harris, and I'm with the Portland Police Bureau." I was getting good at bending the truth.

"Is this about the couple across the street?" she asked, her interest piqued. She stepped out onto the porch, holding the screen door open with her shoulder. "I phoned about them, you know. The missus and I walk together in the morning, and I haven't been able to get anyone to answer the door for days, even though their cars are there. I fear something might have happened to them. Such nice people they are, the Lannisters." She leaned in closer as if to share a secret. "Do you suppose they're all right?"

She'd taken note of their absence. That was a good sign. Technically I *could* answer but thought it best not to, so I glossed over her inquiry as if it'd never been asked. "Did you happen to notice anything odd or out of the ordinary in the last few days? Aside from their absence."

The neighbor, who eventually introduced herself as Mildred, immediately shook her head before giving the question consideration. "I don't think so." She gave more thought. "Mr. Puddles started barking at the door just after ten the other night," Mildred began explaining. "I only know it was after ten because my show, *Riggin's Journeys*, had just ended. Do you watch that show?" Mildred asked. "It's about a man who quits his job as a New York City police officer to become a become a drag queen in a small northern town. It's a wonderful show. You really should try to catch it." When Mildred was finished fangirling, I cued her back on track by asking about Mr. Puddles.

"It's not like him to have to go outside so late, but I figured I'd rather he do his business on the lawn rather than on my floor, so I let him outside. Didn't I? You little stinker." She bent down to scratch the terrier who was bouncing on his front paws at her feet.

"So, did he do his...business?"

Mildred snapped her attention up, away from Mr. Puddles, to me. "Now that you mention it, no. He started barking his yappy bark he does when he's agitated. I didn't know what to think of it."

I believed Mr. Puddles was attempting to alert his mistress that dangerous shenanigans were afoot in their proximity. "In which direction was he barking?"

Realization dawned with wide-eyed horror on Mildred's face when she instinctually looked in the direction of Mr. Puddles's agitation—toward the Lannister property. A worried hand had worked its way up to cover her mouth.

"It's completely possible you saw something that you aren't aware of seeing," I offered, hoping it wasn't a fishing expedition. "We were taught a trick at the academy, a little cognitive exercise to help witnesses recall. Would you be willing to go through this exercise with me?" I had on my kindest, suck-up-to-grandma smile but was conscious not to lay it on too thick.

"Oh," Mildred whimpered, now both of her arthritic hands worried at her mouth, "I don't know..."

I laid a gentle hand on her shoulder, gave it a little rub like a parent soothing an anxious child. "It's a very quick process, and you might help the police department solve a crime." Yes, I was totally playing on Mildred's sense of righteous duty.

"Okay," Mildred acquiesced, "if you think it'll help you with your investigation."

I beamed. "It absolutely might. Now, I'll just need you to close your eyes and take a deep breath." Mildred complied. I took a deep breath alongside her, letting it flow back out through my nose. "One more." We took another deep breath and slowly exhaled. "Okay, picture that night," I prompted in a soft, comforting, guiding voice. "Mr. Puddles is letting you know he wants to go outside. You walk toward the door—do you glance out the front window?"

Mildred stood in the doorway, her eyes closed and her face slack. Her breathing was slow and even. "No," she said calmly, "I went straight to the door."

All right. I nodded even though she couldn't see me with her eyes closed. "You just opened the door and let Mr. Puddles go outside." She nodded silently. "He's out in the lawn. Did you stand on the porch and wait for him, or did you go back inside and wait for him there?"

"Yes." Mildred's answer was immediate and definite. "I waited on the porch."

"Good, you're doing great, Mildred. Now, while you're standing on the porch, does anything catch your attention, even just slightly, and maybe even for just a moment?"

Mildred furrowed her brow in concentration. Her features relaxed when recall struck. There *had* been something that caught her attention, but it hadn't registered as anything needing consideration at the time. "There *were* sounds. Faint," she said, eyes still closed as she raised her hand and gestured toward the Lannisters' house. "There were voices. Gruff ones. Deep. I couldn't make out what was being said. It sounded...angry. Like they were arguing." She squeezed her eyes shut in an effort to hear the past. She gave a frustrated shake of her head and opened her eyes. Tears were beginning to pool around the edges. "I'm sorry I couldn't be of any help."

My expression brightened. "Mildred, you've been a great help! You gave us a timeline to start with." I bent down to give Mr. Puddles a scratch behind the ears. The little fucker growled and nipped at my hand, wagging his tail while doing so. I greatly dislike little yippy dogs. I covered my grimace with another smile (insincere as it was, stupid little punt-puppy), and pushed on since we were on a roll. "You must have given the direction of those sounds a quick glance. What did you see there?"

Mildred gazed toward the Lannister house and held it there for a long moment. I thought I'd lost her when she snapped her attention back to me. "There was a vehicle. A van. I could tell it had writing on the side, but I couldn't make it out in the dark. I do hope the family is safe."

I thanked Mildred and turned down her kindly offer to come in for a glass of lemonade. I couldn't help but accept her chocolate chip cookies though. I tried the next viable option, the house that sat catty-corner with the Lannisters'. The owner was home and not at all in a chatty mood, having pulled a double shift. I apologized and left my card in the mesh of the screen door. For good measure I knocked on the rest of the doors on the street but came away with no more information.

I returned to my rig and dropped the baggie of cookies on the seat before turning my attention to the Lannisters' house. They weren't wealthy people, and they didn't live opulently. Their postwar cottage was well-kept with tidy flowerboxes and loads of curbside appeal. I walked around the entire yard. It wasn't a postage stamp, but it was small by the East Coast standards I grew up with. Short evergreens defined the property's backyard perimeter. Raised beds of herbs and cold-weather greens dotted the sunniest part of the yard. There were no signs of children—no swing set, no molded plastic lawn toys.

Three plank stairs led up to the elevated wooden deck. A sliding glass door off the deck led into the house. I peeked through the sheer covering the sliding door and could make out a small kitchen with a pronounced liquor cabinet above the far counter. I tried the slider's handle. Locked.

I walked around to the front of the house and jiggled the door handle that I knew was locked. Yellow tape printed with Sheriff Line: Do Not Cross was strung across the entrance. Of course, that didn't pertain to me. Using the metal tools I kept in my glovebox, I picked my way through the Lannisters' front door. No alarm went off. The entryway was modest, as was the rest of the house. More of those black-and-white linoleum tiles graced the unassuming entry; low tan shag ran through the living room and down the hall. Much of the furniture, though in good condition, dated from the mid-1990s, when rounded-edged oak tables, brass accents, and floral-patterned upholstery were a thing.

That's about where orderly ended. A cyclone had moved through the home, leaving no door unopened, no book on its shelf, no contents in cabinets, closets, or trunks. Someone, or several someones, had tossed the entire place. They were definitely searching for something. I moved carefully through the house, careful not to disturb things any more than they already were.

It seemed the focus of the search had been in the bedroom. The floor was littered with the contents of the closet and drawers. They'd taken a knife to the memory-foam mattress. Several floorboards had been pried up. Holes had been bashed in the drywall to expose the inner wooden framework.

The toilet tank lid lay shattered in the center of the master bathroom, the contents of the medicine cabinet among the debris. I picked up an orange pharmaceutical pill bottle and turned it around in my hand. The prescription was for beta blockers used to treat high blood pressure and anxiety. It'd been filled for Anthony Lannister.

Further down the hall, a second bedroom doubled as an office and yoga space. Inspirational posters plastered the walls, each of them with flowery prose to spur the reader onward toward some goal. I put crime scene photos on my walls. I guess for the same reason.

I backtracked to the kitchen. Dated appliances and Formica countertops. Black-and-white checkered linoleum flooring. Brass handles on cabinet doors that mismatched the silver-plated faucet. As I had observed earlier, the Lannisters kept their liquor cabinet well stocked, and by the looks of it, someone had a penchant for whisky. Whoever tossed the place had been trained in efficiency. Bags of frozen veggies, swollen packages of cello-phane-wrapped now-rancid meat, paper tubes of thawed juice concentrate, and empty ice cube trays littered the floor. A mismatched collection of pots and pans hung from a wire rack over the Formica-topped island in the center of the kitchen. Along with no signs of children, there were also no signs of pets.

I ventured out to the Lannisters' cars, a Dodge Neon and a small red Toyota truck from the mid-1990s. Both were unlocked. Nothing seemed to have been disturbed in them. I opened each. Both had CD players, and out of habit, I hit eject on both. Empty.

I felt there was nothing more to garner at that point from the Lannisters' house, and no other potential witnesses to interview. I locked the door before pulling it closed and ducking back beneath the police tape. Mildred's curtain moved aside again, then fell back in place when I waved. I backed out of the driveway and onto the street just as Deputy Quinn rounded the bend in his county-issued truck. I didn't slow. He rolled his window down and motioned for me to pull over. I kept my eyes forward and concentration on the road ahead. We passed each other. I didn't give him a glimpse, a nod, or the finger.

Quinn flipped his truck's roof lights on and whipped a tight U-turn in the center of the road. Blue-and-red LEDs flashed in my rearview mirror. I ignored them and hung a right onto the highway. Quinn took the turn and fell in behind me. He blipped the siren. I took my time moving onto the shoulder.

I shot him a *whatthefuck?* look through my raised window when he came to stand on the other side of it. I didn't care much for Quinn. I wasn't sure what it was about him that I found off-putting. If he hadn't been so good-looking, with those soulful eyes and that sideways smile, it would be easy to strongly dislike him. Maybe I should give him a chance. *No*, my inner voice warned. It knew where my thoughts wanted to wander before the rest of me did. *Look, but for the love of God, woman, do not touch. We do* not *sleep with cops!*

"Roll down your window, Harris," Quinn ordered. He seemed a little peeved.

I zipped my window down all the way, sat back, and waited for him to speak.

"Did you not see my crime scene tape back there?"

"Of course I did. And?"

"What do you mean, *and*? You were once police, so what—now that you're the mayor's golden girl, the rules don't apply to you?"

"First off, I was never with the police—I was with the FBI. Secondly, I was invited in by Wickowski, so if you have a beef with that, take it up with the precinct. And thirdly...*golden girl*? Grow a pair, solve something, and maybe he'll like you too."

Quinn was unyielding. "I don't care if you were with Her Majesty's Royal Guard. *Do not cross* means exactly that. You want to contaminate the scene?"

"If you guys already got everything you needed from the scene, there's nothing my looking around is going to destroy. Chill."

Quinn looked at me disbelievingly. "Did you just tell me to *chill*?"

I knew in that moment that our exchange would continue one of two ways: cordially, or someone was going to be pissed off. I opted to force the former by zipping my window back up and pulling away from the curb, careful not to run over Quinn's toes. He didn't make any official moves to stop me, not even a scowl. The expression on his face was almost more humored than anything else. He didn't jump into his vehicle in pursuit.

I helped myself to two of Mildred's chocolate chip cookies on the short drive home. There was an empty parking spot at the curb directly outside my front door, so I swiped it in lieu of taking my designated parking place underground. I hopped out and wiped crumbs off my shirt. Wickowski pulled up behind me in the yellow zone of a fire hydrant. He was driving his own truck, a six-year-old Honda Ridgeline. He threw a police lanyard around the rearview mirror.

"Cookie?" I offered and held out the bag in his direction.

Wickowski paused and peered inside the baggie. He must have deemed the offering safe because he dipped his hand in for one. One bite and he nodded in satisfaction. "Like my *abuela* used to make," he said around the rest of the cookie. His tongue worked the remains from his teeth with a closed mouth before he asked, "You officially on the Lannister case?"

"Am I? Nobody's formally asked," I said with a shrug (as if I'd never invite myself), "but I'll give it some thought. You know, just in case."

Wickowski's brows knit together like he was working mental math. "What do you mean *just in case?*"

"When and if the sheriff's department decides they need me, they can call me. I might consider it." I popped another half of a cookie into my mouth and motioned to Wickowski as if asking whether he was coming upstairs or not. He begged off with a shake of his head then went serious. "The sheriff's office lost their captain yesterday. He's going to be out for an undetermined amount of time. Quinn and McBride are filling in, but the sheriff's office has asked the mayor for support during the investigation. He's given Burnell permission to use you as a resource."

I bet that smarted for Burnell. Wickowski urged me to keep him in the loop should I do anything, then got back into his truck. He threw a casual half-wave my way as he pulled away from the curb into the evening.

I went upstairs and filled the clawfoot until everything but my head and shoulders were submerged. With a deep breath, I let my head go under. The sound of the bathwater in my ears was quickly replaced by thoughts flowing through my head. Two dead. Missing journals worth killing over. No witnesses. A pissed-off cop. Yeah, that all penciled out.

I was right on track.

CHAPTER FIVE

I WAS UP THE NEXT MORNING AND OUT THE DOOR BY TEN. I WANTED to make a personal visit to Anthony Lannister's place of employment. I walked the handful of residential blocks under the canopy of trees that overhung the sidewalks to NWiT's front doors. The receptionist, a young blonde thing who was the definition of *perky*, greeted me with a melodic good-morning and a veneered smile. She tossed her hair over her shoulder as if it were a nervous tic, and she actually smelled like bubblegum. I flashed her a set of bogus credentials that she wasn't sure how to translate but was too polite (naive) to question, and I was escorted to Lannister's cubicle.

It was a typical eight-by-eight space with fabric walls, a desk, and a wheeled chair. Lannister's personal effects were already boxed. Fifteen years with the same company fit into a single recycled paper box.

"I didn't know it was the FBI who was picking this up," Bubblegum said. Then she leaned in and whispered, "Is Anthony in trouble?"

I ignored her question. The deaths hadn't yet been released to the press, pending notification of family. I thanked Bubblegum, who took the hint and returned to her post with a disappointed pout. I think she was hoping for dirt to share at the water cooler. I pulled open the empty desk drawers, not to see if anything had been left behind but to run my hands along the concealed surfaces. I checked the underside of the desktop. I struggled to get the furniture away from the cubicle wall and found nothing hidden.

With box in hand, I thanked Bubblegum (whose name was Tiffany, according to the nameplate on her desk) and walked out. I didn't know what I'd expected to find at Lannister's office, but I was walking home with a boxful. And I had beat someone to the chase.

Back home, I spilled the contents onto the living room floor. There was a small framed photo of Mrs. Lannister taken in Mazatlán, Mexico, a handful of years ago; a gag fiftieth birthday card likening aging to winos; a ceramic cup from the same birthday; a desktop calendar, the kind you peel away to reveal the next day. The last day to be ripped away revealed the day he went missing. I thumbed through the remaining days. No future plans had been noted. The rest of the stuff was just...stuff. An old Darth Vader Pez dispenser. An empty Zippo lighter with the NWiT logo on it. A nylon and plastic-mesh trucker cap with the same logo. A wood-and-brass award that would hang on the wall. Nothing was of any interest with respect to my investigation.

I scooped everything back into the box and set it by the door to drop at the dumpster later. I made a turkey sandwich and cracked open a beer. I spent the rest of the afternoon adulting (doing domestic chores) and rewarded myself with a soak in the tub and another cold one.

I'd just slipped into the sweatpants and braless tank top I planned on lounging in when there was a knock at my front door. I wasn't expecting any visitors. Nobody had buzzed from downstairs. By habit I grabbed the HK and chambered a bullet. I kept it chest-level as I eased up to the door and peered out the security peephole.

Deputy Quinn smiled back from the hallway. I reset the safety and laid my gun inside the table drawer beside the door. I dropped the chain and pulled open the door.

"Can I help you with something?" I asked with perhaps too much artificial politeness.

I'd never known Quinn outside of his deputy's uniform. He was standing in my doorway wearing a red short-sleeved t-shirt devoid of any insignias. The cotton fabric stretched across his chest, defining his physique. He wore running shoes with his 501s. His hair looked naturally windblown. He'd taken his intensity down a notch. Everything about Quinn was more relaxed. He carried something wrapped in brown paper between his elbow and the side of his torso. I really didn't want to acknowledge it, but good God, Quinn was a fine example of eye candy.

"Are you going to ask me in?" he asked with that sideways smile of his.

I cocked my head like I was giving his question serious consideration. I wondered what was in the bag. It was about the size of a bottle. I was curious, so I held the door open invitingly.

He stepped inside. For as relaxed as he was, he also seemed anxious. Like a teenager picking up a date. "I didn't like how our last conversation ended."

"We had a conversation?" I tried to soften my challenge with a smile. "Or were you just defending your territory?"

Quinn didn't react. Instead, he pulled the bottle he was carrying from the paper bag and set it on the coffee table. It was a bottle of Glenlivet. Twenty-one years old. The good stuff, and spendy on a deputy's salary. "You're a hard person to profile," Quinn said. "I had to dig deep for intel. The sheriff's department information systems director owed me a favor."

"And what did you find?" I asked with genuine curiosity. Mostly I wanted to know how deep he'd gone. I had my secrets. I bet my computer nerd was better than his computer nerd. God, he filled that t-shirt out perfectly in all the right places. His dark eyes were the same deep brown as freshly tilled earth.

He flashed another disarming, lopsided smile. "Just paraphrasing from memory, you understand." He began ticking my attributes off on his fingers. "You don't particularly appreciate rules, you take issue with authority, your tenacity is your worst enemy, and you haven't called home in a long time. You also"—he turned the bottle around so the label was facing me—"prefer your Glenlivet barely legal and neat."

Impressive. Quinn *had* done his homework. I saw rules and laws as...mere suggestions. I didn't have a problem with authority—authority had a problem with me. My obstinacy was a double-edged sword. The rest was redundant. God, he smelled good. Freshly showered. Woodsy. Spicy. Parts of my anatomy tingled. *What are you doing, Sam?* my inner voice interrupted when I willingly let myself be distracted. I probably should've listened to it.

Instead I heard myself ask him, "What else did you find?" *What the actual hell are you doing, Sam?!*

Quinn cleared his throat and shifted his weight to the other foot. "Heckler & Koch 9mm is your favorite firearm. You're partial to your Glock as well."

Walk away, Samantha! my inner voice screamed. I continued to ignore its protests. *We do not entertain those in law enforcement!* I took a step forward, closer to Quinn. My inner voice fell silent. I think it knew when it'd been defeated.

Quinn matched my step, and we were nearly toe-to-toe.

He'd been spot-on with the HK but a little off where the Glock was concerned. Sure, I had one of my own, but I rarely used it. I found my eyes creeping slowly along the contours of Quinn's torso. I wouldn't hold the Glock mistake against him. I'd rather hold something else against him. My body. His gaze met my gaze, and I quickly averted my eyes to the floor.

Teasingly, Quinn raised the bottom of his shirt several inches to expose the lower section of chiseled abs and pointed to a narrow scar to the left of his belly button. "Knife fight in Kabul." My eyes absorbed his sculpted abs. *I'm warning you,* my inner voice said as it found itself again.

I stretched the skin of my lower lip over my bottom teeth and pointed to a faded crescent shape. "Business end of a stainless-steel ring." Quinn screwed his face up in question. "Drunken brawl in a biker bar," I answered, a little sheepish.

Things got heated when Quinn whipped his shirt off over his head in one motion. He pointed to a puckered scar on his left shoulder. "Meth head on the eastside of Burnside. Through-and-through." He inched down the waistband of his jeans and pointed to an angry-looking pucker in the fleshy part of his side. "*Not* a through-and-through."

I winced as I ran my fingers over the rough landscape of the scar. Having taken my fair share of shrapnel, I was familiar with the pain of removal and healing. Quinn's body reacted to my touch. I knew it was all over when I pulled my tank top off in the same over-the-head motion he had. I wasn't wearing anything under it. "Two to the chest from a high-powered rifle." I gestured at the still angry—but healed—furrowed scars of my own.

Quinn closed the gap between us. His fingers were gentle as he walked them over my chest. His touch was warm and electric. My body responded in kind. It didn't matter who made the first move, the inevitable was a foregone conclusion at that point. Quinn slid my sweatpants over the curve of my hips. I knocked the remote off the couch just in time to keep it from imprinting my butt.

A couple of sweaty hours later, I rolled over and propped myself up on an elbow. It was almost midnight. At some point we'd moved into my bedroom. I couldn't tell if Quinn was awake or sleeping. His eyes were closed, his head cradled comfortably in his backswept hands. His chest rose and fell in a slow tempo. I had one hard, fast rule in my adult life. Okay, maybe a few more, but Do Not Sleep with Cops was at the top of that list. I gazed down at the lead investigator in my bed. *How do you feel now?* poked my annoying inner voice. If Quinn were any man other than a cop, I'd do him again in a heartbeat. But he *was* a cop, and that left a foul taste in my mouth. Like I was shitting where I ate.

My stomach gurgled and moaned, having gone beyond simple hunger to outright starvation. I got out of bed and padded into the living room, where I used my cell to speed-dial a late-night dive bar that I knew delivered until two in the morning. I took the liberty of ordering burgers, fries, and a couple of ice-cold colas for both of us. I assumed Quinn had worked up as much of an appetite as I had. I walked back into the bedroom but paused at the door. Quinn hadn't moved, and I still wasn't sure if he was awake or not. I couldn't help but let my eyes linger across his form. Surprisingly, my inner voice was silent.

"You're creeping me out, Harris," Quinn said good-naturedly, catching me staring at him. His eyes were still closed.

I pulled on a pair of jeans and an oversized sweatshirt from a pile of mostly clean clothes on the floor at the foot of the bed.

"So, no chance for a round three?" Quinn asked shamelessly. "Or would it be four?" He sat up and let his drawn-up knees rest in the crooks of his elbows. I forced my attention to settle on his chiseled abs and not venture any lower—*oy!*

"I ordered food," I stated. "You should get dressed."

I retrieved his clothes from the living room and dropped them into his open lap. He pulled on his jeans but kept the top half naked. We made awkward small talk until a knock at the door saved us. My stomach answered its own appreciation with a perceptible growl. I reached for the wallet on my kitchen counter, but Quinn was already pulling open the door and handing the middle-aged delivery man a couple of twenties and telling him to keep the change.

"I had that," I explained once he was setting the lock on the door. It hadn't been locked before. Was this an anticipatory move? *Eat and send him on his way,* my inner voice scolded. *You've done enough damage.*

Choosing not to hear my protest, Quinn opened the bag. He tossed me a burger, set his aside on the table, then split the bag wide along the sides and laid it out flat. He dumped both paper envelopes of french fries onto the flattened bag and ripped open several ketchup packets with his teeth.

"You can get the next one," he said as he peeled the wrapper back from his own burger. That seemed presumptuous. Who said there'd be a next time? The scent of bacony-cheesy-burgery goodness made my stomach growl again, which made Quinn smirk. "You should feed that thing before it embarrasses you."

He had a point. I tucked in to my burger and slurped my cola and tried not to make eye contact with Quinn. I was still having mixed feelings about the last couple of hours. I took another big bite of my burger. Grease and pink juice began running down my chin. I chased it with a thin paper napkin.

"Are you having regrets right now?" Quinn asked to break the silence.

"Not at all," I said and gave a shrug. "I love a good greasy burger now and again." I knew he wasn't referring to the meal but the fact that we'd just done the nasty. The horizontal mambo. Reenacted the four-letter F-word. To be honest, I was torn between what I knew I should do and what I wanted to do. I could sense he was waiting for a straight answer. "It was something that happened at the end of an otherwise not-stellar day," I said and hoped he'd leave it at that.

The sudden eruption of text messages on my cell phone interrupted the moment. Blessed disruption. I saw it was Mole. Perhaps more distraction than I needed. When Mole sent flurries of texts, it was usually over something random he was either enraged over or vexed by. Without bothering to read his messages, I turned my cell off and put it back down.

"Beer?" I offered and turned for the fridge without awaiting reply. I returned with two bottles of a locally brewed porter and passed one to Quinn.

"Porter?" he said, turning the bottle in his hand. "Got anything lighter? Maybe a Budweiser?"

I shot Quinn a look far more withering than intended. I'd only meant to press a defense for my choice. But I was in a too-familiar headspace where I lensed everything through a questionable attitude. My softened smile was a passable attempt at apology. I needed some refresher courses on how to interact with people without coming off defensive. Or offensive. Wickowski would say I needed a reminder about patience. Whatever.

"Sorry, I only drink the good stuff."

"Ouch." Quinn flashed that damn smile again then took a long pull from his beer. He grimaced as it went down like he was taking one for the team. He smacked his lips. "You're not like normal women, Harris."

"I have no idea what you mean by that," I said innocently.

Quinn pushed on, "Yeah, I think you do." He took another bite of burger then moved it to the side of his mouth. "Most women can't list their scars from gunshot wounds or fights. Most women don't scare me—not even a little bit."

I shrugged. "I shouldn't be judged poorly for the rest of my gender's shortcomings." I put the rest of the porter away in one long pull to prove my point. A respectable belch escaped. "Besides, if I don't terrify you just a little bit, then what's the point?"

"Seriously," Quinn insisted, "how many of your girlfriends even own a gun, let alone an arsenal?"

That was easy. "None. I'm not a people collector."

Quinn screwed his face up. "You don't have any friends?"

I gave that a thought. "I have acquaintances." Never would I allow Mole or Wickowski hear me say that. They were both so much more to me than casual associates. But in the context of Quinn's question, I didn't have friends, girl or otherwise. I'd never formed relationships like that after my best friend, Cindy, was murdered when we were twelve. The therapist my parents sent me to had been particularly concerned about that aspect of my healing—the inability to trust, the yawning incapacity to open up to vulnerability. Personally, I thought the ubiquitous *they* put way too much emphasis on victims returning to pre-traumatic condition. It had been a little over two decades, and I was still not there. I accepted a long time ago that I never would be. It made me who I am. And I liked me. How many people can say that about themselves?

The expression on Quinn's face altered when he thought he understood what was going on. "You've been hurt by someone—a man," he observed. "Who was it that broke your hea—"

"Don't!" The force of my tone surprised even me. It cut Quinn off and suspended him in silence. My next words were a fierce whisper: "Never ask me about the things I don't offer up myself. *Ever.* You don't know me."

His brown eyes softened into pools that beckoned. They offered me solace, a place to throw all the weight of my own existence. "No, you're right. I don't know you." His voice was little more than a gentle vibration on the air. "Not really. But I'd like the chance to." He wasn't being smarmy or even flippant. He was being authentic.

That activated a panic alarm in the center of my own chest, where feelings liked to hang out in ambush. A jumbled rat's nest of emotions that I couldn't straighten out even though I knew each of them was inexorably rooted in fear. Fear of losing control. Fear of losing the people I cared about. Fear of never finding Cindy's murderer. Fear of letting my guard down. Fear of failure. Fear was a four-letter word that wore many cloaks, but they were all the same prison. I wasn't going to face my jailer, not tonight. My pulse racing, I slipped back out of my clothes, pulled Quinn to me by his beltloops, and changed the subject for the rest of the night.

CHAPTER SIX

THE LOFT WAS SILENT WHEN I WOKE UP LATER THE NEXT MORNING. Silent and blessedly empty. Quinn had roused early, just about the time the morning's rush hour was getting underway. I had feigned deep slumber, and he'd tried to be as quiet as he could in leaving so as not to disturb. Off to work in the same clothes he'd worn the night before. I wondered if anyone at the station would notice. God, I hoped I stayed out of the conversation.

I sat up in bed with the understanding that last night, sleeping with Quinn, had been a one-off. An event with no encore performance. No, I was not going to beat myself up for having slept with him. For breaking my own rule. Sex with Quinn hadn't been an unpleasant experience. But it was something I needed to discipline myself against.

The bedroom felt empty. I slipped a t-shirt over my nakedness and wandered into the kitchen to find...something. Coffee. That's what I needed. The pot in the corner by the refrigerator had been a gift from a former lover whose proposal I'd turned down. I'd let myself develop deep feelings for him, and someone used that against me. I rarely used the stupid thing but couldn't bring myself to get rid of it.

I moved back into the bedroom and pulled a sweatshirt over my head and jeans over my bare butt. I was on a mission. Steam was the nearest coffeehouse. I crossed the street against the light.

The interior of the coffeehouse had a steampunk theme to it, with exposed pipes and lots of copper. Framed portraits of Jules Verne and Edgar Allan Poe graced the walls. Seth, artist and barista, lifted his chin in greeting. He was already pulling the last shot of my quad Americano.

"This is going to eat a hole in your stomach one day," he quipped cheerfully.

"It'll match the hole in my soul," I countered.

Seth raised his brows. "Bad morning?"

"No." I sighed. "Bad decisioning."

He passed the paper cup, banded around the middle with a thicker cardboard heat-resistant sleeve, over the counter and let his fingers linger against mine a second longer than he did any other customer. He wasn't flirting, he was being...supportive. There was no attraction between Seth and me. At least on my end there wasn't. Seth was simply my caffeine dealer.

"If you need to talk," he softly offered, "you know where to find me." I appreciated the sentiment and let my soft smile say so. Seth was a good guy.

I took the elevator back up to the loft. The metal box had its usual Pine-Sol scent. The door slid open with a ding. Mole, who'd been pacing outside my door, startled at the sound. He rushed over to speak in a hushed tone.

"We need to talk."

I put my key into my door and let myself in, Mole in tow. The alarm system he'd had installed a year ago didn't go off. I'd disengaged it months ago. I figured if there were an intruder, I had, as Quinn put it, an arsenal. I could tell by Mole's body language, the way he kept shifting from foot to foot, that he had something to share with me. Or he had to pee. I assumed the former.

"Have something for me?"

"Who was the guy?" Mole blurted.

"Excuse me?"

"Last night. I texted you a dozen times. Then I called, but it rolled over to voice mail." Mole sounded genuinely put off. "I saw him leave this morning."

"He was nobody." Well, that sounded sort of catty, even to my ears. Quinn wasn't a *nobody*—he just wasn't anybody I wanted to talk about just then. "Do you have something related to the case I'm working on?"

Mole cleared his throat before he spoke. "I started digging into Anthony Lannister's background. Found some points of interest. To begin with, what his grandfather had was family money. Railroad. Old money."

"Old money," I repeated. "Was there some sort of a feud or grave misgivings around the family fortune?" Money and loved ones were always a volatile combination.

"Anthony was an only child, but there was no extended family drama that I could tell." He dismissed my question with a wave. "But what I did find was a very dark hole into a very dark spider's web." Mole leaned in and added, in a very mysterious tone, "The dark web."

"Oh," I said flippantly, "your happy place."

"Don't—" He leaned in even closer, and for a second, I thought he was going to plant one on my cheek. He was only positioning closer to my ear, as if he were about to spill top-secret intel into the unsecured room. "—don't ever poke fun at the dark web." He pulled back and stood straighter. "Imagine what one might find in the part of the internet that isn't indexed by search engines. Now imagine the individuals who put that stuff up there." He gave a shiver.

"You make it sound like a comic book villain," I joked, "like a personified monster in the machine."

Mole put his hands on his hips. "I mean sure, the dark web has its legitimate users. Investigative journalists. Researchers. It's also the marketplace for some seriously bad people, Sammy." He sat heavily on the couch. "A person is able to purchase another human being, hire a hitman, plot against a government—you name it, and every one of those transactions is wholly untraceable." He leaned forward with his elbows on his knees. "I can download an app on my phone that would allow me access to any smart television, any baby monitor, or any electronic virtual assistant to give me eyes and ears inside your home. One can buy lists of bank account numbers, social security numbers. And porn. Not just the kiddie-diddly kind, but rape porn. It's a disgusting and dangerous place."

Feeling completely dressed down and scolded for my illicit-internet ignorance, I didn't dare push on with another *So what did you find*. I blew over the top of my still-scalding coffee and waited for Mole's inevitable presentation that he would eventually deliver when he was ready. In his own time.

"Google had plenty to say about Grandfather Lannister." The buzzing of a kitchen timer interrupted him. It was coming from down the hall at his place. He'd left both our doors ajar. "Come with me, and I'll fill you in. I've got a soufflé in the oven, and I think it's done." He stood and made for the door.

"A soufflé?" I questioned his retreating back. "But you don't cook," I said to myself as I followed him.

Mole's home had always struck me as a place where sci-fi movie sets and memorabilia went to retire. His latest fascination was with Japanese animator Hayao Miyazaki. I'd been made to sit through the animated film *Spirited Away* only the weekend previous. A white-masked, black-veiled figurine I recognized from the film occupied a corner of his desk.

"Pull up some couch," Mole offered, coming from the kitchen. It smelled good. He took a seat at his computer and swiveled to face me. His presentation began like a report. "Anthony Lannister Sr., Grandfather, was one of the good guys. He was a family man with an extreme sense of moral obligation and duty." He swiveled back around to his monitor and began scrolling through his finds. "After graduating from the Virginia Military Institute in 1933, Lannister Sr. received a direct commission in the Army

Reserve as a second lieutenant and was assigned to field artillery. He went on to attend Harvard Law School. After graduating in 1937, he was promoted to first lieutenant and landed a job with a law firm as a litigation lawyer—"

"Wait—so Lannister Sr., *Grandfather*, was a reservist in the army and a litigation lawyer at the same time?" Multitasking level: ninja. Sometimes I couldn't read the newspaper and eat a Danish at the same time.

"Yeah," Mole scoffed, "as well as being a new husband, Lannister was also a young father by that time. In addition, he'd received orders for active duty in the Office of the Assistant Chief of Staff, G-2, War Department General Staff by then," Mole rattled off the position from his research. "Initially Lannister Sr. was assigned to the Investigation Branch of the Counter-Intelligence Group."

Mole shifted in his seat and interjected his own thoughts. "You have to remember that even though WWII wouldn't break out for another two years, Russia was, from an intelligence standpoint, considered an enemy of the state. Now, Lannister Sr. wasn't really about policing people, but he did find it was ignorantly believed, on our side, that those exhibiting extreme liberal political views were also our enemy. Until Lannister Sr. got involved, the army's response toward a suspected sympathizer was swift and reactionary." Mole rolled his eyes. "The military believed that if you weren't openly against the Commies, you must be with them." He sat back from the keyboard. "I'm getting the perspective that Lannister Sr. wanted people to think a little more critically and understand that liberal views, or even membership in a Communist front for that matter, wasn't enough evidence of one's taking an active part in the Communist Party. Did you know the League of American Writers and the American Student Union were believed to be Communist fronts? Lannister Sr. believed they were still innocent and loyal until proven otherwise."

"Amen, brother," I whispered under my breath.

Mole went silent for several moments. "The world was in turmoil at that time, and tensions were high. The United States needed to take steps against Japan and Germany to beef up our domestic defenses, which had been on a steady decline since WWI. The race was on to create a weapon that would set a precedent and end the war. Lannister Sr. was assigned the position of overseeing security for the Substitute Materials project. America wanted to beat the Russians and Germans to the punch. They recruited the top scientific minds. Dr. Ludwig Wolff was one of those scientists and the leading physicist on the project. Wolff was of German descent living in America and was a staunch ally. Lannister Sr. respected Dr. Wolff and befriended the man and his wife, who was a member of the American Student Union. This membership caused the American government to question Wolff's allegiance, even though that suspicion was wholly unfounded. Once that Little Boy was dropped on the unsuspecting populace of Hiroshima, the rest of the world tapped out of the war. But they revoked Wolff's top-secret clearance and ruined his career." Mole came up for breath and took a sip of water from an earthen mug. I had a confused look on my face. I'd never known Mole to be an outright history buff.

"The History channel runs late at night," he explained.

Everything he'd described about Lannister Sr. was all good and well. But how did it help me figure out who killed his grandson all these decades later? "You've got to have something else, something more related to here and now. Like who killed Mr. and Mrs. Lannister?"

He swiveled in his chair to face me. "There's a lot more to discover, I'm sure, but I'm just throwing a preliminary thought out there: Is it possible you're dealing with a professional cleaning crew?"

There were few real motives for murder. Love, money, jealousy, revenge, and power were about it. Money and power were the only motives that might involve a cleaning crew. A cleaning crew leans to military or political involvement. That still checked out. Lannister Sr.'s involvement in something was the catalyst to the Lannisters' murders. Sins of a grandfather. But why lash out all these decades later?

"I guess it's possible," I said.

Mole's mental wheels were turning. "An antiquities dealer came around looking for journals? What was Lannister Sr. keeping track of that made everyone so nervous? Now that you're involved, does that make you a loose end? A target by proxy?"

That was a question I couldn't answer and didn't need to. I won't live my life afraid of something that *might* happen.

I shrugged. "Anyway, I'm going for a run." I went for the door.

Mole catapulted from his chair. "Did you not just hear the words that came out of this hole in my face? Loose end. Target. Bang bang. Deadsies." He paused, blank-faced and shaking his head. "Nothing?"

I turned back to him and dropped a reassuring hand on his shoulder. "I heard you. But I need to think, and I do that best with sweat. Besides, I really need to work off some...aggression."

He looked at me oddly but didn't question me further, other than muttering under his breath, "Your funeral."

Back home, I geared up for a casual run through Forest Park. A hydration belt that held two small water bottles at either hip went around my waist. To this I clipped a discreetly holstered compact Kahr PM9. I took the stairs down to the lobby two at a time. Nobody lurked menacingly outside the door under the warm Portland spring sun. I took off west.

It wasn't that I loved running. Or that I even liked it. Deep down I thought it was a ridiculous pastime. I simply found it the best way to get my sweat on without having to socialize, as

I'm forced to do at Ring, my boxing gym. That, and beating my feet against the ground worked off the hostility that persistently simmered just below the surface of my being.

Forest Park was one of the largest urban forests in the country. It stretched more than seven miles and overlooked both Northwest Portland and the junction of the Willamette and Columbia Rivers. There were over eighty miles of trails crisscrossing 5,200 acres; it was a small wilderness in the city. I'd never heard of anyone getting lost in there.

I entered the park at the end of Upshur Street via the Lower Macleay Trail that followed shallow Balch Creek. The opposite side of the creek shot up a steep embankment topped with expensive homes. Erosion and gravity appeared to have been an issue in the past, evidenced by the steel pilings and concrete used to shore up the hillside. The trail was well travelled by runners, walkers, and bikers, but the gravel base kept it from becoming a mud pit.

I hung a sharp right at the Witches Castle, a roofless stone cottage that sat at the switchback, and headed up the Wildwood Trail. That stretch of trail was heavily forested and lined with dense underbrush. Ferns and Oregon grape crowded both sides. The track climbed a short elevation before leveling out and winding through the second-growth forest. The only people I encountered were a middle-aged gay couple hiking with their twins. Each man carried an infant in a sling contraption that rode across his torso. Two attentive dads. The scene made me smile inside. Lucky kids.

I kept running, encountering no one else. The sounds of the city were swallowed by the forest. I'd be lying if I said the wild places of the earth didn't creep me out. Didn't totally give me the heavy heebie-jeebies. I'd had to learn how to be amongst the trees, to see the setting as something other than a great place to dump a body. I wasn't to the point that I could say I "enjoyed" it, but at least I no longer drew down on anything that made a sound in the thicket.

Sun dappled my skin as it fought its way through the leafy canopy overhead. A nearby creek running in a low ravine was perfect habitat for a grove of cottonwoods whose foliage sweetened the air. Birds sang their territorial songs from the boughs above. The slap of my feet was a steady, meditative rhythm. I settled into the pace and let the details of the case flit through at will. *We still don't have a crime scene.* I was aware of every bug buzzing, every variant in the wind. *Lannister made a report about...journals? His grandfather's, or something he was involved with?* I felt the humidity change on my skin as I gained and lost elevation, moved in and out of the sunlight. *I'm sleeping with a cop.*

The trail ran on for thirty miles. I only followed for the first three, to the top of a rise overlooking the city to the north and Mount Saint Helens in Washington just beyond the Columbia River. I'd pushed myself farther than my usual two miles (four miles round trip) because my mood hadn't really improved until my legs really began feeling it. I paused in the center of the trail to catch my breath and drank most of the first water bottle. Half of a desiccated protein bar I found in the side zipper of the hydration belt went into my mouth for some energy. My quads burned so I stretched them, taking turns holding heel to butt cheek. Heel extended before me, I was bent deep in a forward hamstring stretch when I sensed quiet movement behind me. I spun, hand on the butt of my holster—

A whine brought me up short. The Oregon grape along the side of the trail quivered. I saw a flash of white with brown. I made a kissy sound, and a fuzzy head popped up from the foliage. "Come on," I coaxed. A dog that must have been lying down in the brush stood up. It was a mess of matted, dirty fur and visibly underweight. By the looks of the brambles and twigs woven into its coat, and its overall condition, it had spent several weeks on its own in the wild. I could also discern he was a male. What was he doing out here, and why had no hiker or runner rescued him?

"Hey, buddy," I said, keeping my distance because frightened dogs are dangerous dogs. But he didn't seem too scary. The dog answered me with another whine. He kept his head low and his body turned slightly away from me. He was curious, but cautious.

I crouched down to my knees. The dog acted like he wanted to approach but shied away. I wondered if someone might have tried to capture him. Patience, something I normally lacked, came to me as I kneeled in the dirt, coaxing the animal with a soft voice. Nobody happened upon us. The silence of the forest seemed to reassure him. Slowly, with his ears up, the dog crept out of the bush on his belly. I didn't grow up with a dog, but I had friends in school who had them. I recognized this belly crawl as submissive behavior. Hell, I'd dated men who acted the same way. I reached out to give him a scratch behind the ears. The movement made him shrink away from me. Somebody hadn't been kind to this animal. I eased myself back, my butt on the damp trail. I sat patiently and didn't move. I kept my hand extended, palm down, and unthreatening. Several minutes later I felt a warm lick on the back of my hand. I didn't react, just let him explore my hand. Then my wrist and up my arm. "Hey, buddy," I whispered. Then a nose inched under my hand so that my fingers could give a scratch.

That touch was all that was needed to break down the barrier between us. With a series of throat noises that were neither whines nor growls but a happy combination of both, the dog came to life with an animated series of jumps, midair spins, and happy barks. His floppy ears were perked high, his canine smile wide.

I gave the dog a good double-handed scratching around his neck, looking for a collar lost in all that fur in the process. There wasn't one. I ran my hands along the barrel of his chest and got a good feel for how malnourished he really was. "How did you get out here?" More to the point, why hadn't anyone gotten him out? I rustled the other half of the protein bar from its wrapper and offered it to him. He sniffed the morsel then turned away from it. "Here," I broke off a corner of the bland fruit and nut bar, and showed it to him. Then I dropped the scrap into my mouth and chewed it, giving it an appetizing *mmmm* that it didn't really deserve. I held the bar out again. This time he sniffed then softly took it from my fingers with gentle teeth. He swallowed without chewing, the way dogs often do when handed snacks.

I patted my knees. "You want to come home with me?" I asked him in the animated voice that people tended to use with their pets. "You wanna come with me?" This earned me a leap/spin/happy bark. "Who's a good boy?" Another leap/spin/happy bark. "You're a good boy?" Leap/spin/happy bark. His antics were doofy as much as they were excited, like he was experiencing kindness for the first time.

"Come on," I coaxed as I began to run back in the other direction for home. "Come on." I patted the side of my leg. Another series of leaps/spins/happy barks. "You're kind of doofy when you do that," I told him when he ran alongside me like a kid brother. When the path narrowed, he respectfully fell to my six, directly behind me, but stayed close. I was afraid I was going to heel him in the chops!

We met only three others on our way back, near the entrance gate. Two women hiking together with sticks and backpacks, and a man jogging alone with a small dog that was requisitely leashed. The doofy dog wasn't. The little dog barked. The doofy dog didn't. The jogger glared at me long and hard as he passed. I assumed it was due to the fact that the doofy dog didn't have the mandated leash. Neither did he have a collar. "Come on, doofy dog," I said only to myself. "Haters gonna hate."

The doofy dog stayed with me all the way to my street. He sat at the corners while I caught my breath and waited for lights to change, he yielded to other pedestrians on the sidewalk, and he didn't bark at other dogs regardless of how much drama they threw his way. He must have sensed something in me that signified the gate in front of my building was home and that he might be invited in when he started a series of leap/spin/happy barks before I even punched in the key code. "Who's the bestest boy?" I asked when he sat politely waiting for me to key into my front door.

"What's that?" asked Mole from his doorway.

I pushed my front door in, expecting the doofy dog to make himself at home. He made no move to do so. I turned my attention back to Mole. "Three guesses," I snarked.

"Is it yours?" Mole sounded a little anxious.

"Maybe," I said with a shrug.

He narrowed his eyes. "Does it have a name?"

"I'm thinking of calling him Doof."

"Not a very dignified moniker."

I cocked my head in judgment. "Maybe not, but I think it fits him. It's a good name."

Mole backed up a little into his transom. "Does he bite?"

"Mole, all dogs bite. Hell, I bite."

Mole didn't say anything else. He only lowered himself in the doorway and stared, eye-to-eye, down the distance of the hall with Doof. A long silence stretched out between them. I was a curious bystander waiting to see who would blink first—human or canine. Turned out, it was the human.

"It's like he's made of stone. I wonder what he's thinking."

"Probably the same as you. Hey, Doof," I said, and the dog snapped his head up to look at me. I gestured toward the open door with my chin. Forgetting all about the odd human at the end of the hall, Doof bounded inside, gave one of his signature leap/spin/happy barks, and settled himself beside the couch.

"That was the coolest thing I've ever seen," Mole marveled. The look on my face said, *What?* "It's like he knew exactly what you said." Mole followed Doof inside. "Who's a good boy?" he asked the dog.

I followed Mole in and kicked the door shut behind me. "Not this guy," I said, dropping to my knees and taking both sides of Doof's fluffy face in my hands. "The world is full of good boys. Doof is the *bestest* boy. Huh, Doofy-Doof?" I was aware that my voice had mimicked that singsong pet-owner voice again, but I didn't care. The four-legged beast was a hot mess—shaggy and in need of both a bath and a grooming. Both of which I was happy to provide.

"Are you going to take him to the vet and get him scanned for a microchip?"

Why hadn't I thought of having him checked for a microchip? I guess because I'd assumed whoever dumped the dog in the woods wouldn't be concerned for his well-being. That was an awfully large assumption on my part (I knew how I felt about assumptions). It was entirely possible Doof, or whatever his name originally was, had gotten separated from his human and wound up lost in the middle of urban nowhere. If that were the case though, one would imagine his human would be frantic. Frantic owners of lost pets tend to plaster the last-place-seen with full-color xeroxes they purchased in bulk from the nearest copy shop. I'd seen no such LOST DOG fliers anywhere near the park. I suspected Doof was a drop-off. A discard. A stray.

Now he was mine.

"You're thinking about keeping him, aren't you?" Mole sounded skeptical. "Did you ever own a dog as a kid?"

"No. Mother believed they were dangerous and might maul you in your sleep." My mother wasn't a fan of warm and fuzzy.

"Well, I did. Her name was Luna—a black Lab. She was the best. She was technically the family dog, but she was really my dog. She picked me as her human." Mole misted up for a half-moment in recollection of his late dog then collected himself with a sniff. "You're going to have to walk him several times a day, you know."

"Yeah."

"And pick up his dookie when he lays it in someone's yard or in the park."

"Yep."

"Even in the frigid Portland rain."

"Got it. Anything else?"

"I'm just saying, having a dog in the city is a lot of work. A big responsibility. You're not always available."

"But what are you *really* saying?"

Mole let out a long, exasperated exhale. He looked down at Doof, who was smiling a big goofy canine smile up at me. "I think you might be his hero." He straightened up and dug into his pants pocket. "Which brings me to my next point." I wasn't aware Mole had a point to make to begin with. From his pocket he fished out a thumb drive. "While you were scampering through the forest and rescuing impressionable dogs, I made more discoveries regarding Lannister's grandfather—"

Human was interrupted by canine when Doof began whining and circling near the front door. "What's up, boy?" I asked as I crossed to his side.

Mole snorted and said, "Remember what I said about having to take a dookie at all hours?"

Another walk? Already? We were just in the woods and had passed how many lawns, and the urge to take a poo was just now hitting him? This was going to get real old, real fast, living in a city apartment. Maybe it was time to start looking for a real home, a house with a fenced yard. The real American Dream. Didn't that dream also involve 2.5 children, a sum I'd never fully understood? How do you get half a kid? Maybe keeping a dog in a city loft wasn't such a stretch after all. I'd take daily dookie patrol over diaper duty any day.

"Okay, mister, but you stay with me until we get you one of those collar-and-leash setups everyone's so fond of. Okay, Doofy-Doof, you big fuzz-butt." I realized I was baby-talking again, and nuzzling his big face with my own. Mole couldn't suppress his grin. "Shut up," I warned as I straightened.

Mole put two defensive hands up and chuckled good-naturedly. "Don't worry; animals turn even the stoutest personalities into simpering puddles."

I was laughing with Mole when I pulled the door open and two things happened simultaneously: Doof shot out the door, all snarls and flying spit, and the elevator door slid open revealing two suppressed AR-15s. There was no sound other than airy *ppfftts* as the first rounds were loosed down the hallway. I screamed for Doof to come back while scrambling for the PM9 still holstered at my waist. Doof didn't wait to be asked again and shot back through the door with his tail tucked firmly between his legs. Mole ducked behind the couch with his arms crossed over his head. I went down on one knee and snuck a peek around the doorjamb. There were two of them—big and broad and tactically outfitted. The one on the right blasted another silent round, taking out a chunk of my door's transom.

"Mole," I hollered to get his attention, "bedroom closet, green chest. Bring me the small, round canister with all the holes in it!"

"On it!" he answered and was already heading into my bedroom. I could only assume he knew my expectation. He returned with exactly what I wanted: an M84 stun grenade. I pulled the pin and tossed the flashbang down the hall. The delay was only 2.3 seconds, not enough for either intruder to take cover. At 180 decibels, the noise was deafening. The flash part of the grenade went off with blinding luminous intensity. Our building was a refurbished textile mill—all brick masonry and thick plank flooring. It was loud inside, but the neighborhood shouldn't be dialing 911.

Fortunately Mole and I were the only occupants on our floor. I stepped into the hallway and put a bullet into the first form to step from the smoke. He went down hard. I ducked back into the doorway just in time to avoid return fire from the second intruder. One down and one to go.

Doof whined, then lowered himself to the ground, panting. He was anxious, and the loud noises frightened him. I gave him a reassuring pat on the head and told him to stay. He whined again but obeyed. The same couldn't be said for Mole, who crept closer to the door like he was going to attempt a panicked run for it.

"What are you doing?" I hissed.

"I don't do firefights," he hissed back, his face taut with anxiety. "I just want to go home."

"Fine." I peeked out into the hall. The smoke from the flashbang had dissipated, improving visibility. The second intruder had hunkered behind a potted palm by the elevator. I grabbed the object nearest me, a running shoe, and tossed it out into the hall. It hit the wall opposite, drawing the shooter's attention and giving me a clear line of sight. I took the shot. He went down as hard as the first. I turned back to Mole, who'd gone pale. "There you go, all clear," I breathed.

He stared at me wide-eyed. "Why are they *here*?" Mole's tone was accusatory.

That was an excellent question. They must have been watching the Lannisters' house and followed me back. That was all I could think of.

"Great. Now I have to move." Mole had a flair for the dramatic.

I shook my head. "No, nobody else will be coming for me. If anyone does make a move, it won't be here."

"Reassuring," Mole said with sarcasm. "Go find Wickowski," he urged. "I'll clean this up." Doof gave a leap/spin/happy bark, happy to leave all the drama lying in the hallway.

Wickowski. He might still be at the precinct. I dialed his cell, but it went straight to voice mail. Busy. I hung up and dialed his desk directly but only got his automated message. I hit zero, which took me back to the main switchboard. I identified myself (everyone at the precinct knew who I was) and made a request for Wickowski's location. He was reportedly somewhere in the building. I tried his cell again, this time with success.

"Wickowski."

"Wick, where are you?"

"At the precinct."

"Yeah, but where?"

"I'm in the john on the fourth floor. What the hell's going on, Harris?"

I was already taking the stairs down two at a time to where my Mercedes Geländewagen SUV was parked. "I'm on my way to you right now, and I promise to explain when I see you, but, Wick, I need you to stay right where you are until I get there."

"In the can?"

"Yes! And lock the door. Don't let anybody else in with you."

"This is sort of a solitary event."

"I mean it. Lock the main door. Bar it if you have to. Just make sure you stay alone."

"What the fu—"

"Stay put!" I hollered into the phone. I wasn't aware Doof had followed me until I opened the car door and he jumped in, hopping over the console to the passenger's seat. The little voice in the back of my mind mentioned something about exploding bombs that had me popping my hood and looking under the dashboard for foreign or incendiary devices. There were none.

We made the ten-minute drive to the precinct in six, running a number of red lights in the process. I parked underground in the precinct lot. Doof jumped out before I could tell him to stay and followed me to a private entrance reserved for high-profile suspects. I used the passcode the mayor had given me (another perk) to let myself in. Doof at my heels, I raced to the fourth floor and pounded on the men's room door. Wickowski stepped up behind me where he'd been hanging out by the vending machines—right there, an open target. Officers and civilian employees busied themselves up and down the hall. I eyeballed each of them suspiciously.

"What happened to stay put?" I whispered harshly.

"I'm not camping out in the men's room without explanation."

Doof barked his dissatisfaction at Wickowski's answer. Who's the bestest boy?

"Explanation? Fine, here's two." I ticked them off on my fingers. "Hit. Men. As in plural. I know because two of them just paid me a visit."

"Do I want to know what happened to them?" I wasn't sure if Wickowski was being sincere or sardonic. Either way, he had me by the elbow and was steering me toward the elevator.

I settled on sincere. "No, you probably don't." I wasn't even sure what happened to them in the end.

We boarded the empty lift. Wickowski waited for it to move before pulling the stop button, pausing us in the elevator shaft. Doof looked confused. No alarm went off, so I figured this was how these guys got a moment of privacy. Much more effective than the empty stairwell trick. Nobody was going to walk in on them in here.

"Okay, you've got thirty seconds." Wickowski made a show of checking his wristwatch. "And...go."

I took a deep breath. "Two guys armed with suppressed AR-15s paid me a visit. With the Lannisters dead, you and Quinn are the only other loose ends."

I could tell Wickowski wasn't sure if I was being for real or overreacting. Maybe I was pulling a really tasteless joke. When I didn't give in with a chuckle, he eventually accepted what I was saying. I let Wickowski take charge of alerting Quinn. I don't believe any of us knew just how real shit was about to get.

CHAPTER SEVEN

AFTER MUCH DELIBERATION AND ARGUMENT ON WICKOWSKI'S PART, Doof and I followed him to his SE Salmon Street home in the Hawthorne district. His house, which he was able to keep in his proceedings with the latest former Mrs. Wickowski, was a cozy 1920s Craftsman-style bungalow fenced by a low split rail. The yard was simple and tidy and devoid of ornamentation.

Doof bounded from my rig, over the split rail, and promptly dropped a pile on Wickowski's lawn. Wickowski and I looked at each other, sizing up who was going to pick it up. It ended up being me (just as well), and I deposited the offensive shovelful directly into the trash bin at the curb, much to Wickowski's vexation. Apparently you're supposed to bag it first.

Wickowski let us all in through the side deck door. Doof made himself at home in the middle of the floor with his belly against the cool hardwood, hind legs stretched out behind him.

"What kind of name is that anyway, Doof? Doesn't sound very distinguished."

I looked down at the dog, who'd rolled over and was bicycling the air with his back legs, tongue lolling from his big, doofy dog grin. "I dunno." I shrugged. "I think it sort of suits him."

Something outside piqued Doof's attention, and he flipped himself over onto all fours, hackles raised. I went to the window and moved the shade aside just enough to peek out. Two teens walked past on the sidewalk, lost in a heady discussion about something I couldn't hear.

"It's all right, boy. It's just teenagers." Doof gave another of his leap/spin/happy barks then sat back down expectantly. I dropped a head scratch between his ears.

"I hate to break up the bonding, but have you given thought to bringing Burnell into this particular loop? The shooters loop, not the dog," he added to clarify.

Though I wasn't prone to doing anything that involved Burnell, I had been asking myself the same question since I'd left Mole behind to clean up. My reactionary answer was not to inform the captain because of my personal opinion of the blowhard. But not doing so might create a lot of drama down the road. And then the mayor could get involved, and that was a lot of cowbell I'd prefer to avoid. Still, I hated the thought of talking to Burnell, let alone being nice about it. I admitted as much to Wickowski.

"I agree with your perspective of my boss, but at the end of the day, there's protocols we have to follow. Even for civilians. Especially you. With enough leverage, Burnell could have the mayor pulling your business license." He wasn't being melodramatic. It was entirely possible that Burnell could ruin me. Not plausible—the mayor was a fan of mine because I'd closed a few cases for the city, but the opportunity was there nonetheless. The cell at my hip began to vibrate.

"Hey," Quinn said when I answered. "Wickowski left a message to give you a call when I got out of my meeting. What's up?"

I caught him up with what had gone down in my hall.

"You do understand that if you'd left one of them alive, we could've questioned him. Hell, we might have been able to close the entire case."

"Yeah," I scoffed. "I'll remember that next time I'm being shot at. I'll try the hug-a-thug approach."

"You didn't even call me directly to warn me." He honestly sounded a little hurt by that.

"I'm speaking to you now. Watch yourself. Mix up your routine. Don't let yourself be a target."

"I know how to evade and survive, Harris," he sneered. "I have been to war."

"Good," I shot back. "So do it."

Wickowski motioned for the phone, and I handed Quinn over. "Keep your head on a swivel, brother," he told Quinn and then hung up.

Since I'd seen Wickowski home safely—no single-car accidents, snipers, or hitmen—we did a walk-through to ensure there were no hidden surprises lying in wait.

"I'll call you later," I promised. I knew Wickowski was humoring me, letting me follow him home, go through the house, and secure the place. I also knew he was going to do whatever the hell he wanted the moment I pulled away from the curb. I knew this because it's what I'd do, and the two of us weren't that dissimilar.

Doof loaded up the moment I opened the passenger-side door. I gave Wickowski a wave. He gave me a short militant salute off his forehead. I went against traffic on my way back across the river. Doof stayed in the rig while I went inside Fred Meyer to pick up a bag of rather expensive dog food made with organic sweet potato and salmon. I figured Doof had gone without for long enough and deserved a little of the good stuff. A few human foodstuffs went into the cart as well, and a twelve-pack of porter. I was going to convert Quinn to the dark side of beer. I also outfitted Doof with a heavy-duty red nylon collar with matching leash. I threw a box of dog treats made of human-grade turkey jerky into the basket, along with matching stainless-steel food and water bowls. We arrived home without any further interaction that might have need of cleanup. The elevator opened up onto pristine new carpet replacing what had been leaked on.

Mole opened his door and poked his head out before Doof and I made it to our door.

"Yeah?" he nodded, arms wide in presentation, gesturing at the hall floor. "Like new. No one will ever be the wiser. They even got the sticky up from between the floorboards. These guys are good. Top-notch. Professionals—they could disappear a dead guy in, like, three hours with potassium hydroxide. It destroys everything, from identity to touch DNA, trace evidence."

I eyed Mole with a certain unease. "That's a creepily odd set of skills your friends have." I unlocked my door and let Doof enter first. Mole followed, and I trailed him.

Mole ignored my comment and plopped heavily down onto the couch. He found the television remote and began channel surfing. Doof looked to me for permission (though he didn't wait for it) before jumping up and joining Mole on the couch. I washed Doof's new bowls with hot soapy water before filling one with kibble, the other from the tap. Then I excused myself for a shower.

When I returned to the living room dressed in a fresh pair of sweatpants and a Carlos Santana concert t-shirt, Mole and Doof were snuggled together watching Scooby-Doo reruns. I had to wait for the episode to end before I could get Mole's attention. Doof's dinner dish was empty. He saw me looking and slid off the couch to stand beside it, his upturned eyes seeming to plead, *Please, ma'am, I want some more.* I obliged. "No barfing on the hardwood, though, Oliver."

Mole unfolded himself from the couch. "Oh, yeah, I came over because I have something to share with you." He fished a thumb drive from his pocket and used my workstation to open its files. "So, I did as you requested. I ran traffic cams from the surrounding area of the Lannisters' house, caught an image on this one at US 30 and the St. Johns Bridge." Mole fast-forwarded the video then slowed to a frame-by-frame pace when a dark SUV entered the screen. The video was in color and of good resolution, with a clear view of the license plate and rental agency barcode above it in the window. When Mole played the video at full speed, the SUV roared through the intersection.

"First off, it turns out these rigs were rented by a dummy corporation, a smokescreen that doesn't exist. It's actually quite ingenious how these guys go about it. First off, they scam a credit—"

I interrupted Mole with a wave of my hands. "I don't need to know how they do it. Is it at all traceable?"

"Not a chance."

Dammit. "Is there any clear shot of the driver?" I asked hopefully.

"I'm getting there," Mole said. "Watch this." He slowed the video to play it frame by frame again. "Watch as that oncoming truck passes in the opposite lane, right...there! Did you see that?"

I wasn't sure what I saw. "Play it again."

Mole rewound then inched forward one more time, pausing at the moment in question. "There—see how the light from the oncoming truck's headlights pass over the windshield right there?" He hit play, then pause in fast succession.

I saw what Mole was referring to. The headlights hit the SUV's windshield at just the right angle to fully illuminate the driver and his passenger. It wasn't the same two that I'd shot in the hallway, but they had the same blocky, muscular build. Mercenaries. Hired brawn. Professional soldiers employed solely for material gain at the expense of ethics. The resolution of the traffic cam was pretty good, but getting a positive identification off it might be a whole other story.

"Big guys, brunette or dark blonde, I can't tell," I said. "Larger-than-average build. Anything you can do with that fancy facial recognition program you've been working on?"

Mole gave his head a disappointed shake. "It's a clear image, but the angle's wrong. Not enough points of reference to be converted and compared. I wasn't able to get a match, and

believe me, these guys will be in the system. Likely ex-military."
He leaned closer to the screen, then used the ring around the
trackball to zoom in on the image. "Look what they're wearing,"
he said, pointing at the screen.

I leaned in to better make out what he was seeing: adjust-
able shoulder straps and multiple pockets of tactical body ar-
mor. If these soldiers of fortune had been hired to eliminate the
Lannisters, why? Better yet, by who? Million-dollar questions: I
was full of them.

Mole kept scrolling through the video frame by frame. We
watched the SUV's slow, halting crawl past the on-ramp from
Bridge Avenue and then out of the frame until it was picked
up by the next traffic camera just west of downtown on I-405
where it exited onto NW Couch Street. From there the SUV
disappeared.

"I thought I'd lost them. I hacked into doorbell cams and
storefront cams and got nothing. But then I realized I was over-
thinking it. It took me a few minutes before I was finally able
to locate them again when they passed the traffic camera at the
intersection of West Burnside and Tichner out near Arlington
Heights in the West Hills. From there I really did lose them."

I clapped Mole on the back of the shoulder. "But at least you
were able to track them. Good job, Mole. I don't know if you
hear that often enough."

"The loudest gratitude comes in increments of twenty," he
said, his fingers clacking over the keyboard.

Mole was right. His services were invaluable to me. But then,
my gratitude was often extended in hundreds. I looked over his
shoulder. "Now what are you doing?"

"I accessed the State Department and found a cache of transcribed recordings Lannister Sr. was cc'd on. It's very tedious
work because I'm dealing with ancient technology. Hand-
transcribed notes—in shorthand, no less—from reel-to-reel

tapes. I'm searching for copies of the original audio recordings, but so far I've found bubkes, just these transcribed copies."

"You did mention Lannister Sr. had been involved with a few projects that required top-secret security. If we could track down that list..."

"Oh, you make it sound so simple."

I knew Mole was already chasing down every angle. If what we were searching for existed, he would locate it. Mole prided himself in retaining his top spot on the FBI's Most Wanted for white-collar cybercrimes. If the Feds ever did catch up with him, they'd likely offer him a position on their team, deep inside the bowels of the Hoover Building where they could keep a watchful eye on him. I understood that to some, Mole's and my working relationship was ineffable, impossible to understand. It didn't make much sense, me being former FBI and all. But I got what drove Mole. Like how I had a fundamental issue with the red tape and bureaucracy that stood between bad guys and prison, Mole had a difficult time accepting that there were secrets in the world and agencies who worked really hard to keep them from the world. His hacktivist perspective was that information was fair game for all the people, not just the elite—if you knew how to access it. Fair point.

Mole gave a low whistle just under his breath. "There's a lot to go over, Sammy. I'm going back to my place. Give you a shout-out in a bit?"

"Drop it onto a thumb drive, and I'll go over it myself. I have a feeling I'm going to be on Doof-walk duty all night. I'm not even sure yet if he's housebroken."

After Mole left, I took Doof for a walk around the block with his new collar and leash. He seemed to know the drill and didn't pull me, didn't zigzag across the sidewalk in front of me, but stayed at my side. He stopped for a wee against a light pole but didn't drop any bombs along the way, which was just as well. I didn't have a dookie bag with me.

The hall was empty when I returned. Unless Mole found something earth-shattering, I wasn't expecting to hear from him again until morning. I locked the door and set the alarm for the first time in long time. Doof followed me to my room. I couldn't stifle my yawns any longer and crawled into bed, where I wriggled under the down comforter. Doof stared at me longingly.

"No dogs on the bed," I instructed.

He whined but lowered himself to the floor anyway. Doof waited until I was asleep before he hopped up and snuggled against my back sometime in the night. I didn't shoo him off. He lay between me and the door. First line of defense. It was kind of nice.

Something cold and wet pushed against my face the next morning. I stirred and wiped at my cheek and mumbled incoherently. This was all the sign of life that Doof needed. Leap/spin/happy bark. Now I was wide awake, my ears ringing from his sharp yelp.

"Doof, not so loud." This earned me another leap/spin, but no bark.

I got out of bed and reached for the nearest articles resembling clothes: a pair of jeans with the knees ripped out and a black t-shirt I got in Cabo during Sammy Hagar's birthday bash at his cantina years ago.

"Who wants to go for walkies?" I asked rhetorically, taking both sides of Doof's furry head in my hands and giving it a shake. White fluffy hair flitted on the air and attached itself to every surface like it was magnetic. I saw a dismal future for my t-shirt. I pulled away from the dog with the shirt slathered in long, stray, brown-and-white Doof hairs. He nudged me again with his cool wet nose. That was my cue to get my shoes on.

"Then we could stop and get coffee from Seth on the way back, huh, Doofy-Doof?" I found myself using that annoying pet-owner voice again. *Geesh, please don't let it become a habit.* I grabbed the plastic grocery bag his dishes had come home from the store in and stuffed it into my pocket. Dookie bag.

When I pulled open the door, Mole's closed hand was poised and ready to knock. He had a thumb drive in one hand and a surprised expression on his face. "Hey!"

"Hiya. Doof and I were just heading out for his morning walk and constitutional." I held up a plastic grocery bag layered inside another plastic grocery bag as evidence of our intention.

Mole gave Doof a head scratch. "I was up most of the night and compiled this for your reading pleasure." He handed me the drive, which I set on the table just inside the door.

"Can I get you anything while I'm out?" I offered. I read his t-shirt, which had a depiction of a classic large-headed gray alien with Humans Don't Exist printed beneath.

"Full disclosure," he deadpanned. I was fairly certain he was referring to his t-shirt. I'd learned long ago to not engage in the topic with him if I didn't want to be waylaid for an hour.

Could a person really tell what's going through a dog's mind? I liked to think Doof was able to communicate to a certain degree. I knew he was proud of his bright-red collar by the way he stoically stood with it on, and he accepted the leash without hesitation. We waited for the elevator, and he obediently hopped on. Through the front door's glass, I could see Deputy Quinn waiting at the security gate at the sidewalk.

Doof uttered a low, guttural growl, along with an enthusiastically wagging tail. Mixed messages. I wasn't sure if he was going to bite Quinn or give him sloppy kiss. I totally understood Doof's varied emotions. Quinn was holding a venti cup from that green-and-white corporate coffee shop around the corner and down three blocks.

"I took you for strong and straight up," Quinn said as he passed me the cup. "Any new developments in the investigation?"

He didn't even mention the previous night's discussion. I wasn't yet ready to have the conversation anyway.

"Does this mean you're officially inviting me in?" I asked.

"What," Quinn scoffed, "official invite? I presumed you were in the moment you showed up at the river with Wickowski."

"I don't want to step on any fragile egos, that's all." That sounded harsh even to my ears.

The three of us walked along the empty sidewalk. It was an overcast day. The 405 overhead created an omnipotent dull roar. Doof marked the first tire he encountered at the curb. I sipped on the coffee from Steam's corporate competitor. It tasted like disloyalty. Doof found a broad-leaved bush in a lawn in need of a clipping to back his hind end under, where he politely did his business. A quick glance around told me nobody had seen Doof's offense. I left the pile hidden under the bush where it was and kept walking.

"You're not going to clean up after your dog?" Quinn asked, probably not as judgey as I thought I heard him being. I held out the plastic bags I'd been carrying in my pocket.

Quinn took a breath to say something, then must have thought better of it because he stayed silent for a beat. I could tell from the set of his mouth that he was arranging his words. "Have I gotten myself involved in a pissing match that I'm not aware of?"

I ignored his question. What he sensed wasn't attitude. He was detecting an intentional brush-off.

"Look, if you'd rather I take off..." He let his sentence hang in midair.

"Yeah," I said much too immediately. "I've got some things to attend to." I kept walking away from him. "Call you later when I have something?" I offered over my shoulder.

"Yeah, sure," Quinn said awkwardly. "Sounds great." He started off in the opposite direction.

I turned and watched his retreating form. The jeans he was wearing fit him just right. I cocked my head in admiration. Turned out I had a thing for muscled butts.

Doof and I continued with our planned excursion. We ended up on the north side of Vaughn Street where we hooked a left on Twenty-Third. We kept on through the vintage neighborhood of Slabtown to Front Avenue, which ran along the west bank of the Willamette River. The streets near the train tracks had few cars, and the sidewalk along the river was vacant.

Empty, that was, save for one other pedestrian walking toward Doof and me. He wore a bulky jacket over cargo pants. Booted feet. A low growl rumbled from Doof's big barrel chest. It was a different tone of growl than he'd given Quinn, and his tail wasn't wagging but held straight down in a defensive posture. His hackles were raised along his bony spine, and the scruff around his neck expanded like a fighter puffing up, an attempt at making himself appear a bit larger than he was.

For the most part, I wasn't a reactionary person. I preferred to observe and take action in the moment if and when needed. The man walking toward us was closing in at ten yards, his stride quicker than a stroll, like he was trying to make an appointment on time. Doof had the same uneasy feeling I had. His growl grew deeper, more insistent. We crossed the street in front of a five-story apartment building, not waiting for a corner or a crosswalk.

The man stopped and creepily stared at us from the opposite sidewalk. I waited for him to make a move, and when he did, it wasn't what I expected. He turned on his heel and began jogging back in the direction from which he'd come. I sighed in relief prematurely.

Another cargo-panted, booted stranger stepped out from between two parked cars in the lot of a flooring company just ahead. I didn't jump to conclusions, but I did loosen my grip on Doof's leash, a mistake I immediately regretted.

"Doof, no!" I screamed.

He ripped the leash out of my hand and launched himself in the man's direction, all spit and snarl and teeth. Ears perked, eyes fixed on his target, Doof tore after the man with vicious intent. I sprinted after the dog. A glint of sharpened steel flashed, coinciding with Doof's pained yelp. He tumbled, still, to the concrete. He didn't move again. The man disregarded the bleeding animal at his feet and turned his attention to me.

Pure adrenaline coursed dangerously through my veins. I wanted nothing more than to kill the bastard. I vowed to myself right there that if my dog died, this scumbag would too. I closed the gap between me and the man and brought my arm back for a brutal overhead punch. Doof's attacker widened his stance, ready for the attack. I jumped and concentrated all of that rage behind the force, my bodyweight backing up my fist. The inertia of the punch spun his head down and around, twisting his legs out from under him as gravity pulled him down into an immobile heap. He'd never had a chance to raise his blade against me.

The concrete beneath Doof stained red. The knife had taken him in the chest. I didn't want to turn him over; I didn't want to move him, but I knew I had to. His attacker was knocked out but would eventually regain consciousness. I didn't want him to escape, but I couldn't wait around for Doof to bleed out either. I scooped my dog up in my arms and cradled him against me like I was packing firewood. *My dog.* An animal someone had thrown away like so much trash but who'd chosen me as his human. I could tell he was still breathing by the red-tinged bubbles at his nostrils, but that also meant he was bleeding internally.

DoveLewis, the emergency veterinary clinic, was less than a mile away. Doof was underweight but he was still heavy, at least eighty pounds. It was my own adrenaline, determination, and rage that kept me running with Doof in my arms.

"Help," I called out as I pushed through the vet office's front door. "Male, age unknown, knife wound to the left-side chest," I began rattling off details relative to triage. The receptionist, Becca according to her name tag, hustled around the desk and showed us to an exam room, where I gently laid Doof onto the stainless steel examination table. The doctor came in, introducing himself as Dr. Saunders as he moved to examine Doof.

Dr. Saunders was a thin, wiry guy with bright, kind eyes beneath expressive brows. His gentle, easy bedside manner came naturally. I could tell he took his profession seriously, but he also had a bit of a joker vibe. You could tell a lot about a person by the lines on their face. The veterinarian's deep laugh lines said he was someone who'd spent his whole life laughing and smiling. A cheerful guy. The class clown. But he was all seriousness as he bent over Doof. The set of his mouth and furrow of his brow gave me the worst news. The good doctor assured me he and his staff would do everything in their power to save my dog. Then he asked me to step into the waiting room while his attendants prepped him for surgery.

My shirt was tacky with Doof's blood. I used the washroom next to the waiting room to rinse most of it off my face, neck, and arms. *He's just a dog*, I tried to convince myself. It was purely an emotional-survival mechanism. I can't process huge emotions. Or rather, a part of me refuses to. *He's just a stray you found. Don't be attached. It's just a dog.*

When I was five or six, my grandmother had a cat to whom I was attached. It got run over by a car, but my parents tried to sell me the story that she'd been adopted by a little old lady. I knew my parents were feeding me a line of bullshit at the time, but to acknowledge the truth, that Fluffy was killed by a speeding car, created an uncomfortable pit of tears in the core of me, so I bought the fictitious tale and pushed the truth from my mind. That would become a theme throughout my whole life. Persistent redirect.

I used the office phone to call Wickowski for a clean shirt as much as for support.

"You're where?"

"The emergency vet on Pettygrove. Doof got stabbed."

"*Qué mierda,*" he swore. "What happened?"

I brought Wickowski up to speed from the moment Doof and I had hit Front Street all the way through to my pushing through the animal-hospital door. "They've got him in surgery now."

"But where's the guy you dropped?"

"I'm sure no longer where I left him. He either rallied or his buddy scraped him off the walk. Either way, I wouldn't bother sending a squad car around."

"So why are you calling me?" Wickowski asked.

"I don't know, Wick," I said, rather incensed by the question. "Maybe a clean shirt and a hug?"

"You're not a hugger," he said, still with the attitude.

Until yesterday, I wasn't a dog owner either, so things change. "What's up your ass?" I asked him.

"The mayor called me into his office this morning. He wants to know the status of these two homicides. The press is pushing on his office for a statement."

"He's aware it's in the county's jurisdiction, right?" I asked, feeling like I might be poking the bear. "How much faith do you have in them?"

Wickowski didn't answer straightaway. "Quinn has you, so I suppose I have some faith."

Not quite the pep speech I was expecting. And Quinn did not *have me,* thank you very much. Wickowski explained he was in the middle of something and would come by as soon as he was able to get away. I hung up feeling like I'd gotten the brush-off and tried not to take it personally.

I didn't want to talk to Quinn, but I needed...someone. I swallowed my pride and made the call I was avoiding.

"Where's the suspect now?" Quinn asked in an as-expected perturbed tone when he picked up. "And is he alive?"

"I have no idea," I said honestly. "I left him in an unconscious pile on Front. I had to make a judgment call: get the bad guy or save a life. I chose the latter."

"Then get your ass back there and make sure he gets picked up." Quinn's arrogance really put me off. He may have known me in the biblical sense, but he clearly hadn't gotten the memo that I never do what I'm told, and I don't entertain other people's attitudes. I had enough of my own to deal with.

"I'm sort of busy here at the vet's. I'm not going anywhere until I get an update about Doof," I stated resolutely. If Doof wasn't going to make it, I didn't want him to die alone. Not after what he'd been through the past few weeks.

Quinn hung up on me with an exasperated huff.

I took a seat in one of the molded plastic chairs arranged in two rows and picked up a two-year-old home improvement magazine from the stack of expired journals. Six chairs faced each other. I sat catty-corner from a thick man with a soft-sided dog carrier settled on his lap. A small, long-haired pooch with beady black eyes stared out. Across from him and to my right sat an older woman. At her feet was a hard-sided cat carrier with slots for windows and a hinged metal door. A perturbed growling came from within. I began absently turning magazine pages, not really seeing any of them.

My thoughts were on Doof. I was too aware of the fragility of my affection for him. A psychotherapist might hint that my inability to trust humans and the level of affection I had for the nonhuman were tied together. What would I do if he didn't make it? *Of course he's going to make it, Sam. He has to.* I did my best to convince myself while mentally preparing for the worst.

The office door slid open, and the heavy footfalls of booted feet entered. The sound registered in my mind and triggered an internal warning bell a fraction of a second too late. The soft *ppfftt* of a suppressed bullet was followed by the thud of a body hitting the floor. Becca, the receptionist who'd helped me with Doof, lay on her side, lifeless eyes open and staring sightless into the waiting room. The woman with the cat carrier screamed, drawing the gunman's fire. The elderly man with the little dog toppled from his chair, clutching at his weak heart. I'd reached for my firearm in its usual place at the small of my back with sickening realization and visualized it on my bedside table. God dammit! I tumbled out of my chair, taking down the empty seat beside me and rushed to nest them together, doubling the plastic wall that would do nothing to stop a bullet but might slow it enough to survive being hit. I'd been distracted with needing to take Doof for a morning walk; arming myself slipped my mind. How was that even possible?

The shooter's back was to the receptionist's desk, where a scrubbed vet tech stood, paralyzed with fear. Her eyes locked on mine. Her face was a wash of terror. She was frozen, but I knew she was going to make a break for it. The gunman took a menacing step toward me. The vet tech slipped off her shoes. She must have believed they'd give her away. She broke away from her hiding spot, stockinged feet slapping across the sage-green linoleum. Her whimpers and sobs drew the gunman's attention. She almost made it to safety. The suppressed gunshot was audible in the enclosed space.

The violence up front must have registered to the animals in the back rooms. A series of frantic barks and terrified whines erupted where the patients' kennels and cages were housed. The vet tech stumbled forward with the impact, dead before she hit the floor, just a yard short of safety.

"Over here, asshat!" I taunted to draw his attention to me in case more staff made a panicked run. The gunman turned and fired. The bullet chunked the wall just inches from my head. I ducked through an examination room door and slammed it shut behind me. The lock wouldn't hold him back for long. With my elbow, I smashed the locked glass case used to secure controlled substances. The doorhandle behind me jiggled violently. I perused the labels until I found what I was looking for: Nembutal, a name brand of pentobarbital, commonly used to euthanize animals. It was also used as a presurgical sedative in humans. The door shuddered when the shooter threw his body against it. Hurriedly, I filled a 12-cc syringe.

The door suddenly splintered open, and the gunman burst in. I put the steel exam table between us. He leveled his gun at the middle of my forehead. I didn't flinch.

"On your knees!" Spittle flew from his mouth.

I refused to move. I wasn't bleeding yet. That meant he had orders to take me alive. Not necessarily undamaged, but alive. He grabbed the back of my head and forced my face against the wall, pinning me there with his body. He wasn't aware of the hypodermic in my hand until it was buried in his thigh. I shoved the plunger with my thumb and emptied the syringe, delivering a fatal dose.

I pushed back away from the wall and watched him struggle to breathe. He fell to the ground unconscious. I made the mindful choice not to call 911. To let him die on the floor. His chest rose and fell once, twice, then didn't rise again. Did I feel guilty for letting a man die? Not in that moment. Ask me later. He'd pushed me too far. I pushed back.

I spun at the sound of rustling fabric in the doorway. Dr. Saunders was there, his mouth agape, face blanched white. When he recovered his professional composure, he said, "My associate, Dr. Reiner, was able to barricade the door to the operating room and carry on with surgery. She was able to suture the main bleed. Fortunately the knife missed all major organs and arteries. I expect Dr. Reiner will be closing soon. The patient will be in recovery, and you will be able to see him for a moment." Dr.

Saunders turned on his heel and walked stiff-legged to his office. He was obviously still in shock. I'd make sure he got medical attention before I left.

Another voice came from the open doorway. This one was terse and seemingly not at all surprised, "What the actual hell, Harris?"

"Hey, Quinn." I wiggled my fingers at him and followed with a shrug. "You left me unattended." I could tell by the way his brow furrowed deeper that he was unimpressed.

Quinn pushed into the room. His eyes landed on the syringe still dangling from the guy's thigh. He reached down and checked his pulse. He found none. "COD?"

"Cause of death was self-defense. Mode of death was overdose."

"By?"

"Pentobarbital."

"You put the guy to sleep?" Quinn asked incredulously.

"At least there's no blood to clean up this time."

"What haven't you told me?" Quinn sensed I was holding something back.

"Now isn't really the optimal time."

"Harris," he said sternly.

"Quinn," I replied, mimicking his deep voice.

Instead of standing for a lecture, I righted one of the upended molded plastic chairs and took a seat. My head in my hands, elbows on knees, I tried to think of something other than worrying about my dog. I mean, I'd just offed a guy—I might want to take stock of my karma and weigh it against my kill rate. Or not.

"Harris." Quinn got my attention. "I need your statement."

"Can it wait? I mean, I want to check in on Doof—"

"He's a *dog*. Focus on the human being." He seemed more stressed than usual.

The ME arrived and officially pronounced the receptionist, the two in the waiting room, the vet tech, and the shooter on the exam room floor all deceased. Their bodies were zipped into their own black body bags and loaded onto separate gurneys.

I got to see Doof momentarily before I left for home. He was lying in a blanket-padded kennel with an IV in his shaven foreleg. His eyes were open but unfocused.

"He's a very lucky pooch," the vet tech commented. "A fraction of a hair's breadth in any direction, and the knife would have severed a main artery." The woman was impressively professional despite her coworkers and two clients having been gunned down in the lobby. She steadied her hands in each other when they began to shake.

"Is he going to be okay?" I blurted both my concern and my priority.

The white-coated assistant gave me a kind smile. "He's going to be fine. He's going to have to take it easy—no ball chasing or strenuous hikes—and the doctor will prescribe some antibiotics and some pain medicine, but other than that, he should make a full recovery. He'll be back to normal in no time."

I'd only just met Doof. I didn't know what normal was for him. I supposed when he returned to his leap/spin/happy bark, that might be a good indicator. I gave the top of his head several scratches, then added a kiss.

Quinn was helping oversee the removal of the bodies. News vans were already showing up on the scene. Someone had turned off the neon Open sign. My intent was to quietly exit without notice. I wanted to go home. I hadn't had enough coffee yet that day, which was adding to the rapid deterioration of my mood and general outlook.

Wickowski had shown up while I was with Doof. He asked one of his officers to retrieve the footage from the office's security cameras mounted in opposite corners of the lobby. This shooting was under the Portland PB's authority, as was my part in the self-defense death of the shooter, who was part of the county's ongoing investigation. And I belonged to neither the city nor the county but had sure stepped in the middle of their toes.

"He started it," I said and motioned to the body bag on the gurney heading out the door. "And he almost killed my dog, so no, I'm not issuing any apologies."

Quinn joined us and put his hand on my waist to get my attention, a move that didn't escape Wickowski's notice. I shifted my weight to the other foot, effectively moving myself away from Quinn's touch. He must have gone out to his car while I was in back with Doof, because he was now wearing his blue sheriff's department windbreaker. "I'll give you a lift home if you're ready to go." He leaned over and offered. It felt too intimate. That didn't escape Wickowski's notice either.

"I need to get your statement before you get too distracted," Wickowski reminded me. "We can do it at the station, or I can drop you at home and get it then." His offer of dropping me at home felt more territorial than meant for my convenience.

"Thanks for the offers, boys, but I'm going to walk home on my own."

"You're covered in blood," Quinn pointed out.

"So give me your jacket." I held my hand out expectantly.

I could tell by his reluctance that Quinn wasn't sure if I was serious about the coat and walking home or if I was just being difficult. In his defense, he'd gotten a pretty good glimpse at my obnoxious side. Deciding I was serious and, wiser yet, not to argue with me about my decision, Quinn sloughed off his jacket and put it into my eager hand.

"Harris," Wickowski called before I could successfully slip out the door, "try to keep your head down."

I eyeballed both Wickowski and Quinn. "Don't call me. I'll call you," I said, then turned and walked out. The sun had broken through the clouds just enough that I felt its warmth on my shoulders. There should have been happiness in those rays. All I felt was emotional vulnerability.

I jammed my fists into the pockets of Quinn's jacket and sulked all the way across town. I was alert for a tail, a slowing car, or footsteps falling in sync with my own. None of those things happened.

My first priority was an attitude adjustment. Seth threw an extra shot into my quad Americano on the house. If my mood didn't improve, I was going to be one wired, grumpy bitch. Thankfully he didn't notice the blood on my shirt when the jacket fell open, or he didn't say anything about it if he did. Nor did he mention my attire, team SHERIFF splashed across my back, or the county insignia on my chest.

Coffee in hand, I unlocked my front door and went straight for the shower, where I stayed until the hot water turned my skin bright red. I settled in the middle of the bed wearing frumpy sweats and opened the thumb drive from Mole on my laptop. I settled back against a pile of feather pillows and began reading.

I had no way of knowing the unringable bell I was tolling.

CHAPTER EIGHT

FIVE HOURS LATER I WAS STILL IN THE MIDDLE OF MY BED, BUSY with the files from the thumb drive. My printer had gone into overdrive. I'd had to swap out toner cartridges three hours in. All four walls of my bedroom were papered with reports. I'd had to use string to help me visibly connect my thoughts. It was a tangled web with all strands leading to one name: Lieutenant General Richard Coppice.

When I googled his name, I learned the lieutenant general had been an officer with the Army Corps of Engineers who'd overseen the construction of one of Washington's major defense buildings. Coppice later became director of the Substitute Materials project. He personally placed Lannister Sr. in charge of security for the project (pre-Homeland, but they would have loved him). After the war, Coppice's paper trail disappeared. With the elbows he was rubbing, he may not have disappeared but taken himself underground. Or he was taken off grid.

"Hey, got a minute?" I asked when Mole answered his phone.

When he ducked under the web strands that crossed the doorway and stepped into my bedroom, he gave a dramatic whistle. There was a blank space by the foot of my bed where he stood and pivoted around on his heel. My room had become a maze of identifying photographs from personnel files and printouts of declassified reports. The web of yarn wrapped around the room connecting characters to each other, reports to timelines.

"I can't tell if this is an art installation or what goes on in your mind."

"I'm following something."

"This is why I do the computer stuff and you do the bullet stuff."

"Perfect. I need more information on this guy." I pointed to the culmination of several web strands: Lieutenant General Richard Coppice. "So far I've found he was connected to the Development of Substitute Materials as project director. Lannister Sr. is mentioned under him, but then he just sort of peters off into obscurity."

"Scoot over." Mole moved onto the bed and nudged me with his elbow. He sat cross-legged beside me and pulled the laptop onto his lap. His fingers moved in light blurs, the clacking of the keys a rhythm all their own like an obscure beatboxer. "Compliments of the dark web." The printer hummed to life and began spitting out pages.

I took the first one, a photo of Lieutenant General Coppice, who was a tall, rotund man, way over regulation by today's standards. He bulged above his belt and strained the zipper of his khakis. His merits must have outweighed his physical burden for the army to utilize him as they did. Coppice directed several top-secret projects regarding covert operations, like remote viewing, the military's bid to use psychics to spy on their enemies from afar, as well as weapons development and advanced technology not originating from our planet.

"I'm trying to find where his trail picks up after the war. Nobody really disappears. Especially back then, when a person left an indelible paper trail."

Mole silently kept at it for several more minutes before claiming, "I'd be more comfortable digging into this on my own more secure computer."

I stared at him hard. "What do you mean, more secure? I run my life through that laptop."

He shot me a withering look. "As if I'd allow any form of hacker, other than myself, into the sanctity that is this building.

I'm just more comfortable at my own workstation." He slid off the bed and gracefully retraced his steps through the yarn web, turning back at the door. "Stay close to your phone." Then I heard my front door close behind him.

Mole had left a cache of transcribed audio recordings open on the laptop. They were copies transliterated from the original shorthand transcriptions from wiretaps. The Office of Counterintelligence of the War Department, and Lannister's grandfather. The words were in English, but it was in science-speak, all neutrons and uranium. That I found odd. Not that I was a buff on the subject of WWII bomb jargon, but because I'd read earlier that the Office of CIWD did indeed wiretap as a means to find individuals engaged in Communist activities or recruitment stateside. I scrolled through what made no sense to me, stopping when I came across an exchange about weaponizing concentrated, high-powered energy bursts. There was doubt of plausibility in the reply. Another transcribed wiretap was between a chemist and a physicist regarding biological agents and propulsion systems. Both sounded like they were working on specific tasks.

I admittedly knew next to nothing about WWII. My parents hadn't even been born yet, and they never really explored it in high school. My public school years covered the Revolutionary War and the Civil War, mentioned the two World Wars, and taught contemporary US government structure. The more distasteful parts of our history, like the slavery years, the slaughter and systemic oppression of Indigenous peoples, and the business of war, were ignored. And we wonder why we're doomed to repeat history.

When my stomach growled, I figured it was enough for the day. I ordered in another spicy pizza, then filled the clawfoot and let it cool while I waited for the delivery guy. When the front door buzzer sounded, I thumbed the button by the door to let him in. I had a wad of cash and some change in my hand when I answered the door.

Quinn was standing there in the hallway balancing a pizza box in one hand. "You know," he purred, "the best way to a man's heart is through pizza."

"No," I corrected, taking the pizza box from him, "the best way to his heart is through his upper thoracic ribs."

Quinn followed me inside without my inviting him. Who was I kidding? Of course I was going to invite him in. The question was, would he still be here in the morning?

Quinn caught sight of the yarn web from where he stood by the kitchen. "I never figured you as the arts-and-crafts type," he said, pointing in that direction. Why had I never noticed until just then the soft, warm timbre of his voice? *No, Sam!* my inner voice scolded. *Bad Sam!* It knew better than I did what was good for me and what weaknesses I was prone to. So then why did the primal part of my brain so frequently override the part that knew better? If I ever answered that question, I would have solved all the ills of my personal world. Until then I'd continue to fall victim to my own bad self.

I opened the pizza box, which was still steaming hot, and offered Quinn a slice. He eyed the box suspiciously. I'd had them add extra jalapeños and red pepper flakes. "It might burn a little, but it'll be worth it."

I fetched a couple of porters from the fridge and passed one to Quinn. We sat side-by-side on the couch, the pizza box on the coffee table in front of us. We ate our first slice in silence.

"Going to tell me what that's all about?" Quinn asked with a nod toward the bedroom as he reached for his second slice. I knew he was referring to my yarn web.

"Just following the narrative," I told him, "seeing where things connect."

"What have you come up with so far?"

Part of me, the catty part that I didn't like to acknowledge even though it had influence over my mouth, wanted him to go do his own damn footwork. I caved to my more personable side and brought him up to speed. See? I play nice.

"Just give me the name and location of the triggerman so I can make the arrest," Quinn said as he sat back and drank his beer.

I sighed and finished the last half of mine in one long pull, then burped myself through the alphabet all the way to S. It made me smile. I'd once been kicked out of homeroom in junior high when I'd belched the entire alphabet from A to Z. Though my classmates were impressed, Mr. Beane, our geometry teacher, was not. My talent had cost me three consecutive lunch breaks, but I was known among my classmates from that day on as the girl who could belch the alphabet. I bet I still was in some circles.

Quinn wasn't interested in my prepubescent talents. Nor, it turned out, was he interested in discussing dead bodies, killers, or life in general any more than I was when he laid his hand on my inner thigh. His forearm was muscled and flexed when he moved his hand. My breath caught in my throat. I didn't even bother to make sure the door was locked. In that moment, I didn't much care.

One thing I appreciated about Quinn was that he didn't linger in the morning. No waylaying showers. No loitering offers to make breakfast. He simply got up, got dressed, and left. Don't get me wrong—I've known the pleasure of a slow-burning romantic love affair. I also knew what kind of liability that sort of relationship inevitably became. There was just as much satisfaction in the simplicity of unencumbered, emotionless sex. A repetitive one-night stand.

It was midmorning when I finally threw the blanket off. Quinn and I had spent the night on the couch—spooning when we were trying to sleep, stacked horizontally on one another when we weren't. I could still taste him. A scrap of paper peeked out from beneath the pillow. Curious, I opened it to find a quickly jotted message on the back of a fuel receipt: *Gotta run but I'll swing back by later.* Later? That was irritatingly nonspecific. I blushed when I thought of his return. My inner voice remained silent. "Focus on the case, Sam," I chastised myself.

A quick shower that I ran cold at the end and I was out the door. The sky overhead was a typical moody mix of heavy clouds with thinning spots where the sun battled to peek through. I'd lived here long enough to know it wasn't going to make it. My first stop was at Steam for my usual fix, then on to see Doof. I was hoping he might be released soon. I couldn't wait to get him home. His forever home.

Caffeine fix in hand, I kept my head down and tried to keep my thoughts focused on Doof and his recovery. Then they slid to my billing and the electronic filing that lay on my desk back home. I should hire an assistant. The thought of having someone literally in my business sketched me out. Besides, I could use the busy work *because* it kept me busy while I worried about Doof. There were a couple of phone calls from prospective clients that I needed to make appointments to interview. I didn't work for just anyone, and my services weren't inexpensive. I'd discovered early on that white-collar businessmen were willing pay any fee to ensure their investment and its intellectual properties were secure. I knew I should be making some charitable donations. My free-spirited Aunt Zelda was always recommending I take my karma a little more seriously—whatever that meant. *Maybe I should give her a call and clarify? Maybe I could call home while I'm at it.*

Out of self-preservation, I shifted my thoughts to things I was actually going to do. Quinn's image was suddenly there. That wasn't really what I'd meant, but there I was. I could have changed the subject. I didn't. I let the image of him come into detail. His body. I appreciated the care he took of it. What he could do with it. His eyes. There was more depth there than I think he even realized he was capable of. I'd searched in there for answers, how to make sense of what I was feeling. It had only confused me more.

Quinn challenged me, and I respected him for that. But could he take care of himself in my world? I may not have a lot of friends, but I have a buttload of people who'd rather see me no longer exist. Therein lies my quandary—where lovers become liabilities. Might I still control the narrative if I lowered my guard, backed off with the aggression? Maybe this was one of those existential growth opportunities I'd heard about. A test of character. I appreciated Quinn had the self-confidence—and the balls—to push back when I got in his face about something. I felt an unbidden smile take over my face. He could handle me.

The sound of rubber slowly rolling over asphalt crept up on me. I tossed a peripheral glance over my left shoulder. A delivery truck. Not an uncommon sight in that part of the Pearl, which was dotted with eateries. It passed me, and Quinn was there in my thoughts to pick up distracting me where he'd left off. How serious was my personal rule about not dating cops? I mean, I'd already done it, already broken my own rule, so there's that. Maybe if I just didn't make it a habit moving forward.

The delivery truck eventually pulled to the curb at the back door of a bistro further up the block. I hadn't paid attention who'd gotten out. The back door was partially rolled up. I was just passing when a pair of hands suddenly fell down on me from behind. One covered my mouth, the other caught me by the throat, forefinger and thumb squeezing my trachea, making it hard to draw breath. It all happened so fast—one minute I was on the sidewalk, the next I was in the back of the delivery truck, the door already rolled down. I was on my back. A single bare bulb fixed to the ceiling threw a cone of light. Two metal chairs were bolted to the floor several inches across from each other. An anticipated face-to-face. But with who?

A foot to my stomach stunned me momentarily immobile. My hands were quickly captured and zip-tied behind my back. I got a good look at my abductor—that was to say, at what he was wearing. His face was obscured by a full balaclava. Black cargo pants. A black tactical vest. Gloves. His actions were swift and efficient, like he'd taken someone from the streets before. Adrenaline flooded my veins and fueled my actions. I fought, legs kicking out wildly, when he grabbed me by the front of my clothes and hauled me up into that icy-cold chair. That's when I realized the truck was refrigerated. Federal interrogators would oftentimes use soft torture methods, one of them being to douse their subject with water and lower the air temperature to extremes. My heart was already racing at an unhealthy pace. I held my teeth against the chattering.

My abductor stood behind me, smelling of intimidation and gun oil. I was relieved of my cell phone and HK. The truck bumped along the streets. I tried to memorize our movements but soon lost track. I could tell we'd taken a freeway on-ramp. We were travelling at highway speeds. We could have gone either north on I-5, west on the Sunset out of the city against inbound commuter traffic, or south on any number of outbound routes. I focused on my breathing.

There were three of them: my abductor and the one behind the wheel, and the third was hidden in the shadows outside the cone of light. I picked up the faint fragrance of expensive cologne, not aftershave or the cheap stuff you get on a premoistened towelette from a gas station men's room. I stared into the dark corners, daring whoever was there to make themselves known.

A knife point dug painfully into the hollow in the base of my skull directly above my cerebellum. One reactionary twitch of the knife, and I would never walk again. I breathed against the dread that was building inside of me. Situations such as these rarely played out in favor of the abductee. Where fear should have been, a rage-driven pressure began to dome inside me, an imminent eruption that threatened to destroy...everything.

My challenge thrown at the dark corner was met by a genteel voice from out of the shadows. "I've read your FBI jacket, Ms. Harris." The man let his statement sink in. He knew exactly who I was. That meant he knew my past, my connections. Where I lived. Mole's subsequent exposure was my first concern. That said something about our relationship. "That's why we're here."

Movement came from the corner, and the man with the genteel voice stepped forward from the shadows. At first glance he didn't look all that threatening. His light-colored suit was crisply pressed and well tailored. Expensive. It was a brave choice for that early in the spring. It also denoted he didn't do his own dirty work. Salt-and-pepper hair worn short. His face was clean-shaven. Age naturally lined his features, but they were lines earned by years spent on the planet, not battle born. I'd put him in the same age bracket as my father, in his mid-sixties.

He took a seat in the other chair. Our knees were nearly touching. He took a deep, assessing breath. "You are a very driven individual," Genteel commented. I wasn't sure if it was meant as a compliment or an accusation. He leaned forward, elbows on knees, fingers twined, index fingers steepled. His eyes were soulless pits that held no warmth. "Because I respect your...tenacity, I'm going to issue you this single warning to step away from your investigation into the Lannisters' deaths. There are things in play here that are much larger than the deaths of two civilians."

He said it so nonchalantly, "the deaths of two civilians," like he was commenting on yesterday's weather.

"Why did you kill them?"

"Alas, Ms. Harris, I never met the two. It is an unfortunate turn of events, however. I should like to have made their acquaintance before whomever arrived at their door before me." I eyed him suspiciously. He was telling the truth. He'd never met either of them. "As I said, Ms. Harris, there are things in play that are beyond any of this." He gestured at everything around us. "Go on about your life. Get married, raise a family. Just cease your investigation."

Yeah, that probably sounded like sage advice from his point of view. But when had I ever listened to anything other than my own gut? He may not have known the specific individual who'd ended the Lannisters' lives, but he knew who they were connected to. I wasn't ready to let things go.

"A guy like you doesn't have unknown adversaries."

That earned me a gracious nod. "I do suspect a foreign operative. An enemy of the state."

"Terrorist?"

"Perhaps."

"What do they want?"

Genteel narrowed his eyes. "Power." Something washed over his face when he said that. It was there, then gone just as quickly. Had I just caught a glimpse of humanity's greatest flaw, an ego out of control and drunk with desire? It sent an involuntary shiver down my spine.

We'd left the highway. Our speed decreased, and we began stopping intermittently. Stop signs. That meant we were in a residential area. There was the *tat-tat-tat* of heavy machinery breaking up concrete and the throaty rumble of diesel engines. Residential near road construction. The truck took a sharp right, bumped up over the lip of a curb, and drove several more feet before stopping. The knife moved away from my skull, leaving a tiny painful indention. The back door slid up halfway.

Genteel broke the silence. "Give me your word, Ms. Harris. Give me your word that you will cease and desist your actions in regard to the Lannisters. Their deaths are inconsequential to the bigger picture. Think of them as having made the ultimate sacrifice in keeping our nation secure."

"Cease and desist. Do you have a court order for that?" If their deaths were so trivial, why was he still in Portland making threats?

I didn't even see him nod or give any signal, but the knife was back, making its point in my skull. I didn't cry out when it penetrated several layers of flesh. I wouldn't give Genteel the satisfaction of reacting to the thin streak of blood that ran down my neck.

"If I think you've betrayed me, I will wipe everyone dear to you from the face of the planet." Nothing about his threat felt empty. "I will begin with Detective Wickowski. Then your deputy friend. Next I'll move on to your family back east. Am I making myself clear?"

"Go fuck yourself," I said loudly enough to be heard over the pounding noise outside.

The air grew tense. Genteel gave a good-natured chuckle. Nothing had ever sounded so ominous. Nobody said anything. The knife eased up. Genteel flicked his eyes toward the door, and I was roughly unseated and dragged out by my elbow. My abductor forced me to the ground on my knees, and I braced for whatever came next. Turned out there was no real way to brace against a pistol-whipping that you didn't see coming. Everything went black for a long second, and I was unable to break my forward fall. I crumpled and landed hard on my shoulder. My face scuffed concrete that smelled like piss and old garbage, a typical back alley. Before I could rally, a boot caught me square to the stomach and had me dry heaving and gasping for air. Still I struggled to get my feet under me. Something hard struck the side of my head from behind, knocking me off balance again.

"Stay down," instructed Genteel, now standing in the alley beside me. His shoes were Italian leather and buffed to a shine. "Stay down, Ms. Harris, or God help you."

His divine threat made little impression on me. God and I had tried and failed at a relationship when I was a kid. I blamed Him for what happened to Cindy as much as I blamed myself. My parents had dragged my sister and me to church every Sunday morning. It wasn't that they were devout, but they were afraid of what others might think of them if they didn't make the requisite appearance. It hadn't escaped my notice how my parents drove past the homeless and turned a blind eye and deaf ear to ignore panhandlers asking for change on the sidewalk outside the church doors. It seemed odd behavior when we were essentially going inside to learn how to live more like Jesus.

The zip ties were cut before one last kick to my stomach for good measure. "Stay down," someone growled, and something heavy hit the ground beside me. I heard the truck door being rolled back down. With a chirp of tires on asphalt, they sped away.

Nausea rolled through like a tide. I breathed through it until it passed. My head throbbed. I forced my eyes to focus. They'd dumped me on a narrow dirty alley between two aged apartment buildings. They'd left me with my phone and HK. Insult to injury, I'd been whipped by my own gun. It took two attempts, but I finally picked myself up from the ground.

I felt like a stranger in a strange body. I ached. My face hurt. I was nauseous. My head felt likely to explode with each heartbeat. Multiple priorities presented themselves: Get home. Get help. Protect Mole. Find the bastards and make them pay. I didn't say they were all rational.

I stumbled my way out of the alley amid questioning stares from road workers. The side street led out to the main thoroughfare. They'd dumped me on Sandy Boulevard on the northeast side of town. I was technically within walking distance of home if I were in the condition to do so. I called an Uber and was told it would be at least a half hour wait, so I swallowed my pride and dialed Quinn.

"You're where?" he asked doubtfully.

I was in no mood to repeat myself. "Just come get me. Please," I added, figuring that might get his attention. He told me to hold tight. He was on his way.

I slumped on the sidewalk against a concrete light post to wait for my rescuer. Quinn. I wish I could claim plain, pedestrian commitment phobia where he was concerned. The intricacies of male/female relations were confusing to me. One-night stands made complete sense. Then I'd met a man, an artist, and we'd begun to hang out. Nothing about Vin had made sense to me, but I'd found myself inexplicably drawn to his gentleness, his sensitivity. Vin was a painter and poet who possessed a peaceful, Zen-like quality that was a comfortable balance to my fire. And he wasn't ugly. Or boring or boorish or any number of other turnoffs that often presented themselves in men. I hadn't even realized it was happening, that I had fallen in love. When realization reared its head, it was the beginning of the end. Lovers become liabilities. Now Quinn was twanging those same strings.

But Quinn is a cop. He knows the life. We share the same dangers, live the same risks. Maybe he's safe. Jesus—was my inner voice on Team Quinn now? I had to assume it was, for the sake of personal growth through vulnerability. Sneaky bitch. That seemed terribly dangerous. There was a lot of trauma and drama locked away in there. Compartmentalization doesn't even come close to describing my internal process. Most people have a metaphorical box in which they can put their feelings or experiences, and they place that box on a shelf in the back of their mind to be forgotten. I didn't have a metaphorical box, but I did keep a mental scorecard.

I sat on the warm concrete with my knees drawn up, my head resting on my arms, shielding my eyes from the bright glare of daytime. My body had begun aching in delayed reaction. I closed my eyes against it and fought to stay present, in the now, as Aunt

Zelda had tried to teach me. Every bad thing that had happened to me in life was in the past. There was no such thing as the past, it no longer existed—there was only now.

A car stopped at the curb in front of me. Quinn. He was driving his own car. Red and blue lights mounted in the back window and front grille. Traffic flowed around him. He got out to crouch at my knees. I looked up and heard his breath catch.

"Who did this to you?" he asked as he gently helped me to my feet.

"I don't know" was all I could muster for an explanation. It wasn't a lie, and I would have elaborated if vomit hadn't risen up the back of my throat. I leaned forward and spit it into the roadside gutter. Quinn took my hand and laid a comforting arm around my shoulders until I was ready to stand.

When the threat of being sick passed, I let Quinn guide me into the passenger seat. When he got back behind the wheel, he goosed his siren and whipped a U-turn in the middle of Sandy Boulevard.

"I'm taking you straight to the ER," he announced. He wouldn't hear my resistance. "This isn't up for debate, Harris. I can't work with someone who I can't trust not to pass out from a concussion," he said plainly.

I acquiesced because I didn't have any fight in me at that moment.

CHAPTER NINE

DON, A MIDDLE-AGED TRAUMA NURSE, MET US AS SOON AS WE cleared the sliding doors of Legacy Emanuel Medical Center in North Portland. I was no stranger to the emergency room. Don sat me in a chair and wheeled me into triage where he took my vitals, gingerly prodded my stomach and ribs, and shone a light in my eyes. He had the bedside manner of a saint and the soothing voice of a grandfather. He cleaned the crusted blood from my face, dabbed some ointment, and softly applied a butterfly bandage across the open cut on my cheek. I didn't argue against x-rays. I didn't make a fuss when the doctor gave me something to relieve my pain. My cooperation ended when he began the admittance process. Quinn was more of an obstacle between me and my own bed than the doctor was. But I was able to wear down even him with my obstinance.

By the time Quinn helped me through my front door, my pain levels had simmered along with my rage, which was at a semi tolerable smolder. Still dangerous. The possibility of explosion still very real. Quinn drew all the blinds, darkening the loft against the bright, overcast day. Two ibuprofen and a couple shots of whisky was my usual go-to healing method. Quinn wouldn't let me drown my pain in drink. Asshole.

He sat with me, refusing to let me fall asleep, rejecting my opinion that I was fine. He had me hold an icepack to my cheek. When I told him some street tacos from a specific eatery downtown would make me feel a lot better, he reached for his car keys. I wasn't really hungry. I just needed space. Dirty pool, I knew it, but I did what I needed to do when I needed to do it. That's something everyone should know about me by now.

I shook another pain pill from the hospital pharmacy into my hand and chased it with a swig straight from the bottle. The whisky made my belly warm. I was just getting comfortable back on the couch when a sudden succession of heavy knocks fell on my front door. I knew who it was, even though he'd forgotten to use his signature knock. Infiltrators didn't knock—they stormed in.

Mole entered when I hollered the door was open. His wall-eyed expression told me he was about to deliver some news. "Where have you been?" he asked, hands animatedly emphasizing his concern. "I've been blowing up your pho—" Mole stopped midsentence to gape at the condition of my face. I could feel the puffiness around my eyes, the shiner growing on my cheek. "Jesus, Sam, again?" he muttered, more to himself than to me.

"Did you leave a message?" I asked.

"No."

"If you didn't leave a message, I didn't miss a call."

Mole stared at me, still wide-eyed. "That's the most ridiculous logic I've ever heard," he said plainly, "yet annoyingly accurate." He was quiet for a short moment and then said, "What happened?"

"There was a disagreement" was all I confessed.

Mole raised his brows. "Are they still alive?" It was a legitimate question.

I didn't have an answer for that. They were alive. For now. The question behind the question was, how and when would that change? I gritted my teeth as I adjusted my posture. "What's going on with you?"

Mole winced as he looked me in the eye. "Maybe now isn't the best time," he offered.

It wasn't like Mole to get so excited over something that could be easily put off. "What is it?" I urged.

He took half a breath to order his words. "You're under attack." He dropped his announcement like a bomb. "Hackers are trying to get into your accounts, but so far I've been able to deflect them. Your online presence, not that you had much of one, has all been erased. They've taken down anything pertaining to Harris Securities. Their bots are trying to gain access to your cloud..."

My stare might have been blank, but that smolder that had been there earlier, the one that I'd worked to tamp down, flared up with a vengeance. I took the next three minutes to bring Mole up to speed with my morning. Up to and including my visit to the emergency room.

"They could have killed you," Mole whispered.

I reached out and took his hand to comfort him. "But they didn't, and cracked ribs heal, broken skin knits back together." I gave his hand a squeeze. He squeezed back.

"Please tell me you had your phone on you at least?"

I fished the cell out from my pocket. "Yeah I did. Why?"

The grin that lit up Mole's face was endearing. The chuckle that followed was downright disturbing. "They think they can come at my family and get away with it," he swore under his breath. "Let's find out who you are."

Mole swiped screens and pressed buttons on my smartphone. He disappeared out into the hall then returned with a wire connector and what looked like a heavily modified laptop computer. One end of the wire went into a port on my phone, the other end into the laptop. My head always swam when Mole worked his hacker magic. It was a language I didn't speak. I was fluent in search engines, but this was a whole other ball game I left to Mole.

He began thumb-scrolling through my phone. "I'm accessing the cellular data on your phone to get your geographic location history. Then I'll use this GPS data and load it into Google Maps, using your browser's geolocation feature along with the Maps

JavaScript API." As if any of that made sense to me. He took a seat on the edge of the couch. "Now all I have to do is see what cell phones were near your phone."

I watched over his shoulder as he worked his craft. "Burner phones?"

Mole nodded. "Most likely." A burner phone worked by forwarding calls through it to your main cell number. So the person you're calling only sees the burner number on their caller ID, a number which can't be easily traced back to your real number. "However, these numbers can be traced to the store that sold the device. Retailers have to keep a log of phones sold, but to who is completely anonymous."

"So how does that help me?"

"Oh, ye of little faith." Mole was right. If he couldn't track these guys down, they couldn't be traced. "I'm going to find these guys, Sammy, but it might take a minute."

That was fine by me. I really wanted to find these assholes. Mole retreated to his own place to continue working his angle.

I was still in my dirty, blood-stained clothes. I changed into a pair of loose-fitting sweatpants and a plain white t-shirt. I helped myself to another swig from the bottle then retreated to my bedroom, where I sprawled on the bed and closed my eyes against the yarn web of the Lannisters' reconstructed life that still clung to my walls. I didn't bother securing my front door against possible infiltration or attack. They'd already impressed their opinion, made their demands. Now they would step back and see if their demands were met. Genteel said he'd read my FBI jacket. Then he should have known he was wasting his breath. While they waited, I was plotting their destruction.

"Sam?" Quinn called from the doorway when he returned with a bag from the taqueria.

I called out from my room, my tone low and guttural, "Now's not a good time."

He completely ignored my hostility and stepped into my room. I was a balled-up mess of foul mood. Being cyberattacked was salt to my physical wounds. I gave a sharp nod toward the door, hoping Quinn might take the hint. He did the exact opposite. He closed the door and then made matters worse by coming at me with the wide arms of an approaching hug. I was *not* a hugger. I did have a penchant for throat punches though.

My energetic shade found its mark. Or maybe it was the daggers-and-danger vibe emanating from my eyes. Quinn brought himself up short. His hands went to his hips in a defensive posture. Or maybe just closer to the gun under his jacket. "Stand down, Harris," he said. "We're all friends here." He took a tentative step forward, his arms down at his sides again. "We can talk about whatever it is, whatever's happened since I left to get food." He shook the bag like he was trying to distract an attacking dog.

My disposition was far too volatile for words. Quinn was the last person I needed or wanted to see at that moment. I was in a dangerous headspace. Being abducted off the street in broad daylight and the violation of my personal life weren't things I thought I'd ever allow to happen to me. They happened to other people. But it had happened to me because I wasn't being vigilant. My thoughts had been preoccupied in places they had no business being. Thoughts I knew better than to let get a foothold. I was taken, and the bastards had threatened my friends. Nobody got to survive that.

"Sam," Quinn's voice was a gentle whisper, "I know you come from a dark place. Shit like that doesn't just go away. It eats at you until there's nothing left but a dried husk where you used to be. It might not be me, and I'm totally okay with that, but you've got to talk to someone." He wasn't talking about what had happened to me that morning. He was going deeper into my past, triggering all those bells and whistles.

I slid my legs off the bed but stayed sitting. "What do you think you know?" I challenged, my eyes narrow slits, a snarl curling my lip.

"I know you were a good agent—a great one—but something scared you away."

"Nothing *scared me away*." My voice was icy and dangerous.

"You behave like a traumatized victim. If you don't deal with the trauma, it's going to keep coming up and tainting everything you—"

Quinn was too close to my most sensitive subjects. "Get out." My voice was barely above a murmur. "Get out," I repeated a little louder.

"Sam—"

"Get out!" When I swung back around, the gun from under my pillow was in my hand and leveled at the middle of Quinn's face. He responded with wide-eyed shock that quickly closed itself down into a sneer that was more betrayal and hurt feelings than anger. "You shouldn't have done that."

We stood there, unmoving, that fateful moment locked in time to forever be etched into the memory of the room. I moved first by unchambering the bullet and resetting the safety before dropping it on the bed. Too little, too late. Quinn turned and slammed the door behind him when he stormed out. No, I shouldn't have done that, but it was what happened in that moment, and I couldn't take it back.

By the time I swallowed my pride and stepped into the hall, Quinn was gone. The door to the stairwell was just finishing its slow fall closed, finding home with a solid *clang*.

Mole's door shot open. "What's with the slamming doors?" Then he caught what must have been a completely foreign expression on my face, a mixture of concern and anger mixed with something a little softer that emanated from the heart. "You all right?" he asked. My moods had a way of telegraphing themselves. "You want to come in for a minute?"

I nodded and followed him silently through his door. I eased aside the heavy tarpaulin covering the tall casement window to try and catch a glance outside. The thick canvas, and reflective sheeting, were meant to shield from both the heat of the direct sun and prying eyes, whether physical or digital. Mole's security was as layered as an onion. With a heavy sigh, I took a seat on his couch and stared at the blank wall.

Mole paced, as he often did, and waited for me to tell my tale. Yet another thing I appreciated about our working relationship: he never rushed me for the details. He knew I'd bring him up to speed with the pertinent information when I was ready. Or, if he knew I wasn't in a talkative mood, he knew to just hold silent space.

I had no idea how long I stayed like that, staring blankly at the wall while the wheels of destruction turned in my head. A plan was taking shape, one that I wouldn't be talked out of regardless of how futile it might seem. Nobody threatened those closest to me and got to continue with their life uninterrupted.

Mole read my intentions perfectly, as if I'd typed them across my forehead. "You're going after those guys, aren't you?" His voice carried an edge.

If they weren't responsible for the Lannisters' murders, then why were they still in Portland? Bauer had claimed their deaths were inconsequential to the bigger picture. I wanted a glimpse at that picture. "No," I answered calmly. Too calmly. "I'm not going after them. I'm going to pay a visit to their families. Let them know I can get to their loved ones too." *Tit for tat*, but I didn't say that out loud.

"That's cold, Harris."

It was no big secret that I suffered from situational ethics. It was something I'd always known about myself. But my intentions were always on the up-and-up, always for the good. Life wasn't black and white. It wasn't simply light versus dark, good versus evil. Reality was a multihued rainbow.

I stood up and began to pace the space between the couch and the blocked window. "I don't need your opinion, Mole. Or your blessing. But I do need the information from that phone." I pointed to my cell still sitting on his desk.

"Maybe you should take a seat and let me call Wickowski. You guys can figure out what to do together."

Mole and I both knew I wasn't going to be bringing anybody in on this issue. Fate had been written in granite the moment they took me from the sidewalk and made threats against the people I loved. Beds had been made. Like graves. They just needed to be filled. "Mole." I let his name hang in the air. It sounded like a threat.

"Sammy." He returned the sentiment.

I let my gaze slip from annoyed stare to that place I go when I'm face-to-face with a breathing target. My mouth became a thin, hard line, my eyes narrowed slits. The masseter muscles flexed as I clenched and unclenched my jaw. I could feel my pulse slowing with my steady, shallow breath. If I were on the range, I'd squeeze the trigger on that exhale. Mole and I locked ourselves in an unflinching, unblinking stare.

"Fine," he blurted and turned toward his desk. He tapped a few keys on the computer keyboard. The printer beside the monitor hummed to life to spit out a single sheet of paper.

"What's this?" I asked as I took the slip of paper from his hand.

"That's the number of at least one of the men that threatened you."

"There were three of them. Well two actually, and the driver."

Mole took a deep breath as his brain dumbed itself down to speak Analog-for-Sam, a form of the English language that is completely devoid of any technology. "I explained the burner and the GPS tracking, et al.? I was able to track those burner numbers to their point of purchase, a big-box store outside of Baltimore. The store was set in one of those strip mall arrangements, multiple facilities, from auto parts to boutique clothing, at the edge of a residential neighborhood. The strip mall's surrounded in front and on both sides by a large parking lot with numerous access points. Using traffic cams, doorbell cams, and individual store security, I was able to construct a log of vehicles as they entered the lot and when they exited it. I wasn't able to account for walk-ons, but I didn't think that was going to matter. Once I had a time stamp of the phones' sale and compared it to the time stamps from the various videos, I was able to track the registered owner of each plate number that fit the time frame. From there it was easy to access government records until I came up with a name and a photo." He spun the photo that had just come off the printer so that it faced me. "Now, this is where things get tricky, so don't go off all cocky and guns blazing. Of the plates I pulled, this guy is the only one with a deep military background, and he's built like a brick shithouse. He's Niles MacKinnon, forty-three, lives with his wife, seventeen-year-old daughter, and fifteen-year-old son in Roanoke, Virginia. He was honorably discharged from the Marines less than twenty-four months ago. So I focused on him."

"You have a home address?" I asked. Niles sounded like he fit the bill for my abductor.

Mole snapped his wrist. Another piece of paper was in his hand on which was scrawled a Roanoke residential location. I plucked it from his grasp and committed the Union Hill address to memory.

"Want me to call Wickowski?" he finally ventured after several long, silent minutes. "Maybe the other boy-toy-with-a-badge?"

I shook my head, but it was the murderous darts from my eyes that had him halting that line of inquiry.

Mole was quiet for a long moment. Then he posed the obvious. "You're going to do the exact opposite of what you were told, aren't you?" When I didn't answer, he added, "Blink once for yes and twice for no."

A slow, sadistic grin spread out over the lower half of my face like a comic book villain instead. I didn't blink. I didn't need to.

"Oh, shit," Mole muttered under his breath.

I left for my own place with Mole peppering my back with questions: "What are you going to do? You sure I shouldn't call Wickowski?" There were more inquiries, but they bounced off the closed door, never to be answered. I didn't even know what I was going to do. Some inner drive seemed to have taken control of my feet and hands and had me packing a bug out kit, in which went a clean set of clothes and tactical gear—guns, knives, ammo. Flying wasn't an option with the way I pack, so it was going to be a cross-country road trip to Virginia.

I zipped a laser scope into a pocket of my bag and couldn't help but note how my hands were shaking. I took a deep breath and let it out slowly through my nose. That fury burned a hole in my soul. It'd been there for as long as I could remember, even before what happened to Cindy. I didn't know where it came from, what its origin story was, but it was an omnipotent constant that everything in my life lensed through. I'd never been able to tame it; I barely had a handle on it at all. Sometimes the power of my own rage scared me. It sat, coiled around my belly like a serpent, waiting. Always waiting, anticipating the next strike. I didn't trust myself when I was triggered. The abduction when I was twelve only served to give it a place to live, a reason for being. Quinn hadn't been wrong. That serpent was going to one day devour me. Or maybe it was already in process. My personal ouroboros.

I took stock of my loft. The couch where Quinn and I had spent the night. The maze that was my bedroom. The walls plastered in the Lannisters' paper trail. *I'm going to find them, the ones who murdered you two*, I silently promised as I dismantled the wall and tapped the photos and reports into a tidy pile. I hinged a wide clip over the end of the paper stack and slipped it into my bag behind the guns. Inside my gun safe I also kept a slush fund of accessible cash. I stuffed both of the brown-banded stacks of fifties, ten grand in total, into my bag. I had no idea if or when Mole might recoup and secure my accounts that had been attacked. I needed to be able to move around and function without worrying about funds.

My Mercedes Geländewagen was parked under my building. I made a quick sweep of it for potential hazards like bombs or kill switches before scrambling in with my bag. I hadn't bothered to say good-bye to Mole. He knew what was up—or at least could mental a pretty accurate guess for what was about to happen. He *had* given me a bad guy's address. I figured I'd phone him a few states from now. I was going to have to reach out to Wickowski sooner than later, though. He didn't often take my extracurriculars-sans-backup very well. They left him moody and volatile. Maybe I'd call him from Virginia. Then again, maybe not.

I'd just pulled out from the parking lot beneath my building when my cell began to ring. My first inclination was to ignore it. I had no intention of furthering discussions with Quinn, I didn't want to talk to Wickowski, and Mole knew better than to attempt any sort of communications when I was in a mood. I was definitely in a mood. The phone stopped making noise when the call rolled over to voice mail. It chirped to alert me of the message.

I don't know why I looked, but I was glad I did. The call had come in from DoveLewis, the emergency vet where Doof was. Dr. Saunders was getting back to me. Doof was clear to come home, with some care instructions. I listened to the message one more time. Doof would need rest and to take it easy, and he had a prescription for pain medication, but he was ready to go home. I was going to be driving—plenty of time for rest and taking it easy in the back of the Geländewagen.

I made another stop at Fred Meyer where I purchased a thick dog bed that fit in the back when I collapsed the back seat. I also bought a twin-size fleece blanket, a bag of kibble, some dog treats, a spill-proof water bowl designed for travelling along with a collapsible food dish, a fuzzy squeaky toy shaped like a water buffalo, and some human snacks from the chip and jerky aisle. Oh, and a case of water and a twelve-pack of my favorite porter. I stripped the tags from the dog bed and laid it in the back. I threw the twin blanket over that to create a cozy travel bed for Doof and stashed both of our snacks on the passenger floorboard beside me.

DoveLewis's front door was locked when I arrived, and a sign had been printed and hung apologizing for the inconvenience. Patients were requested to phone the number listed. I visored a hand over my eyes and peered through the glass. I saw movement of shadow inside, so I knocked. I repeated the rapping several times before someone came to investigate. It was a woman I didn't recognize from the day before. She wasn't wearing the white coat of a doctor or the scrubs of a vet tech but a casual khaki pantsuit with gold strappy sandals. "Can I help you?" she mouthed through the closed door.

"I'm here for my dog," I said, "the big furry one recovering from a stabbing."

The woman flashed a personable smile as she held up a finger. *Hold on. I'll be back in a quick moment.* She disappeared around the corner from whence she'd approached. The waiting room's plastic molded chairs had been stacked and pushed to the far side of the room, probably so that the crime scene cleaners could do their job. The woman returned after a moment, the smile on her face a little less amiable than before. She seemed much more uptight when she unlocked the door. She held it open just enough for me to pass through before she closed and locked it again. "Doctor will be up in a moment," she said, keeping a distance between us like I was contagious.

I couldn't take a seat in the waiting room with the plastic chairs stacked against the wall, so I stood awkwardly in the center of the room and waited. The antiseptic smell mingled with the scent of industrial cleaner was fueling the headache that had parked itself behind my eyeballs.

I spun on my heel at the sound of a door opening behind me. Dr. Saunders stood in the doorway that separated the front office from the holding room where felines and canines were housed post recovery. He looked like he hadn't slept much since I'd last seen him. His bright eyes were dull and hollow. His professional attire was gone, replaced by blue jeans with ratty hems and holes in the knees and a faded flannel. He had the appearance of someone who'd been blindsided by life. I suppose that was an acceptable reaction when your business becomes a crime scene. I was responsible for that, and I knew it. Apologizing didn't seem like it would cut it. He was going to lose business over it, that was the nature of human reactions. Maybe Mole and I could figure out a way to somehow bolster his income. Off the books and unbeknownst to the doctor, of course.

"He's good to go?" I asked as pleasantly as I could without being fake. I knew the second the good doctor recognized me as the one who'd euthanized the bad guy by the way he came up short in his tracks and the color fell from his already ashen face. I held my hands up as a peaceful gesture—or at least to defuse the doctor's anxiety. "The big fuzz butt with the knife wound to the chest. He's mine." *He's mine.* It was still foreign on my tongue. Pets were something other people had.

The vet dug deep and found his cheerfulness, albeit slightly forced. "Doof is recovering better than I originally anticipated when he first arrived." Dr. Saunders stepped into the waiting room, hand extended. He shook mine. "Thank you for stopping those men," he said. "I don't know what we would have done if you hadn't been here." He gave my hand a squeeze before releasing it. His genuine thankfulness made me feel like a heel. He sincerely believed I'd just been a lady in the waiting room. He had no idea that *I* was the reason those guys stormed the place. If I hadn't arrived in his office, then neither would they. I kept my confession to myself.

"Doof. He's good to go?" I repeated.

The professional Dr. Saunders emerged again. "He is a little underweight, but he's parasite-free and hookworm negative. Do you know if he's current on his shots?"

I shrugged. "I have no idea. He found me in Forest Park." A spike of panic hit my heart—was there something wrong? "Is there something I should know?" I felt the catch in my throat when I asked the question. "He is going to be just fine though, right?"

Dr. Saunders put my mind at ease that Doof would make a full recovery. He gave me a quick rundown of dos and don'ts. The instructions hadn't been much different for Doof's stabbing than they'd been for me last time I visited the ER: no exertion, pain medication when needed. I was to keep an eye on the wound site for signs of infection. Keep him hydrated. Let pain be his guide as to what he was or wasn't able to do in the immediate days to come. I paid the bill, which wasn't insignificant, but worth every penny if it meant I got to walk out with Doof.

Dr. Saunders disappeared one more time but came back with Doof on a thin disposable leash. Gauze dressings crossed his barrel chest, which had been shaved for surgery. He smelled like disinfectant, antiseptic, and nerves. I squatted down and gave Doof a gentle hug. He gave me a weak tail wag and licked my hand, and my heart melted. I had a dog. Doof had a human.

With the doc's help, we lifted Doof into the back of the Geländewagen. I could have lifted him up and in by myself, and would be doing so until he was able to do it on his own, but I accepted the help. I thanked the doctor for everything, and he bid us safe travels. Doof turned in a circle until he found the right spot and gently lowered himself with a heavy sigh. His big expressive eyes turned up to me. I didn't speak dog—yet—but I was fairly sure he was either thanking me or sizing up whether I had what it took to care for us both.

I laid a hand on his head and gave him a scratch. "I'm gonna do my best," I said as my scratches moved under his chin. "I promise you nobody will ever be mean to you again." I moved my face closer to his. "If anyone tries to, I'll put a bullet between their eyes and kick their body into a ditch." I sealed my oath to Doof with a kiss on his nose. He reciprocated with a whine, nuzzle, and tail wag—the closest to leap/spin/happy bark he was going to get right then.

We turned the nose of the rig east and followed I-84 along the Columbia River Gorge until it veered south at Boardman, where I filled the tank and used the restroom. I found a shady park and eased Doof out for a bathroom break. The leash and collar were still in the rig. He had enough things to deal with. He didn't need to work around his new accessories. And it wasn't like he was in any condition to bolt and run. He finished his business and nudged my hand to let me know he was ready to go. I bent at the knees and lifted him back into the rig, one arm around his butt, the other around his chest.

We continued on to the Oregon–Idaho border just north-west of Boise. The terrain was flat farmland, apparently perfect for spud farming. Doof and I checked into a pet-friendly hotel in the farming community of Caldwell, just outside of the state capital, where I ordered delivery from a nearby bar and grill. It was steaks for the both of us, medium rare for myself, the other blue rare, or barely seared on either side, for Doof. I had to convince the woman taking the order that yes, I understood what blue rare meant, finally admitting it was for my dog. She called Doof spoiled. Seemed legit.

Twenty minutes later there was a knock on the hotel room door. I crept to the security peephole, HK in hand, as was my habit. A doughy-faced kid in bib overalls and a trucker hat advertising his employer arrived with food. I added a couple bottles of porter to the meal from my truck. Doof ate off a paper plate on the floor, and I ate out of a foam clamshell in the center of the bed.

While I showered, Doof watched the bathroom door from the vantage point of the bed. He'd seemed to know precisely where he wanted to sleep, and it hadn't been on the floor. He sat propped up on his elbows, ears perked, head cocking this way then that as he focused on every sound coming from the steamed glass box. He appeared to lose most of that pointed interest when I stepped from the shower with a towel wrapped around my torso, like he was more curious in my whereabouts and not being abandoned than he was concerned for me.

Of course I let Doof sleep on the bed alongside me. I knew by morning that that decision had, in his mind, been a permanent arrangement. I lifted him from the bed to go do his morning business. He wanted to be returned there when we came back to the room. He was letting me know he was now a bed dog. Lap dog might try to be next.

We were back on I-84 by midmorning after a short walk around the grassy field that bordered the hotel parking lot. We both got a chance to stretch our legs. I wasn't sure how long we'd be on the road that day. I wanted to reach our destination sooner rather than later, but Doof needed to take things a little slower.

The miles flew past the windows at seventy. The scenery was flat and grassy and boring, yet beautiful in its own lonely way. It was after two when we dropped down into Salt Lake City and grabbed some drive-through at a burger joint. I would have kept driving if I'd been by myself. Instead, we found a grassy park to eat in. Doof lapped water from his bowl, and I washed mine down with a couple of porters I kept on ice in a disposable foam cooler.

We needed to put distance between home and us. I needed to get to Virginia, but I couldn't push Doof that hard. The momentary thought occurred to me that I could park him in a boarding facility and retrieve him on the return trip. But I told myself I could never do that for fear of distressing him. He had obvious separation anxiety. That, and I was sort of growing attached to the guy. I was quickly becoming that person who preferred their dog's company to that of other humans.

After we ate and walked around in the sun beneath fluffy white clouds and blue sky, we continued on our way, tacking south on the 80 into Wyoming. We called the Cheyenne Best Western home that night. I lounged in a long, languid bath that I refreshed with hot water several times. Doof had pulled up some linoleum floor against the warmth of the tub and was snoring. The overhead lights were off, and I enjoyed the silent darkness. My thoughts drifted from Lannister, to the case, to Quinn, where I shut all thought down. I focused on my breath moving in and out across my nostrils. Then I focused on the rhythm of Doof's deep, steady slumber. I felt myself drift drowsily. It may have been the first time I'd truly relaxed, both mentally and physically, since becoming involved in the whole Lannister mess.

The jangling of my cellphone shattered my bliss. I could tell by the ringtone, a Latin instrumental of "Despacito," that it was Wickowski. I didn't want to talk to him just then. I didn't want to talk to anybody. But I knew putting Wickowski off was just going to make matters worse. I didn't get out of the tub; I let his call roll over to voice mail. I'd return his call later, after I was toweled and dressed.

"Harris," Wickowski answered on the second ring. It was like calling home and having your dad answer and you can tell from that single word, the way he says your name, that he's both worried and pissed.

"Yo," was all that came out.

By the long silence that stretched out between the phone lines, it was apparent neither of us were in talkative nor acquiescing moods. I could almost say this was becoming a norm between us. Wick plays good cop; I'm that annoying thorn in the good cop's ass who means well but at the end of the day plays by her own rules.

"I got a—"

"I don't want—"

"You go first," I said.

"I got a call from your neighbor friend, the weird one with the glasses." Wickowski and Mole rarely crossed paths. The former didn't even know the latter's real name. So I could only imagine the alarm that call raised on Wickowski's end. "He's a weaselly guy even to talk to on the phone. He makes me uneasy, like he knows something I don't." *You have no idea, Wick.* "He called me up and told me to be careful. I think the words he used were something like, 'proceed with extreme caution and assiduousness.' I had to look up what that even meant. Why couldn't he just say be careful? And careful about what? Was the little freak threatening me?"

"No, Wick, he wasn't threatening you." I found my voice. If Mole was threatening someone, they'd never even know it until after the fact and they had no credit score or there was a warrant out for their arrest in an inconvenient county two states over. "He was doing you a genuine solid. Shit's gone a little off-center. I'm not going to go into it, so don't ask. I'm taking care of it, but I can't be there watching your six, so you're going to have to take precautions to protect your own back until I get home. That's what he meant by extreme caution and assiduousness."

"Where are you?" I could tell by the dubious tone in Wickowski's voice that he wasn't sure he wanted to know the answer.

"I'm not in Portland" was all I gave him.

"Well then, maybe you can shed some light on Quinn for me. I got an interesting call from his office. He submitted for some personal time, then took off before the ink was dried on the request. Said he was following something case related but took his own rig."

"I'm not Quinn's keeper, Wick."

Another long silence stretched out between us. Wickowski was giving me space to open up, and I wanted nothing more than to close down the line of inquiry. "You'll keep me posted," he said. It wasn't a question. "And not just when your back is against the wall or you need an extraction. I mean you will keep me informed of your movements and actions."

"I don't work for you, Julio Wickowski." I'd never called Wick by his full name before, and I didn't like the way it tasted on my tongue—bitterly official with the sour tang of misplaced anger. Deep down, he was just concerned for my safety. He'd experienced my rogue nature before. I think it made him feel helpless when he couldn't protect me from myself. I'd never asked it of him, nor had I expected it. I am wholly capable of keeping myself alive, if not out of trouble. "That came out stronger than I meant it, sorry."

"No, it didn't, Harris. I've known you long enough and well enough to know you say precisely what you mean to." He wasn't angry or even upset. He was just being true. "I know you've got irons in your fire that you didn't invite. Quinn is a good guy. He's a good cop. Just be gentle with yourself about it all. We'll catch up when you call me next. Until then, stay safe and don't get dead." The line went quiet when he hung up.

I stared at the screen of the cell phone in my hand for a long moment after Wickowski was gone as if it were going to come alive. My fingers were dialing Mole before I even knew what I was going to say.

"What's up, chicken butt?" he answered. That was a new one. "Kill, maim, or otherwise destroy any thugsters yet?" Mole knew me so well.

"Did you tell anyone where I was going or give them any intel on my behalf?" I tried to keep my tone and word choice casual and nonconfrontational but wasn't sure how well it came off.

There was a heavy sigh on the other end of the line. It wasn't exasperated or impatient. I could imagine Mole settling down into his computer chair, the overstuffed one he'd had for far too long. When the seat's tweed upholstery became threadbare, I'd suggested rehoming the chair to Goodwill. When the stuffing started spilling out, I'd suggested the dump. He refused to give the thing up, insisting it was saturated in his "mental magic mojo." He'd likened his tattered chair to Samson and my suggestions of discard to Delilah.

"Rat you out and risk a pissed-off phone call in the middle of what is an otherwise pleasant evening from a woman who could make my life a living hell because she's the closest thing I have to family?" Mole countered. "Yeah, what of it? I'm worried about you. Where are you?"

I told him I was in Cheyenne, Wyoming. (No point in being evasive. I could be in an obscure location on the other side of the planet and he'd find me if he really wanted to.) We made idle chitchat. It was good to hear his voice. He asked after Doof. He inquired about my plans. Doof was fine. I wasn't yet sure. Yes, I'd be careful.

We hung up, and I stared at the phone, trying to talk myself out of the call I knew I was going to make.

Aunt Zelda picked up on the second ring. I wouldn't have been surprised if she had been crossing the floor to answer it before it even rang. She was a very grounded, in-tune, aware woman. Frighteningly so sometimes.

"My Darling Girl." That had been her pet name for me since I could remember. Even when I'm packing an arsenal. "You've been on my mind for several days now. I wanted to reach out but knew you would do so in your own time. Tell me your troubles."

Aunt Zelda was that person everyone deserved to have in their life. She was true and wise. Having chosen a lifetime of adventure and learning over the traditional family and career, she had a unique perspective on life. She was the living epitome of a free spirit. My father's younger sister, she had their great-great-grandmother's Irish red hair (something I'd thankfully escaped).

"I feel lost, Aunt Zel." The words poured out of me like water from a failed dam. She listened patiently and without interruption as I revisited the past regarding Cindy and the guilt that drove me. That segued into what I saw as a failed career with the FBI. Then I started explaining Quinn, and I found words difficult. I'd spent so much of my life driving away, or running away from, anything that made me feel vulnerable. Entanglements of the heart were at the top of that list. I'd made it a habit to cut out before things got serious. I told myself I did it to protect others.

"You've always been such a force of nature, my Darling Girl. Even before you were born, you were doing things your own way. You were nearly born breech; did you know that?" Aunt Zelda gave a good-hearted chuckle at sharing the family memory. "The doctor had a devil of a time turning you around, but you wouldn't have it. You flipped your butt back down and stayed there until you decided to go the right way. You had to do it your way, in your own time. In school you stood up for those who couldn't do it for themselves, even though it meant a bloodied nose or fat lip for your trouble." Aunt Zelda's sigh was full of love and warmth—and safety. "You are a warrior, my Darling Girl. Your love for life, and those in yours, is bigger than you feel you can handle. Love makes people messy, isn't that what you've always said? What if Quinn is strong enough to survive even you?"

"What if I let him in and he's not?"

"I can't tell you what to do, my Darling Girl, but I can offer you one bit of advice I received from a very dear friend, Ram Dass, who used to say, 'Zelda—be here now.' He meant to be present.

Be here, now. My Darling Girl, everything you've explained to me has happened in the past, or might in the future. Neither of those scenarios exist, right here, right now. They only happen in memory or thought. Be here, now."

"But—"

"There are no buts, Samantha. There is only now, this moment. Life is a collection of nows. There is nothing else."

Aunt Zelda made a kind of sense that I couldn't explain, could only feel that it was true, if that made any sense at all. When I put her teachings into practice by closing my eyes and turning my focus outward, to the scent and the sounds of the room, truth was overwhelming. The only thing attacking me was my own mind, my thoughts and emotions—none of which were tangible. A foreign sensation of peace washed over me. It was like standing in a blank room all alone. My focus shifted from outside to the inner being of *me*. I saw myself as a speck inside that lonely, blank room and understood at an existential level that that was all that existed. The realization terrified me. It didn't make me responsible for everything in my life; it made me realize I was only responsible for my reactions to life. What the hell do I do with that?

CHAPTER TEN

Doof and I were up before daybreak. I wanted to get as close to our destination that day as possible. An uneasy feeling greeted me as soon as I threw my legs over the side of the bed. Since my talk with Aunt Zelda the night before, I had been fighting against allowing my thoughts to enter into the mire of my own drama.

Quinn was close. God dammit. I couldn't explain it then and still can't, but I felt his presence nearby. How the hell had he found me? I mean, it wasn't as if I was running from him, but I also wasn't leaving a digital trail. All my transactions had been in cash. I'd been using false identifications supplied to me by Mole a few months back when he'd been experimenting with his technique in making them. I wasn't sure if it was a job he'd been hired to do or if he was exploring the darker side of his own curiosity. Never thought to ask him for clarification, and he hadn't seen fit to supply one. *Plausible deniability* was my favorite phrase.

So how was Quinn tracking me?

He could be doing it electronically. I turned to my phone, stripping off the protective OtterBox shell to access the phone's battery compartment and popped the battery out. That was the only way to sever a connection if there was one. Not even I knew how to track through a phone. That was Mole-level activity and something I doubted Quinn had access to. I snapped the phone's cover back on and thought about it.

Leaving Doof locked in the room with the promise of immediate return, I went back out to my rig and used my phone's flashlight to examine the Geländewagen's undercarriage. I wasn't looking for an incendiary device but something smaller. I found a round transmitter the size of a Communion wafer with a thin wire protruding from it affixed to the surface of the rig's frame near the pumpkin, the big round metal part where the gears mesh together and make the wheels turn, in the rear axle. Another wave of volatile emotion washed over me. It felt like betrayal and violation.

I ripped the transmitter from the pumpkin and used my light to peruse the parking lot's license plates. I found the vehicle with the farthest zip code, Manitoba, and wedged the transmitter in its grille. We'd see how far Quinn got before he realized he was chasing his tail. Then I returned to the room to collect my bag and Doof.

After a quick drive-through for a breakfast burrito that I shared with Doof, I set the cruise control and settled back with SiriusXM tuned to an '80s station. I would later regret my generosity. Doof's guts began rumbling. Then his gas hit. Dog farts filled the cab, forcing me to keep the windows down across most of Nebraska.

I heard a wise man once claim, "There's no such thing as the middle of Nebraska; you're either in it, or you're not." I didn't really understand what he'd meant until I was driving across the state. It was just one long, flat, barren stretch that went on, and on, and on until Lincoln. We took a well-deserved break at a rest area off I-70 where Doof showed interest in chasing ground squirrels and I had to intervene, putting the kibosh on his play plan. Doctor's orders. We took a long, languid walk along a dirt trail that ran beside the fence line of a nearby farm. The sun was lowering as the afternoon waned but was still warm against my back.

"Have another couple of hours of travel in you, buddy?" I asked Doof with a scratch behind the ears when we were loaded back up in the Geländewagen. I let him ride shotgun. He wagged his tail and settled his head in my lap with a satisfied sigh. I kept scratching his favorite spot behind the ears as we continued down the highway. With nightfall came a drop of temperature. We checked into the Best Western just outside of St. Louis, Missouri. It'd been a twelve-hour driving day. Personally, I would have pushed on until I arrived in Virginia, but I had Doof to think about. For the first time in my life, it wasn't all about me.

The room was a carbon copy of the one we'd stayed at in Cheyenne, with its contrasting two-toned walls and geometric-patterned, low-pile carpeting. Even the nondescript abstract print was the same mess of primary colors. We settled in with an armful of snacks from the downstairs lobby. I made a soft hill of pillows to lean back against on the bed. Doof occupied the corner end of the mattress. He appreciated the cookie bites, but he wanted nothing to do with the nacho-cheese flavored tortilla chips. I poured a bottle of Evian into his water bowl in lieu of the chlorinated tap water. We'd watched several episodes of *Ancient Aliens* on the History channel when there came an unexpected knock on our room door.

On a normal day I didn't do unexpected well. After the last twenty-four hours, I really did unexpected poorly. Reactionarily. My HK was in my hand, bullet chambered, safety off, when my feet touched the floor. I eased up to the door's security peephole, mindful of the amount of shadow I was casting beneath the door. I kept my gasp silently inward when I saw Quinn standing in the hall. He didn't appear wholly piss and venom, but he didn't look like sunshine either.

I froze and held my breath. *Shit!* Engagement with anyone was the last thing I was looking for. A face-to-face with Quinn, after I'd pulled a gun on him at our last one, wasn't even in the realm of anything I wanted to undertake. If I ignored him, he'd go away, right? I shot a look at Doof, one that was meant to express, *Stay quiet, bestest boy!* But he read my body language as wanting to play, and he gave a series of excited, deep-throated barks that gave us both away. I closed my eyes as I died a little inside.

"It seems a little ridiculous to pretend you're not in there, Harris." Yep, he sounded pissy. And there was an authoritative tone that frankly I didn't like, but that didn't give me any impetus to move. I could hear him outside the door. Still didn't move.

Our silent standoff went on like that for several more minutes until I finally heard him move away from my door. I eased back up to the peephole with its wide lens. The hallway was vacant. I double-checked the lock, rotated the security bracket—an L-shaped piece of thick steel that prevented the door from being forced open—into place, and resumed my lounging on the bed with Doof. I kept the HK on the bed beside me.

Like the room we'd stayed at in Cheyenne, this one also had a side door in the wall that separated the two adjoining rooms. An odd metallic scratching at the door attached to ours got Doof's and my attention. *Son of a bitch!* Someone was picking their way through the lock on the door that opened into my room! Doof started up a protective ruckus the moment my hand was back on the HK. He felt good enough to launch himself off the bed when the door cracked open.

Quinn stepped inside. He pulled his firearm against the animal, just as his training had taught him.

"No, Doof!" I hollered and scurried after him. He was all bark, teeth, and flying spit when I threw protective arms around his neck and shielded him with my body. "Put the gun down, Quinn. You're making yourself a threat."

Quinn holstered his firearm, but he didn't back away. Doof slid his lips back over his bared teeth, but he didn't back away either. Instead, he sat and squared up, like a fighter about to enter the ring. Quinn eyed him suspiciously. Boys and their silent pissing matches.

"I'm going to go sit over on the edge of that bed," I hooked a thumb over my shoulder. "Quinn, you can go, or you can take a seat there on the carpet where you're standing. Doof, come over here." I patted the bed beside me. He made no move, as if he'd not heard me. "Doof, come." I patted the pillowtop beside me again. When he stood up to obey, he'd flexed all his hair follicles to retain his maximum-bulk appearance. He looked about the size of a husky twelve-year-old kid on all fours. With really, really big canines. Reluctantly, and with one last parting glance at Quinn, Doof jumped up beside me on the bed. He turned once, twice, then settled down with his back purposefully toward Quinn as if dismissing his existence.

"First off," I broke the silence that filled the room, "how the hell did you track me down again, and what are you doing here?" My tone was surprisingly more conversational than either Quinn or I expected.

"I knew when you pulled your gun on me back in Portland that you weren't completely rational. You lead with a certain rogue reputation, Harris. My gut told me you'd make a move against your aggressors, and it was going to be as belligerently reckless as how you do everything else."

"You've been behind me this whole time, haven't you?" Again, I would beat myself up later for having dragged a tail across the continent without noticing because my thoughts had been preoc-cupied. I saw a trend there, the common denominator being Quinn.

"I watched you tag that truck from Manitoba. I was across the street in the Denny's parking lot. I'd only rolled in there a couple of hours before you came out. You had some serious bed hair." Quinn's good nature was maddening.

"Shouldn't you be out stalking the Lannisters' killers instead of the woman who told you no?" I wanted him to get defensive. I wanted to start a fight. I needed to hit something. Doof sensed the underlying current of my mood and gave a guttural growl just to remind everyone what the stakes were.

"It's no wonder the FBI turned you loose." It was as if Quinn was aware of my current disposition and wanted to exploit it to see what I'd do. "The Feds did themselves, and everyone else around you, a huge favor. Probably saved a life or two, but they couldn't save them all, could they?"

My heart stopped, then began again in double time, but I let none of that play across my face. "You're cute, Quinn, when you think you've got things figured out, have all the answers, and then try to weaponize it against me. The bureau didn't cut me loose. My parting words were in plain English the last time I was in the Hoover Building: 'I fucking quit.' So have facts, not stories, when you want to use something about me to beat me up." I suspected that fight I was itching for was about to happen. Inevitable.

Quinn shrugged. "I have you figured out, Harris. You're the most dangerous thing in any room, yet you've never outgrown the trauma you suffered as a kid. Now it's affecting your ability to do your job."

"What the hell are you talking about? There's nothing in my life that hinders my ability to perform any task, be it a job or otherwise." I could feel the floodgates of rage losing their hold. Failure was imminent.

Quinn narrowed his eyes, a preemptive reaction to what he was about to say. "Have you found your friend's killer yet?"

That was as low a blow as Quinn could have delivered. My response to his callousness surprised me. I had nothing to throw back at him. Was it the shock of having Cindy brought up in an altercation that no one had any business bringing her into? Quinn had seen a weapon and lobbed it for the sole purpose of causing pain. Or maybe he was using it to wake me up. I tracked down other people's murderers—all of them strangers to me—but I'd yet to find the one killer that meant the most. How many times had I promised her memory I wouldn't give up?

But I had.

Knowing he'd taken things too far, Quinn retreated back to his room and closed the door behind him. I shot up and closed my side, locked it, and wedged the desk chair from beside the phone under the doorknob like they did in the movies. What I really wanted to do was load up Doof and get back on the road. I looked at the giant floof ball laying on the bed, protectively observing my every move. He was panting hard. It was a cool sixty-five in the room. It was anxious panting. I wanted to take my attitude and get back on the road. Doof didn't need any more excitement that evening. I wanted to leave. He needed to rest. *It's not always about me.*

Doof slept on the bed all night. His bulk was a comforting warmth at my back. His dog dreams woke me up with his throat barks and twitches. I patted him reassuringly on the haunches to settle him. In the wee hours before dawn, he whined at the door for a potty walk. I scoped out the parking lot. Quinn's personal vehicle, a Dodge Challenger with a custom matte black paint job and wide tires with matte rims, was parked beside my Geländewagen. I directed Doof over and suggested he pee on Quinn's tires. Like the bestest dog he was, he obliged.

I'd had the forethought upon check-in to order room service for breakfast from the hotel's in-house café. A platter of bacon and toast and a carafe of coffee arrived with a polite wake-up knock just after six. I convinced Doof everything was fine and that he could stand down before I opened the door on the young kid with the tray. I tipped the kid twenty dollars when Doof found it necessary to size him up via a nose stuffed into his crotch with a resulting squeak from said kid. Doof needed as much social training as I did.

There were no sounds from the adjoining room. I peeled the window covering aside and took stock of the parking lot below. Quinn's muscle car was still parked beside my rig. The thought of a quick sneak-away crossed my mind, but only momentarily. He'd track me again. Maybe I was my own foregone conclusion. The one who detested expectedness had become predictable. I supposed there were worse things.

I gave the plate of bacon to Doof and downed the toast and coffee myself. Dressed in the same clothes I'd worn the day before, my bag slung over my shoulder, I left the room key on the counter beside the television.

I pummeled Quinn's room door. "I'm leaving," I said. "Do not follow."

I knew Quinn would ignore my demand—hell, it's what I'd do. To buy myself some time, I used my tactical knife to impale all four of his tires. He was going to be tied up with roadside assistance for a few. Doof and I were back on the highway heading eastbound.

Three hours later my stomach and the Geländewagen's tank were nearly empty. Doof and I pulled off at a truck stop/diner combo and filled both. I got my club sandwich with a small cola to go and shared the innards of one half with Doof. Impeccably timed, a call from Mole jingled my phone. I listened as I ate.

"I've spent the last twenty-six hours submerged in this rabbit hole you call a case, and I've discovered some alarming things. And by *discovered*, I mean I had all three boxes crunching data. Then I hand sifted through every database that pinged," he said in a tired but artificially enhanced voice. "Lannister's grandfather, it turns out, was involved in more covert activity than just keeping major weapon-development secrets. He was plugged pretty deep into military intelligence. I'm getting that he and his commanding officer were involved in projects beyond their common orders with weapon security. After the war, Coppice is mentioned in connection with an individual whose husband was also part of the Development of Substitute Materials project. Coppice was said to be searching for the notes from the scientists whose ideas weren't viable for the project, but on the downlow. It wasn't a government-sanctioned endeavor. He was particularly interested in their brainstorms, out-of-the-box ideas, failed projections, anything from the discard pile, and whomever he was working for was willing to pay for his efforts."

When Mole paused for air, I asked the first question that sprang to mind. "Why? What would he want with someone's failed test answers?"

"Think about it, Sammy: Coppice was working with, and was surrounded by, the world's brightest scientific minds. World-class physicists. Mathematicians. Chemists. Imagine what crazy ideas got thrown on the wall—but also imagine what didn't stick. What happened to those ideas whose time hadn't yet come? With today's technology, imagine the possibilities."

Technology had grown exponentially since the Cold War. When your intention was to build the atom bomb before your Communist counterparts, you would explore the unknown, even if it didn't pan out. The destructive potentials of those failed ideas in today's scientific landscape were staggering to even dwell on.

"I'm still digging through this stuff. I'm coming up against some pretty sturdy firewalls. My spidey senses tell me it's the gold nugget that will buy you all the answers you need. Probably way more than you want."

I thanked Mole for the intel, and he promised to keep in touch with anything else he found. We promised each other to be safe and to watch our backs. He asked what he should do if Wickowski started asking questions regarding my whereabouts. I told him I had faith in his ability to spin a convincing cover story.

Doof and I entered the Roanoke city limits after dark. Instead of a corporate chain, we mixed it up and opted for a pet-friendly mom-and-pop inn. My pack flung over my shoulder, Doof leashed and heeled at my side, I secured us a room with a bathtub and a king-size bed. The desk clerk reached behind her, retrieved a copy of the receipt, and slid it across the counter to me. I scribbled Lannister's name across the top in lieu of a case number. Damn straight I was going to turn my receipts in to the county. Or maybe to Wickowski, who'd gotten me into this whole mess to begin with—see if that got me anything more than a belly laugh and a couple of light Spanglish insults.

Doof followed me down the hall to the room number printed on the keycard sleeve. The room was cozy with framed prints from local folk artists adorning the walls. No adjoining room door. I opened the window and let the breeze billow the gauzy curtain into the room. I tossed my bag onto the bed and told Doof he was welcome to take up residence on it as well. I dropped some kibble into Doof's bowl, kicked my feet up, and dropped my whole body heavily onto the bed with the remote.

I was just getting comfortable and settling on a '70s *Charlie's Angels* rerun when the burner phone jangled beside me. Mole's was the only number I had programmed into it.

"Hey!" I exclaimed into the phone. "Please tell me you have something."

"Hello to you too," Mole said. "I have more on this Coppice fellow. He wasn't just interested in old brainstorms. He was head of a fraternity—that's what they called themselves. The Fraternity. They were anything but party boys. These guys were a group of social-military elites who had the foresight of an unknown technological future and the possibility of a New World Order under their control. Those closest to Coppice called him a raging xenophobe. From what I can tell by his personal life, the guy was a dick. But he was a powerful one. That's irrelevant, though, because he kicked it in 1970." Mole took a deep breath and let it out dramatically. "That's when Roland Bauer joined the Fraternity. He was only twenty-five at the time, a silver-spoon heir born into an old-money military family, but he never served himself."

Roland Bauer. *Genteel.* Now I had a name to write on the bullet I would use on him one day.

"Instead of serving on the front, Bauer was part of the Phoenix Initiative, a program designed and coordinated by the CIA during the Vietnam War. The initiative's sole purpose was to attack and destroy the political infrastructure of the Viet Cong through infiltration, capture, 'interrogation,' and assassination. Bauer was the initiative's golden boy. He had a natural knack for breaking people. He and his project were purportedly responsible for the neutralization of nearly 82,000 people suspected of involvement with the VC. After Coppice's death, Bauer replaced him as head of the Fraternity. Even though he was junior to the rest of the guild by thirty years, his...resolve secured his position." Mole went silent for a moment to allow everything he'd just shared with me to sink in.

"Okay, I'm following."

Mole continued, "I found a passage from Lannister Sr.'s memoir where he talked about going to bat for Dr. Ludwig Wolff, a German theoretical physicist on the Development of Substitute Materials project whose wife had fringe ties to the Communist Party back home in Germany but had had no engagement with the affiliation since her husband took the position in the United States. When our government wanted to strip Dr. Wolff of his top-security clearance, Lannister Sr. stood up in his defense." Mole gave a sardonic scoff. "Wolff was called before a tribunal of the Atomic Energy Commission for a hearing on his past involvement with the Communist Party. The FBI raided his lab and office and confiscated all his work. They were concerned about his continued security clearance and the possibility that he was a Soviet spy. Lannister Sr. testified on Wolff's behalf because he trusted and respected him, but also because Wolff was his friend."

I thought on that for a second. "This wouldn't have been a sudden decision, either, to strip Wolff of his clearance." I was testing a theory out loud. "So, put yourself in Wolff's shoes. You're sort of a rock star in your brainiac world who just helped the United States bring an end to the war. Then that same government begins to turn on you. You hear rumor of raids on your lab. What would you do?"

I swear I heard Mole roll his eyes. "I'd hide my shit!"

"And where would you hide it if they knew everything about you?"

Mole's voice brightened when he caught on to where I was heading. "I might hand it over to my friend who I know can keep secrets. I'd ask him to stash them for me until further notice."

"What if he never came back for them? Wolff wasn't found guilty of anything, but come on—you and I both know the US government never forgot about him, never stopped watching. So if he never felt secure enough to retrieve what he'd given to his friend for safekeeping, in the end, where did those secrets end up?"

My own grandfather had passed back when I was in high school, and my father inherited boxes of his personal belongings along with reams of old paperwork like tax records, forty-plus-year-old documents that were no longer of relevancy, old operation manuals from appliances long dead. In amongst the boxes of immaterial bookkeeping were valid bits: the deed to his house, a love letter from my grandmother penned when he was stationed overseas during the war, an old safety deposit key that had belonged to *his* father (the box was empty save for an old Babe Ruth baseball card that turned out to be a worthless forgery and an obsolete business card from a brothel somewhere in the Bronx). My point being, my parents had to go through every box piece by piece to make sure nothing important got tossed into the garbage. Anthony Lannister may have inherited something from his grandfather that he wasn't even aware of. I thanked Mole for his help. Was this why Bauer and his merry band of mercenaries were still hanging around?

"I took the liberty of downloading the MacKinnon family's personal schedules from their laptops and devices. I also grabbed emails and texts. Momma MacKinnon is attending a bunco party Friday night at seven. The daughter is seventeen. She's told her mother she's going to spend the night at a friend's house, but she's arranged a night of passion with her boyfriend, who's home from college for the weekend. The son is a whole other story. This kid is a lot like I was as a kid—not really sociable, smart but finds school boring. It seems his whole life exists online, so it was extremely easy to get him occupied Friday night by inviting him to join my online League of Legends team. It's my real team, comprised of many of my talented and gifted gamer friends, much like myself. No way that kid is going to not show up, and some of these matches last hours. Once he's online I can keep him engaged for as long as you need. The house should be all yours."

When I hung up with Mole, I settled back into the pillows. Doof had turned himself in circles on the bed until he'd found *the* comfy spot and was now snoring beside me. Not long after that, I fell asleep with the television on. As it turned out, morning came earlier than usual, dictated by Doof's digestion and evacuation system. We took a walk around the block to a nearby construction site. He pooped behind a tree in some rubble of an adjacent abandoned lot, and I figured it was at home there, so I didn't bother to pick it up. I did, however, pick up a steaming cup of coffee and a berry scone at a tiny bakery around the corner, and I ate it on the way to the inn.

We'd made good time on the road. It was only Wednesday evening. If I wasn't infiltrating the MacKinnons' until Friday night, we had some time to waste.

"What should we do for the next day and a half?" I asked Doof, who looked at me quizzically, his head cocked adorably to one side. "I know," I explained as I took his fuzzy head into both hands and gave him a tousle. "We're gonna do some RSI: reconnaissance, surveillance, and intel, aren't we Doofy-Doof?" I gave him several deep ear rubs, which he groaned appreciatively through. "We're gonna bust some ass, aren't we, boy? We're gonna tear some shit up."

Doof smiled his wide canine smile. I liked to think he understood and was more than happy to accompany me. But first, we were going to spend the day hiking around in nature.

CHAPTER ELEVEN

THE GELÄNDEWAGEN WASN'T A GOOD SURVEILLANCE VEHICLE, NOT like the Honda Accord that I rented from an agency in town. Hondas were like belly buttons—everyone had one. Well, not everyone, but they were a dime a dozen and blended into the scenery of any neighborhood, upscale or inner city. Doof slept across the back seat. I sat behind the wheel. The leather seats were levered back, and the tinted windows offered just enough camouflage if I sat still. I'd parked in the dappled shade beneath the canopy of a giant red maple, catty-corner from the MacKinnon abode. Theirs was a corner lot, and from my vantage point, I had full view of the front and side yards, which were surrounded by a decorative iron fence. The fence's spear-topped finials were more than simply ornamental accoutrements. They would easily impale an intruder's body. First line of defense. They were an obstacle, for sure, but not a deterrent.

I sat. I waited. I plotted. Quinn came to mind, but he was chased away when a blue Honda (what did I tell you?) Civic with flared tires and a stereo system bumping 5,000 watts of pure distortion showed up on the scene. "Who might you be?" I asked under my breath. After fifteen seconds the impatient driver revved the engine, making the car's custom exhaust rip and pop with little flames sparking out the back of the pipe. I bet the driver was as annoying as his ride. The front door of the MacKinnons' house flew open, and a bubblegum blonde in a pink jean jacket bounced out, an oversized handbag slung over her shoulder. She texted as she walked toward the curb without really looking where she was going. She skirted shrubbery, avoided flowers in the bed, stepped off the curb, and opened the passenger-side door without ever looking up from her phone. The millennial superpower.

The Civic sputtered exuberantly away from the curb with its tinny exhaust. I turned my attention back to the house. All was quiet from my perspective. I checked the digital clock on the dash. It was only three in the afternoon. Momma MacKinnon wasn't taking off for her bunco night until closer to seven. Mole's online tournament would begin around that time too, so Doof and I had a few hours to kill before go time. I had some strategic planning to do.

"It's never really dark in a neighborhood like this," I observed aloud to Doof. "Too many security and street lights." I was going to need a covert way in without alerting nosy neighbors. I could park the rental at the curb in front of the house on the opposite corner from where we currently sat. From there, line of sight would be obscured by the low limbs of a flowering tree. Satisfied with the evening's plan, I turned the Honda around and used the Maps app on my phone to locate somewhere with trails where Doof could get some gentle exercise. After Doof had his fill of peeing on everything in sight, we took a seat at a pub patio (canine welcoming) and made an early dinner of burgers and a couple of pints. Never pull a job on an empty stomach, especially if silent and clandestine were called for. A growling stomach was as effective for blowing a cover as a cell phone on vibrate.

My cell phone jangled with Mole's ringtone. "Mole."

"Sammy. Everything's set on my end. Your boy is anxious. Little nerd is already online and checking out gameplay. I checked his mom's cell phone; she's still at the house. I'm keeping track of her cell and emails. So far there's been no indication of cancellation this evening. I'll be able to track her comings and goings too. The address does have an alarm system. There's no way of knowing if Mom's going to set it on her way out or not. I've accessed my way into the alarm company's mainframe and redirected the MacKinnons' home phone to my computer, so I'll be able to disable the house alarm from here. I'll also intercede any incoming calls. You should be able to get in, uninterrupted. Anything else?"

"No, Mole, that sounds like everything I need." I thanked him and told him I'd let him know when I was out.

There was still a little over an hour until showtime, so Doof and I drove the rented Honda to a dog park for some dog time. The next couple of hours were going to be potentially stressful. We both needed a stroll.

When we returned to the MacKinnons' neighborhood, I parked on the curb on the opposite corner as planned. I waited behind the wheel to assess the landscape. Blinds were already drawn against the growing night. Children had been called in for the evening. The streets and surrounding areas were vacant and silent. Dogs were kenneled behind chain-link fences. Garage doors were lowered at the end of another day. The neighborhood seemed to have retired for the evening. Twilight was a deceiving period, when the safety of hearth and home was merely an illusion. A time when doors weren't yet locked against the dark night. I took full advantage of that complacency. In fact, I counted on it.

Doof whined when I told him to stay and guard the car. I cut across the MacKinnons' side yard under the cover of shadows offered by clumps of tall, billowy pampas grass. The side yard offered a convenient man gate secured by a simple drop latch. There were no wires or other signs of electronic perimeter security. I slipped through to the other side and waited several heartbeats while I got my bearings through the lit windows. There was no discernible activity within. From Mole's intel I knew the boy's room was upstairs facing the street. Nobody was available to witness my crossing the backyard to the sliding glass patio door. Just as Mole said it would be, this entrance was electronically wired. I hoped he was as accurate with his plan to defuse the alarm when I popped the lock on the door and saw the alarm pad in the hall begin silently flashing red. The panel instantly returned to steady green of all clear.

I stood in place and took stock of the home around me. Mrs. MacKinnon kept an impeccable house. Neat, tidy, everything in its place. There assuredly were no dust bunnies or cobwebs to speak of, not even that fine film of dust that settles in hours. MacKinnon's military background and service were evident by the framed commendation for valor in war. A Purple Heart was framed in a wooden shadowbox that sat in the center of the fireplace mantel. I pulled on a pair of latex gloves from my pocket and fingered the box. It was awarded to Captain Niles MacKinnon in 2013 in Afghanistan.

On the wall above the shadowbox hung an eight-by-ten portrait in a gilded frame. MacKinnon was stern looking in his dress blues, bling littering his lapel. He appeared honorable, but there was no mistaking those piercing eyes. This was him. My abductor. I stared into his eyes on the wall, and my hand unconsciously went to the scab on the back of my neck where his knifepoint had penetrated. A shiver ran down my spine. Asshole.

The video game battle Mole had arranged should already be underway. I wasn't a gamer, but I'd been exposed to Mole's habit, and I knew Junior MacKinnon would be engaged for the next several hours, or for as long as I needed him to be. I also understood the house could burn down around him, hunger could eat a hole in his stomach, and he'd sit in his own filth-filled pants before his attention was yarded away from the game screen. I ultimately had a free pass inside the MacKinnon house—to a point.

I pulled the burner phone from my pocket and dialed the only number programmed in it. "I'm in."

I heard Mole clap and rub his hands together in enthusiasm. "Okay. Even though it would take a bomb going off in his room to break this kid's attention, you still need to exercise caution. This MacKinnon guy went all out on his security package—motion detection, heat-change sensors. These aren't part of the commercial package, but I wouldn't doubt things like biometrics and pressure plating around sensitive areas of the home. There's a large electronic signature emanating from the second floor, master bedroom. Could simply be a secondary alarm system. Just tread carefully."

I kept Mole on the line as I made my way up the stairs, keeping to the edge of the stair tread nearest the wall to minimize any chance of catching a squeaky board. Loud, explosive gameplay came from the room at the top of the stairs. An oversized *Gears of War* video game poster, once an in-store advertisement, now adorned the kid's door along with a plethora of stickers from various game makers. I eased past, stopping first to put an ear to wood for a listen inside. The sound of clacking keys and under-the-breath curses was familiar. I'd heard the same issue forth from Mole's place. What those sounds told me was this kid was fully engaged and wholly preoccupied.

The master bedroom was at the end of the hall. Its door was firmly closed. Mole's spidey senses must have picked up my trepidation through the open line.

"Take a moment at the master bedroom. That energy signature is emanating from the other side. There might be a trip wire on the door. Whatever's inside, Dad doesn't want the kids to get into it."

Great. I was going in blind. I took a moment to run a contingency plan through my head should I set off security. I had no alternative strategy, but that was okay because I worked better on the fly anyway, tackling unknowns as they came without forewarning.

The master bedroom's knob turned easily in my hand. The click of the mechanism disengaging was tactile against my fingers. No sudden alarms blared. No lights flashed. There were no other outward signs of intrusion. That didn't mean a silent alert hadn't been triggered.

Time was of the essence.

The master bedroom was in the same immaculate condition as downstairs. A chunky, high, four-poster bed of solid mahogany sat at an angle in the corner of the room, and a tall, leafy potted palm sat in the triangular negative space behind the headboard. Thin, two-drawered night tables stood flush against the walls on either side. Earth-toned drapes over the windows matched the same soft-toned comforter on the bed. A multihued green Pendleton wool blanket was folded and artfully positioned at the foot. The wide woven rug that covered most of the hardwood floor dampened my steps across the room. Wooden vertical blinds covered a sliding glass door. I peeked through them out onto a small deck adorned with potted plants.

With time on my mind, I turned my attention back to the room. Quickly I riffled through dresser and night table drawers, running my hand along the undersides for anything placed in hiding. Taped to the underside of Mrs. MacKinnon's lingerie drawer was a small packet of something white. I tested it with the tip of my pinkie, then spat it onto the floor. Cocaine.

I lifted the tank lid of the commode in the master bath to discover a hidden stash. Bundled in a watertight bag was, at first glance, close to fifty grand. I stuffed the bundle into my inner jacket pocket. Don't judge. That was the extent of the secrets I uncovered before moving on to the closet.

The light from the burner phone was bright enough for me to discern that I wasn't about to trip any hidden wires when I pulled open the heavy closet doors. The space inside was much smaller than I anticipated. That was because the walk-in had been remodeled and divided. Sort of like what Mole'd done in his bedroom. A pocket door, the kind that slid into the wall, was cut into the back, and a biometric lock had been installed beside it. This seemed like a brazen choice—housing whatever required that level of security in the home proper among your family. Most family men with covert operations in the works tended to keep a distance buffer between their work and their loved ones. Was Mrs. MacKinnon in on her husband's affairs, or was she just a willing participant in her ignorance?

Mole couldn't contain his enthusiasm. "Ha! I figured as much! No worries, Sammy. I just sent you the key." The burner pinged with incoming data. An enlarged, high-resolution photo of an eyeball. "I was able to download MacKinnon's latest DMV photo and enlarge it. When will people realize technology, in the right hands, is as good as a master key? At least try to make me work for it."

I silently appreciated the general public's ignorance while I held the phone's screen up to the security monitor. A red laser moved across the surface as it scanned the image. With an audible click and an electronic whir, the mechanism locking the door released. I slid it open.

Inside was a simple desk with a workstation in the center of it. The walls were bare save for a copy of Anthony Lannister's face and accompanying bio, details of his life pertinent to the task, like home and work addresses, personal schedules, threat assessment, and conclusion that he was a liability.

"I'm inside. I expected it to look like a war room, but all that's in here is a desk and workstation."

"What kind of system?"

"Fuck if I know," I said crudely. I wasn't the technical brain of this duo.

"Is it on?" Mole asked patiently.

That I could answer. "Nope."

"Okay." Mole sounded confident. "So this is what you're going to do. Turn on the monitor first, then the tower. As soon as you see anything appear on the screen, start pressing the F5 button a few times as the system begins to boot up. This will show me information about the computer. But," he said emphatically, "the moment you turn the tower on, they're going to know someone has accessed that computer, so this ends with you running like hell."

I did as Mole instructed, then began explaining what I was seeing. Because I was the brawn and the bullets, none of what I relayed made any sense to me. "Is this bad news?" I pondered.

"Sammy, this is golden!" Mole exclaimed enthusiastically. "This is *excellent* news!"

"How so?"

"Because they have to run their entire platform on a Unix shell."

"And that's important why?" I asked.

I heard Mole deflate his frustration with a sigh. "Umm, okay, how do I explain it... Unix is an *extremely* antiquated system. It's from, like, 1969. But in instances like this, it has to operate inside a contemporary operating system like Microsoft Windows, Mac, or Linux. You with me so far?"

"Sure," I lied, wanting him to continue. It would eventually make sense. Or it wouldn't.

"Most large government organizations, like the CIA, NASA, administrations of that size, run on outmoded systems like Unix that are twenty, thirty years old."

"Why?" I couldn't help but ask the obvious. "Why would they not update their systems with the latest technology?"

"Because their systems were custom written to do specific jobs. They're very bespoke, very specific. Those who originally wrote the systems have mostly died off. The expense in manpower alone to rewrite and retrain on a new system makes it implausible. Basically, if it's not broke, why fix it?"

"But without modern security, how is it at all safe?" I couldn't wrap my brain around what he was trying to explain. "Don't those systems make themselves targets?"

"One would imagine so, but to the contrary. Using such an outdated system offers a pretty good level of security because network traffic between these systems isn't at all unusual. Thousands of transmissions go between them. Most of it's just data. Nothing that's going to catch anyone's attention. The system is old and crusty, not easily modified and not updateable. That itself secures these systems because the general populace can't run them. There'd only be one or two people who would know how, most likely young computer nerds fresh from college looking for a job who could pass security clearance. That's your weak link. But fortunately for you, Sammy, this system offers zero security from someone the likes of me." I could hear his gloating smile.

I knew my clock was running down. I scanned my eyes down the screen. "I'm looking at a screen full of text. What am I looking for?"

"You're looking for that computer's IP address. It'll be a series of numbers, no more than twelve—four groups of three—separated by periods."

Argh. I scoured the screen. "This is so much easier when you do it," I said.

"Well, if you'd told me your plans, I would have sent you with a thumb drive so that all you would've had to do was plug it into the computer, but you didn't do that, so you're going to have to work for it, sister."

"Oh—here, I think I found it. Maybe? 185.230.63.107 sound right?"

A heavy, nearly defeated sigh filled my ear. "Dammit!" Mole cursed. "I was afraid of this. There are both public and private IPs. This one looks to be on a private network. This doesn't mean

I can't get into it, but not in the time frame you're on. Yank the wires out of the back and get the hell out of there. Bring that bad boy home with you."

"The whole tower?"

"If you want to know what's on it. But I suggest getting a serious move on. Two SUVs just turned into the front gates of the neighborhood."

"Can you slow them down?"

"If they had lights instead of stop signs in that gated community, yes. But they don't. So move!"

I already had the cables disconnected. The tower wasn't heavy, but it wasn't something easily tucked under the arm and sprinted with. The hallway was just as empty as when I'd arrived. I took the stairs down two at a time, not giving a rat's ass if there were squeaky treads. Back out the way I came, I almost made it through the side yard gate. Two SUVs glided to a stop at the curb in front of the house. Eight car doors slammed shut. A team no less than eight. The side yard was too exposed. I needed another escape route. The neighboring yards were separated by high wooden fences.

Next door was a hive of social activity. Smoke from an outdoor firepit rose up into the evening sky, deck lights illuminated balloons on strings, and strains of "Happy Birthday" rode the air. No lights shone in the backyard of the neighbor behind, but the fence was tall—too tall to jump with a computer tower. Flashlight beams begin crisscrossing the side yard. I needed to get to that dark and silent yard. The fence was made of a soft wood, stained dark. It had seen a couple of East Coast winters. The wood had swelled and shrunk through the seasons, slowly loosening the nailed boards.

I set the tower down, sat on my butt in the dew-damp grass, leaned back, and used both feet to kick the bottom of the weakest board away. The nails screeched in protest. When I'd created enough space, I shoved the tower through the opening then scrambled over the top of the fence. I landed silently on the other side just as I heard the latch of the side-yard gate. I moved the board back into place as a flashlight beam moved across the fence. I picked up the tower and ran around the house to the street, then circled back around the edge of the block to where Doof was waiting in the front seat of the parked rental. He instantly picked up on my haste, giving me a tail wag and an anxious whine when I laid the computer on the back seat.

"Don't worry, dude. I'll get us out of here." I used my blinker and pulled away from the curb. I didn't peel out or chirp the tires. As we passed the front of the MacKinnon house, I could see two black-clad tactical men standing in the living room, cell phones screwed to their ears. We cruised past without anybody's notice.

The burner in my pocket rang. "The game got cut off between Junior and me. You out of there with the goods?"

"Of course." I didn't go into the details of my escape. That could wait until we were face-to-face.

"You know they're going to know it was you."

"That was my point," I countered.

"You infiltrated MacKinnon's home," Mole persisted, "put his family in harm's way. They're going to come at you *hard* now. You did look for a tracker before you absconded with the hardware, I trust?"

"Tracker?" I asked as I pulled out of the community's front gates.

"Yeah, it's always a possibility MacKinnon took that level of precaution. Always assume the worst and plan for it."

I didn't even have time to contemplate the heaviness of Mole's words. Matching black SUVs with heavily tinted windows skidded onto the street behind me from a side alley. They gunned their engines and flanked me on either side.

"You should have led with that tidbit, Mole," I said calmly for Doof's sake while I accelerated through the next intersection. I instructed Doof, who'd been riding shotgun, to get down onto the floorboards, then ordered him to stay. Bestest boy that he was, he obeyed without hesitation.

"Where are you?"

I gave Mole the street I was on and the upcoming crossroad.

There was a pause then, "I see you now on the traffic cams. Cut hard to the left once you pass that white minivan you're coming up on. Stay on that road for three intersections. Then get in the far left and take it. It's going to be tight, but I'm going to hold the gate up at that railroad crossing. I'm serious though, timing is going to be everything."

I kept Mole on the line but set the phone in the cubby space beneath the stereo. I punched the accelerator to access all two hundred of the Accord's horses. The Honda answered by jack-rabbiting forward. I shot past the minivan and cut a hard left onto the adjacent residential side street. I prayed no pets nor pedestrians were in my way. I laid the pedal to the floorboard, gunning past quaint yards and quiet homes. I chanced a high-speed glance at the rearview. Both SUVs were fishtailing around the turn in pursuit. The gap between us grew shorter.

The flashing red lights of the rail crossing ahead gave warning. The SUVs were at my tail. The oncoming train's horn blared long and loud as it bore down on the crossing. The first SUV pulled parallel to me, the passenger window down, the suppressed barrel of an automatic protruding. The muzzle flashed, and the side window behind my head shattered inward. Glass rained down on the back seat. Another muzzle flash just before my window shattered, covering Doof and me both in rounded shards of tempered glass.

The second SUV rammed the Accord's rear bumper, shoving the entire vehicle forward. I rotated in my seat, one hand on the wheel to keep us on the road, the other wrapped around the butt of my HK. The shot was explosive, taking out the rear window and embedding itself in the SUV's engine block, but doing little to slow their pursuit. Eyes on the road, I raised the trajectory of the barrel and shot twice more. The SUV veered off to the right, careening into parked cars without slowing, then stopped with a crash head-on into a power pole.

One down, one to go.

Then things got a little hairy. A cacophony of action and re-action. The crossing gates began to come down just as the first SUV opened fire again. In an evasive move, I took my foot off the accelerator to immediately slow me. I cranked the Honda's wheel to forcibly bump the SUV's rear quarter panel. The two vehicles collided with a sickening crunch. Doof began to whine. I held the wheel hard to steady it. The force of impact sent the SUV into a spin from which the driver could not recover. When its wheels met with the curb, it rolled onto its side, inertia carrying it onto its roof.

The crossing gate, well into its downward trajectory, clipped the Honda just above the windshield, spiderwebbing the glass as we shot under it. The train's engineer laid on the horn and blasted past. I took a right into a sleepy cul-de-sac, stopped, and wrenched the computer up into the front seat.

"You still there?" I asked into the phone.

Mole was where I'd left him. "That was a lot of screeching and crunching. Is everyone involved okay?"

Doof looked up at me from the floor, and I invited him back up into the seat. He didn't seem thrilled with the offer. "Doof and I are fine, if that's what you're asking."

"And the others?"

I had no idea about the physical condition of any of the SUV occupants, and frankly I didn't care. They came after *me*. Neither I, nor my conscience, were going to give it any psychological time. I said as much to Mole. "Help me find this tracker before the next wave hits."

Mole talked me through getting the cover off. I used the phone's camera to take a few shots of the computer's guts and sent them off to him.

"Umm, Sammy," Mole ventured tentatively, "I don't see anything that even remotely resembles a tracker."

"What?" That wasn't at all what I expected to hear from him. "So where the hell is it? Do I need to start tearing into these circuit boards? Is it one of these little gadget-doohicky-bobs soldered onto the board? How do I even begin to tell which one it might be?" I was well aware that the last few minutes of playing chicken with a train might have maxed out my calm. My voice had risen to a fevered pitch.

"Have you looked along the inside surface of the cover?" Mole asked patiently.

I turned the metal cover over in my hands. A small black box about the size of an old flip phone, but half as thick, was affixed to the inside cover. "Oh, looky!" I exclaimed and attempted to pry the device from the cover. The adhesive was far too strong, so I did the only thing I could think to do and squealed away from the curb. "I hope you didn't need the cover. Or the tracker for that matter. I left both on the side of the road."

"Good girl. Now, this is most assuredly not over. Get back to Portland ASAP. Wickowski came by your place looking for you after I called him to tell him to be careful. I didn't talk to him, only saw him on the monitor." Mole had everything wired. "I'll see you when you get here."

Doof and I retrieved my Geländewagen from the rental agency lot and left the Honda in a parking spot designated for after-hours returns. The windshield was shattered, and both the front quarter panel and the rear had sustained heavy damage. I was sure it was more than the insurance coverage had anticipated. I'd hear about it at some point.

Mole contacted me again in the wee hours of the next morning to let me know both the driver and the passenger of the first SUV had succumbed to their injuries just hours before. He thought I should know, for whatever reason. I hung up feeling nothing. Should that have worried me? My inner voice was supportively silent. Why should I feel bad about killing people who were trying to do the same to me? Should I beat myself up because I got to it first? You come for me, there's only one thing I can guarantee you: death by hostility.

I wanted to get back and resume life on the normal, like taking long soaks in my own tub or having beers with Wickowski and watching the Trail Blazers on the big screen. All that was right where I left it. I just had to get back home to Portland.

Staying on the interstate was predictable, but the backroads seemed exasperatingly unhurried. I split the difference and utilized sideroads when they became available that would eventually wind me back to the main highway. We drove straight through, save for a three-hour nap I caught in a rest area outside Cheyenne.

It had been a long day's drive when we finally arrived back in the city. Doof and I were both ready for a stretch and a walk. I was just dropping over the Fremont Bridge into the Pearl when Wickowski rang my cell. My personal one, not the burner.

"Excellent timing, my friend." I kept my greeting light. "I just got back into town."

Bauer's voice stopped my heart. "An unfortunate event for your friend. You disappoint me, Ms. Harris. I read you as someone who understood, who would choose the welfare of their friends and associates over their own need."

Bauer's words stung because they were true. I hadn't been able to deny my inner need to stick it to someone, to go after what I wanted—retribution. There was a life lesson in there, I was sure, but that wasn't the time to learn it.

"Where. Is. Wickowski?" I menacingly enunciated every word to avoid miscommunication.

"The detective is alive. For now." Bauer took a deep, philosophical breath. "Life is an interactive experience, Ms. Harris. Our involvement is mandatory. Some only entertain minimal participation, and as such they only receive the minimal reward. Each of us is equally responsible for our own survival. This is one of those situations where the opposite rings true. The detective's continued existence relies wholly on your willingness to listen. To do as instructed."

The line went silent. Silent, but not dead. He was still on the other end.

"I don't enjoy making an innocent man suffer, Ms. Harris." Bauer's genteel voice dropped, sounded sincere, like he really believed what he was saying. It was a ploy, of course. Bauer was a snake.

I did my best to keep my voice even. "Why him, Bauer? Why not take me? Wickowski has nothing to do with your quest. You're not even in his jurisdiction."

"No," Bauer agreed, "the poor detective means nothing to me. That's true. But he means something to you. And in that, I find leverage to get you to stand down. Good day, Ms. H—"

I disconnected the call. I couldn't deal with Bauer just then, because I couldn't reach through the phone and pull his spine out through his throat.

CHAPTER TWELVE

My pulse racing and my vision red with fury, I made my way off the bridge and pulled onto the first side street I came to. Parked beneath a streetlamp that was just humming to life, I was hidden from anyone seeing me beating my fists against the steering wheel. I screamed a stream of obscenity-laced threats at the sky, promises to the Almighty of Bauer's bloody fate. I dared Him to try and stop me.

"Bauer has Wickowski," I breathed into the phone the second Mole picked up.

There was a lot of commotion, and I envisioned him shooting out of whatever seat he was occupying. I heard the clatter of fingers furiously working over a keyboard. I imagined him bringing up a series of thumbnails, views from the various cameras he had stationed around the property. "Okay, good." He breathed in relief. "There've been no triggers. Yet."

That caught my attention. "Yet?"

Mole's timbre was solemn as he measured his words. "They've got Wickowski. I don't mean to sound like a dick, but Bauer did warn you to back off, which was the exact opposite of what you did. Who do you think is going to be next? Oh yeah—that'd be you. Or me!" Mole paused for so long, I thought I'd lost him. Finally, "I suggest it's not too late to just...back off." There was a heavy sigh, one burdened with what he wouldn't say to me. What he *couldn't* say to me, because I wouldn't be able to hear him.

"You want me to bow out and let Bauer go," I stated, not asked.

"What I want is irrelevant, Sammy. I love you, but you're always going to do what Sammy needs to do first." My feelings might have been a little raw in that moment, but I really thought I sensed disapproval in Mole's voice and that, itself, stung.

"I can fix this, Mole. I can get Wickowski back and still destroy Bauer."

"Can you? And can you do that while keeping us both safe? And Quinn?" he challenged.

"Yes," I said defiantly. "Will you help me?"

I tried not to read into the space between my question and Mole's answer, which wasn't direct. "You need to get that computer to me without actually coming here. So far, there're no hostiles in sight. But that doesn't mean the building and surroundings aren't being surveilled, waiting for your inevitable return. Your deputy friend taped his business card to the gate outside. You should probably give him a call."

Quinn. I'd totally put him out of my mind since we'd parted. He must have raced back to Oregon instead of chasing me down. Smart move. Maybe there was hope for him yet.

Too many thoughts were swirling in my head. I needed to slow them, examine each of them one at a time, and I would do just that—once I got Wickowski back. I'd get myself sorted with Quinn, I'd formulate a plan to not only get Bauer but also find a way to dismantle the Fraternity. Somewhere in there, justice might be served for the Lannisters. On Cindy's grave, I vowed to tackle all of that. But only once Wickowski was safe and sound.

There was a sound on Mole's end of the line. He had taken a breath to speak, but nothing had come out. It happened again. I was familiar with this behavior—it was Mole processing his thoughts before voicing them. "If they knew about me, they would have already grabbed me." He was confident in his words. "So here's what we're going to do." He launched into a detailed plan: I was to activate one of the unused aliases he'd set up for me a long time ago in case of instances like this (though this current scenario had never been on the board), I was to check into a nondescript hotel (not a chain establishment with a large security budget), and wait. It seemed like a nonsensical plan, and I didn't do *wait* well at all, but simple was oftentimes better than jumping in guns blazing.

Allison Jayne Stuart checked into room number 28 on the second floor of the Lamplighter Motel off of Sandy Boulevard. I chose the establishment because it was cheap, nondescript, and had a back-alley exit. The hotel was essentially the office for the local prostitutes, so the constant in-and-out traffic didn't hurt in staying invisible. The room was at the end of the exterior hall, opposite the stairwell, with an alley-facing bathroom window that was large enough to shimmy out of should the need arise. I parked in the shadows and snuck Doof upstairs to the room.

The room had a suspicious smell, and the comforter was stiffer than it should have been in places. I shuddered and tried not to touch anything while I waited. Mole must have headed out as soon as I messaged him my location via the burner. His knock came less than forty-five minutes later, and he was armed with a backpack and a two-wheeled rolling cart with two zippered carry-ons bungeed to it as if he were headed to the airport. He didn't explain his exodus from home, and I didn't ask him for details. He slipped inside, gave Doof a scratch on the head, then began unzipping and assembling his workstation on the nightstand.

The illicit computer was in the middle of the bed. We both stood back and looked at it as if it were in danger of coming alive.

"Once I crack into this, all sorts of things could happen. It might set off a chain of events we have no idea about with ramifications we're wholly ignorant of. Are we sure this is what we want to do?"

"We're getting Wickowski back," I said as a low, monotone declaration.

Mole held my gaze for exactly three seconds. "Okay, that's all I needed to know." He laced his fingers and cracked his knuckles. "Once I ring this bell, there's no going back." He got to work. First, he examined the innards of the computer tower, making under-the-breath comments I couldn't hear and probably wouldn't have understood if I had. "I don't see anything insidious," he murmured. "Okay, here goes nothing."

I patted the edge of the bed where I sat. Doof understood I was inviting him up to sit beside me. I wasn't sure which was a worse place for him—being on the floor or hanging out on the bed. My imagination probably couldn't do reality justice in regard to the effluence that filled the room on a microscopic level. I didn't want to know. Ignorance in that instance was the better option, as long as I didn't touch anything.

Mole inserted a thumb drive into the computer and, using the keyboard he'd brought with him, began breaking his way into the system. "This is going to take me a few minutes," he said. When I only nodded, he added, "I work better in solitude."

"And leave you here without backup?"

"Leave Doof with me." He gave the dog a pat on the head. "He'll protect me."

Neither Doof nor I looked convinced. "He doesn't have a gun," I pointed out.

"No, but he's got a big bark and even bigger teeth. But seriously—take a stroll, take a drive, go get some food, go see the deputy. I'll be fine. There aren't any more trackers in this computer; nobody followed me here. Go." He waved me out the door.

Doof wanted to follow me. I had to get down on his level and tell him, eye to eye, that I needed him to take care of the goofy human until I returned. I wasn't sure if he really understood what I'd said, but he did give a small whiny groan before turning away from the door. He curled up at Mole's feet, then slid his eyes sideways at me without moving his head and gave a heavy sigh. The canine equivalent of the middle finger.

My eyes darted around the lot before I made my way to the Geländewagen. I got behind the wheel and waited in the dark. I was being vigilant for movement in the shadows or any other sign of discovery and imminent attack. There were none. I used the burner to call Quinn.

"Sammy." He coughed. "You made it back." Quinn's greeting had my hair standing on end. He was working too hard at sounding conversational, like he didn't want any emotion to taint his words. And he'd never called me by my first name before, certainly never referring to me as *Sammy*.

"Yeah," I said nonchalantly, "it was a long drive, but I just got in a few hours ago."

"Where are you?" he asked pointedly.

I needed to make my next move with caution. I knew Quinn wasn't the only one on the line with me and every nuance of our conversation was being dissected. "I'm taking some time to figure things out. I'm leaving with Doof to the beach for a night." It was a lame redirect, but I only needed to get a cushion of time around me and everything that was going on.

Bauer's team had Quinn. I knew Bauer, personally, didn't have him, because Quinn was speaking for himself. Every team I'd encountered to that point had been a two-man tactical squad. There was no reason to think the team holding Quinn would be any different. It would be two of them to one of me. Totally workable odds. The kind I excelled at.

I abandoned the Geländewagen near the hotel, parked in the shadows of a big oak. A Pontiac Grand Am from the early '80s had been sitting in the same spot since I arrived. The hood had gone long cold. Either an overnight guest or a john racking up a hefty bill. It didn't matter to me either way. I made a space between the glass and the weather stripping and slim-jimmed the door open. The interior smelled like bong water, stale cigarette smoke, and cheap cologne. The glovebox overflowed with multicolored condom squares.

I rolled the easily hotwired Grand Am out of the lot and stuck to the side streets. I made my way through industrial Southeast Portland and skirted residential streets. I stayed far away from traffic cams, doorbell cams, and store security cams. Trust me when I say hanging out with a hacker might make me a little paranoid about who's watching and from what angle, but it also gives me the advantage of knowing how to avoid those same eyes by knowing their perspective.

Much of the population surrounded itself with the latest technological gadgets—voice-driven devices that are always listening for commands, cameras in our doorbells that record all our comings and goings, even our cell phones that constantly listen, always keeping tabs. Yet nobody thought to ask, "Who's listening?" That wasn't Mole's rhetoric being parroted but pure fact, something the federal government doesn't talk about and doesn't want you thinking about. I've sat with headphones and hours of recorded data from a suspect's digital personal assistant. Listening to everything from the strain and flushing of their morning constitutional, to their most intimate moments, to every personal detail of every second of their day while inside the assumed privacy and sanctity of their home.

Armed with his address, I parked two blocks from Quinn's and approached from the east, sticking to the shadows of the overhanging elms along the sidewalk. The HK was down at my side—bullet chambered, safety off. I watched the front of his house from the driveway across the street, where I crouched beside a truck. I saw no sentinels, no lookouts set in place. I focused on the surrounding cars. Quinn's was kept in the garage. The SUV in the driveway was empty. I crept up on the driver's side, staying low and where vision was obscured by the deep darkness, away from lamps and lights. Quinn's front porch light was off. A speedy peek up into the SUV's window, and my suspicion of a set alarm was quickly verified by the blinking red light on the dash. I put a pin in that knowledge and moved on to the side of the house and the utility panel.

Before I cut the main breaker, I needed a plan. Once severed, it was only going to be a matter of time until one of the two-man team looked out a window, saw the rest of the neighborhood still lit, and sent the other out to investigate. Problem was, they were going to come out armed. An ancient elm tree offered the only real opportunity for cover. I scouted the climb route, and then I cut the power at the main panel beside the electric meter. I made the rapid climb up the tree using the trash bin as a leg up. The general hum of the house stilled.

Like clockwork, the first of the two-man tactical team came out to investigate. Weapon drawn, he searched the side of the house for trespassers. Finding no one, he gave the breaker box a cursory once-over, looking for the culprit. I used the thundering approach of a passing Harley-Davidson to cover me when I dropped down from the tree's branches onto his shoulders. He recovered from the shock of the drop quicker than I'd anticipated and fumbled to get a firm grasp on my torso to pull me off of him. In the tussle, I slid my KA-BAR Straight Edge between his fourth and fifth ribs. He fell silent before his body slid from my knife.

I didn't bother dragging the body out of sight, though I did pick it clean of firearms and ammo. He had no identification on him, so I moved on to number two.

Lucky for me, he'd left the door open when he'd come out, so I slipped in silently. I stood in the deep shadow of the lightless foyer to allow my eyes to adjust. Even at night, outside was much brighter than inside, especially in a drawn house with the electric cut. My eyes adjusted easily, but it was my ears that had become hypersensitive. I picked up the presence of another human being just inside the doorway of the adjacent room. They were inching forward toward the open door. Inching, pausing, listening. Their breath wasn't labored, but it wasn't silent either. Not anxious, but his deep, even breaths were much louder than my calm, shallow breathing. I was invisible to him both visually and auditorily when he unknowingly stepped into the space in front of me. The KA-BAR made a silent slice across his throat, sending a rooster tail of blood across Quinn's wall. The scent of pennies and loosed bowels filled the space.

I waited exactly four heartbeats before calling out Quinn's name. I heard a muffled groan from the other room, where I found him hogtied and bleeding on the living room floor. I cut the zip ties then made a quick sweep of the rest of the house, clearing each room as I went. There was nobody else on the premises.

I returned to Quinn with a warm damp towel and the first aid kit from beneath the kitchen sink. I dabbed the towel against the cut over his brow. He touched a corner of the towel to his split lip. Blood was crusted under his mashed nose, a coagulating drip suspended from his chin. He'd taken a beating because of me. Wickowski could lose his life because of me and my inability to stand down. My ego was writing checks that others were cashing in blood.

I caused this.

I was going to fix it.

Once his appendages were free, Quinn was on his feet. I followed him into his study, a bookshelf-lined side room just inside the front door, off the foyer. The floors were a dark hardwood. The room definitely had a bachelor vibe to it. Two walls were lined with bookshelves that held more boy stuff than actual books. An extensive collection of artillery shells, both contemporary and vintage, took up one entire level. The shells were organized in neat rows, pointy ends up. Clusters of framed photos were scattered on the shelves amid the artillery. Photos of Quinn at the shooting range, hunting in the mountains, riding motorcycles, and driving ATVs. There were several antique guns set on display stands.

A heavy desk was situated to face into the room so that it, and the wall behind it, were the first things that demanded your attention when you entered the room. A long table with a printer sat against the wall behind the desk. Mounted on the wall above the printer table were framed accolades and marksmanship awards from the Portland PB. Quinn didn't strike me as the throw rug type, so it didn't surprise me there were none.

He crossed the room to where he stored his service revolver in his desk, top right drawer. I separated the blinds with my fingers and peered through the window overlooking a dark side yard. I detected no threats lurking in the shadows, nothing in the street beyond.

I turned back to Quinn. "We've got to get out of here. When these guys don't check in, backup is going to be dispatched."

I didn't wait for Quinn to agree or not. I stepped over the body in the foyer. Quinn tried to make a statement, but it was cut off by a coughing spasm that had him holding his ribs. "Other one?" he finally managed to get out. He'd taken quite a beating.

I nodded. "Beside the house. We may want to move him before the sun comes up and he's in full view."

"Any idea what your personal kill count is?"

"To date, or this case?"

Quinn held his ribs and stifled his chuckle. "Ouch!" He took a slow, tentative breath. "Ow...don't make me laugh." When he got his breathing and rib pain under control, he pointed toward the door. "After you."

I was glad he hadn't pushed on with his inquiry. I knew exactly how many lives I'd ended. How many scores I'd evened. I just refused to allow such thoughts because most people felt some sort of conscience twinge, if not outright guilt, when they took a life. That might be true for drunk drivers, but it wasn't an affliction of the feels that I ever had to deal with. The way I saw it, each life taken equated to justice served. Maybe that was an arrogant tactic, but it helped me sleep just fine at night.

Quinn and I made it to the Pontiac without incident. I helped him into the passenger side. I wasn't shy about leaving rubber on the road when I left the curb. Using the burner, I phoned Mole, who was still deep inside MacKinnon's computer. He was on the trail of something he wasn't comfortable discussing on the phone, even if we were using burners. Doof was sound asleep on the bed beside him, and all was quiet on his front. He suggested Quinn and I not return to the Lamplighter and instead find somewhere to lay low for the rest of the night, or until he reached out.

I wasn't thrilled about leaving Doof behind, even less excited about leaving Mole unattended and without guard. But Mole knew how secure he felt, and I knew without inquiring that there were exterior security measures in place (outside of myself) that he never spoke of.

"So now what?" Quinn wheezed.

I should have taken him to the emergency room, returned the favor. But nothing could be done for broken ribs, so what would be the point of getting x-rayed to find out how many broken ones there were? If he kept spitting blood, we'd revisit the conversation. I was glad we were on the same page about it all. For the record, it'd been his idea to nix the ER. I only supported the suggestion.

"Now we find a place to hunker down and get some shut-eye," I proposed. "I know just the place."

Still in the stolen Pontiac, we drove in silence over the Burnside Bridge, back into the west side. We followed Burnside Street up into the hills to where it became a two-lane road. I hung a right onto Skyline and found a quiet street with no cars but plenty of overhanging trees. I parked beneath the outstretched limbs of an old oak and cut the engine. I helped Quinn into the Pontiac's back seat, where he could lean against the door and stretch his legs out along the seat. I got behind the wheel, racked my seat back, and closed my eyes.

Oddly, I found listening to Quinn struggle to breathe through his ruined nose reassuring. It meant he was still with me. Still alive. I didn't feel there was any way I was going to sleep. It wasn't the situation. It wasn't my conscience. I'd never killed someone who didn't deserve to die. Was I too callous in my beliefs? Too heartless? By whose measure? I couldn't live my life through the opinions of others. I couldn't be who everyone thought I should be. I couldn't adopt society's boundaries. Screw insomnia and those things that kept my mind active. I closed my eyes and drifted off to the whistling of Quinn's nose.

CHAPTER THIRTEEN

IT WAS A FITFUL COUPLE OF HOURS' NAP AT BEST. SLEEPING IN A car was never comfortable, regardless of how bone weary I might be. This had been no exception.

Wickowski was my first waking thought. *Is he still alive?* He wasn't a part of any of this. His life was in danger because of me—because he was my friend. One thing I'd learned long ago: personal relationships of any kind are opportunities to become leverage to the wrong people.

The burner phone on the dash lit up and began to ring. "I have something, Sammy, and it ain't pretty. No"—Mole paused, not for dramatic effect, but for cold, hard emphasis—"this is not pretty at all." There was a long, labored sigh, and when he spoke, his voice was full of anxiety and fear. "Where do I even begin?"

"At the beginning," I cued.

"Not over the phone," he said. "I don't care if these are burners. This is for your eyes and ears only. And Sammy?"

"Yeah?"

"My spidey senses tapped out on this one. Too much. Peril overload. And"—he cleared his throat—"I'm demanding hazard pay. In fact," he pressed, "I think you should make a bank transfer into my account before I go any further. You may not be alive to pay up when this is all over."

"I'll be right there. I'm only a few minutes away. Coffee?"

"No, thanks. My anxiety is all I need right now."

I'd already pulled from the curb and was heading back toward town. "I'm on my way," I reassured him.

We made the six-minute trip back to the Lamplighter in twice that time, after I doubled back through residential streets to verify we hadn't picked up any tails. I left the Pontiac in the alley behind the dive motel, out of the line of sight of Sandy Boulevard. The owner may or may not have even been aware of its absence.

Mole was surprised when I walked through the room door with Quinn in tow. Doof jumped from the bed where he'd been sleeping and greeted me with a mild version of his leap/spin/happy bark. His antics lacked their usual exuberance while he was healing, but he'd be back to his puppylike energy soon enough. For now, he was all whines, and lapping tongue, and wide canine grins.

Mole was jumpier than he was excited. "You brought friends," he said with an edge of irritation. Mole was less of a people person than I was, if that were at all possible. And like me, he could count the number of people he trusted on one hand, and he didn't like surprise meetings.

"Deputy Quinn, this is my...associate. Associate, this is Quinn."

The two men exchanged questioning looks. Quinn extended his hand in what I knew was going to be a moot gesture.

Mole looked at Quinn's proffered hand disdainfully then addressed me as if Quinn wasn't standing there at all. "You know I don't do cold introductions."

"I didn't have time to give you a heads-up," I explained with a shrug.

"He's seen my face," Mole whispered ominously.

"He's right here." Quinn leaned toward Mole and dropped his voice to a whisper to match his. "And he doesn't care what you look like." Quinn straightened. "But I will need a name to run a warrant search." Quinn shot me a wink.

Though normally full of guffaws and inappropriate humor, Mole was uncharacteristically sullen. "The Associate is not amused." Mole leveled his response at Quinn in such a way that it chilled even me. Quinn's chuckle faltered, and the good-natured grin slid from his face. This could turn into a pissing match real quick if I didn't intervene.

"Play nice, boys," I warned. "Mole," I began, revealing not his true name but the only one I'd ever known him by, "Quinn is with me. He's one of the good guys, and if things prove otherwise, I will personally put a bullet in his knee." I turned to Quinn. "I hope you appreciate this extremely rare opportunity you find yourself in." I weighed my words for exactly 4.2 seconds. Under normal circumstances, I'd never do what I was about to do, but that moment was anything but normal. We were facing well-trained mercenaries. It was no time to pull punches. To beat around bushes. It was time to get real. "Quinn"—I hoped I was making the right decision—"Mole is...how do I best phrase it...extremely gifted with computers. With technology in general. And as such, he sits at the top of some important lists."

I could feel Mole's burning glare as he stared at me, mouth agape. Color had drained from his face, but his hands were balled into fists at his sides.

I'd been extremely cryptic, but Quinn wasn't an idiot. He knew by "some lists," I was referring to the kind the Feds kept regarding the people they're most interested in. "But that's not to say he isn't one of the good guys," I went on.

Mole uttered a sarcastic "Aww, shucks."

"And aside from that, he's my business associate, my friend, but most importantly, he's family. *My* family. And I would take it as a personal insult should anything befall him as a result of our conversation here." I bounced my finger back and forth between Quinn and myself. "I protect my friends, my family, and my assets with lethal force."

Once I felt everyone in the room understood the stakes, I cued Mole to explain his recent digital discoveries. It took him a moment to gather his thoughts through the panic of becoming "visible" to Quinn, someone he'd just met.

"I've been working on this all night. Actually, I farmed out half of it to Sneak—"

"Sneak's been released and is back up and running?" I said, skeptical. Last I'd heard, Mole's black-hat associate had been shut down by the FBI. He must have had a gifted lawyer, or Mole might have had something to do with Sneak's speedy release.

Mole took off his thick, black-framed glasses and rubbed at the lenses with a soft cloth he kept near his keyboard. "Sneak was exonerated. He was scrubbed and back underground by dinner that same day. All the evidence they had against him mysteriously disappeared." Mole slid his glasses back on and gave Quinn and me an innocent shrug. "I guess it pays to have friends at the top of lists." He shot a warning glare at Quinn that said, *If I could do that, imagine the plethora of ways I could destroy you*, before continuing, "I was really just using his boxes to crunch data, sift it for repeated patterns, you know...digital shit neither of you would understand."

"Please, just cut to the chase."

Mole exhaled through puffed cheeks. "Sammy, I think you've got a problem, and its bigger than I believe you're prepared to deal with. I'm not a hundred percent positive, and confirming is proving to be difficult." He ran a nervous hand through his hair. "I came across a code name mentioned several times in correspondence between Bauer and MacKinnon. I can't help but wonder if this isn't affiliated with the Agency."

I cringed. The Agency was shorthand for the Central Intelligence Agency. The CIA—those bastards had zero sense of humor. "Okay."

"I'm not sure. I'm running a search algorithm, looking for that code name inside the set parameters. So far, the only lead I've found is actually no lead at all."

I waited for him to elaborate, but he didn't until I asked him to. "You've driven east on the I-84 out of downtown, out past

Hood River and The Dalles? Do you recall seeing those massive warehouse-looking buildings on the north side of the highway, along the Columbia River? That's a Google datacenter where they house all manner of online data like Gmail, Google Drive, YouTube videos, etc. You know when you back something up to the cloud? That's where it goes. It's a perfect place to stash your business, your secrets, your black ops."

"Okay, I don't see the problem yet."

"The problem is, if you're going to find more, it's going to be on a file buried deep in that datacenter."

"So, world-class hacker," Quinn mocked lightheartedly, "go get it."

Mole scoffed, "If it were that easy, don't you think I'd be handing you all I'd found instead of sitting here telling you we might have hit a brick wall and can go no further?" He made a frustrated sound with his throat.

"I need to be somewhere other than this hotel room. I've been sitting in the same spot for too long, way longer than I'm comfortable with. I feel exposed. I need a real workstation in better accommodations and a faster connection."

I knew I was thick when it came to computers and denser still when it came to the magic that Mole did with them. He'd hijacked the president's SOTU address, for crying out loud! It simply didn't compute that Mole was stumped. I ran a hand through my hair. "I don't get what the issue is."

"The issue—" The pitch of Mole's voice began to rise. "The issue, it isn't just grandma's recipes, birth announcements, term paper research, or digital family photo albums that are stored at sites like this. It's also the perfect place to stash top-secret files, black ops intel, and private, off-book banking and tax information for organized crime, and such. The issue is that because datacenters in general are target-rich environments, and the average cost per data breach to the facility is $5.5 million, security is top-notch.

It's cutting-edge and usually comes with bullets. And a federal sentence. The issue," Mole sardonically pushed on, "is that even if I were able to infiltrate the facility, billions of bits of information flow through a single server in a day, and there's 164,000 square feet of servers. The issue is that unless you know precisely what it is you're looking for—*and* where to locate it—you're walking away empty-handed. If you walk away at all."

"So what you're telling me is that I need to find someone who can get me in and can help me gain access to what I need once I'm inside?" I smiled broadly. "That doesn't sound so difficult."

"You're possibly talking about a CIA black site, Harris." There was Quinn again. "I've never met them personally, but the CIA doesn't strike me as the type of organization that cares much for outside influence."

Admittedly, I'd never personally met the CIA, though I'd had a tumultuous affair with their little brother, the FBI. Alphabet agencies as a whole weren't my thing. But I had to get Wickowski back. Sometimes the best way out of a hole is to keep digging yourself deeper and hope you finally emerge out the other side.

Both Mole and Quinn, who'd remained quiet through most of the former's monologue, stared at me with wide-eyed, brow-raised expressions. Taking down an established covert organization was a challenge. The ultimate challenge. It wasn't something one could do alone. You needed the resources and support of a team behind you. Potentially, I wasn't after just a single person. I was after dozens of people—all of them cloaked. Invisible. All of them with resources and skills. And all of them with a stake in my assured silence.

"If I can't go through the front door, and you can't gain access through the back door"—I looked at Mole—"then I'm going to have to find someone on the inside who I can convince to do both."

"What if Wickowski can't hold on that long?" Quinn asked. Now who was being devil's advocate?

I didn't like the implications of his question. I had to believe whoever was holding Wick wouldn't kill him unless I made a move. Forced their hand by an act of aggression. A declaration of war. They had me over a barrel, and they knew it. I wouldn't gamble with Wickowski's life. Not until I knew my move couldn't fail. Some twisted sense of hope believed my not rising up and slaughtering everyone involved was the olive branch I was bringing to the table. My way of calling a truce. For now. I *would* burn it all down one day.

Olive branches made great kindling.

Unspoken or not, I understood the question behind his question. What he really meant to say but didn't have the courage was: How far was I willing to push things? Could I live with myself if my decisions backfired and Wick paid the price? I couldn't answer that last part, but I was going to put my head down and lean in to the propellor blades. We'd all see how it came out in the end.

CHAPTER FOURTEEN

I RECEIVED A CONCERNED PHONE CALL FROM BURNELL THE FOL-
lowing morning regarding Wickowski's prolonged absence. I told
him I hadn't heard from the detective (not a lie), and that I didn't
have any idea of his whereabouts (also not a lie). In addition, I
informed the department that I'd do everything in my power to
locate him, and that I'd drop a call to the precinct when I did
(all truths). I almost included a heads-up to put the coroner on
standby, but I wasn't sure who might need the ride—the bad
guys or Wick. I didn't want it to be Wick.

We relocated Mole's workstation from the Lamplighter to
a private residence in the Hawthorne district on the east side.
The house belonged to a contact of Mole's, a safe house of sorts.
When I asked why we hadn't bypassed the dive motel and landed
at the safe house from the beginning, he got a little sketchy with
his answer. I got the feeling our presence wasn't as welcome as
he'd anticipated.

There'd been some tense, raised voices—Mole's and a
woman's—coming from the vestibule when we'd first arrived.
I couldn't make out what was being said, but when Mole came
back out to the porch, his face was set in a mixture of frustration
and consternation. Quinn and I were denied access. The raised
voices had been Mole catching hell for his having exposed the lair
to us, two outsiders. "Spamela insists on cloning your phones, for
safety's sake." I told Mole to relay the message to Spamela that
she could suck my butt—but he reminded me we needed her

assistance. Grudgingly, I complied and handed it over. Hackers were a moody, paranoid breed.

"I have twelve hours—then she's kicking me out. You're too hot right now, Sammy." Mole shook his head. "Someone has flooded the dark web with your name. There's a reward for information leading to your custody. That, and she doesn't like dogs."

I completely ignored the bit about dogs. "Whose custody?" I inquired.

"I asked her that exact question. She said there's no indication who's looking to put you in lockdown, but it's enough to spook her, and Spamela is a tough broad. She doesn't spook easily."

"I'm coming in with you," I stated and followed him inside. He was reluctant to lead the way, but Mole oftentimes had a hard time telling me no. Quinn stayed outside with Doof.

Mole and I ran into his anti-canine friend the moment we cleared the foyer. She was a fifty-something hippie throwback who gave both of us dagger eyes.

"What the hell is she doing in here?" Spamela had a lot of drama in her voice. "I gave you my specific conditions! I don't need the kind of attention someone like her could rain down on me!"

Spamela and my Aunt Zelda would get on well, at least as far as their shared fashion sense was concerned. Spamela was dressed in a flowing blue peasant skirt paired with an oversize red flannel and Birkenstock sandals, my aunt's favorite footwear.

"Calm down, Spamela," I said. "Nobody's going to be raining anything down on anyone. We came here for a simple task. We accomplish that, and we're out. No harm, no foul, and you will never hear from the likes of me ever again." How does one talk down a melodramatic nerd on the edge of a meltdown? I had no experience with these kinds. Shooting her—my first thought—wasn't an option. I mean, who doesn't like dogs? My expression had already settled into that flat, highly focused, and pointed glare I got when pinning down a target on the range. It wasn't the first time I'd led by facial intimidation.

Spamela's stance faltered when my pointed glare pricked her sensibility. Suspect, but the fight clearly out of her, Spamela ushered Mole and me toward the back of the house and down a steep flight of stairs to a basement. The stagnant air down there was heavy. Dark and oppressive, it was the ideal setting for a B-rated horror film. Flickering fluorescent tubes along the ceiling added to the overall creepiness of the space. I kept catching Spamela sizing me up from the corner of her eye.

"In there." Spamela gestured toward a windowless room built in the center of the basement space. "144 square feet of total privacy," she explained. "Lead sheets laminated to 5/8-inch sheetrock to prevent digital and physical eavesdropping. This is an air-gapped room," she added, "a Faraday cage of sorts for those of us who are digitally inclined."

"That means there are zero physical connections to the outside world, no network interfaces, either wired or wireless, connected to outside networks," Mole clarified to the tech-challenged in the room (me).

I stepped over the concrete lip of the Faraday room's doorway. Where the basement outside was worthy of a pedophile or a murder scene, the interior of the Faraday room was comparatively cozier. Drier and warmer, with taupe walls and plush beige carpet, the space also sported a table, a hot plate, a single chair, and a cot. At 144 square feet, it wasn't a lot of room, especially when you took up a chunk of that real estate with a small bathroom complete with toilet, sink, and shower. The windowless room presented more as a place to stash a hostage than it did a hacker pad.

Spamela pointed at Mole. "I trust you informed your friend of the process we use." She took his silence as a no and proceeded to enlighten me. "Once I close the door, it does not open again until his allotted time is up, not a moment before, not a moment after. There are no in-and-out privileges, hence the toilet and cot."

"I can't be locked in here," I stated up front. "I'll be wholly ineffectual if I'm trapped." Maybe someone should have led with this extremely significant point and saved us the exchange at the front door. "You have to let me go if I need to run."

Spamela had already crossed her arms defiantly across her chest. She stamped her foot as if to punctuate her position and said stoically, "As they say, Miss Harrison, them's the rules."

"Harris," I corrected, unthreateningly. I looked to Mole, who only shrugged and turned his attention to the ground at his feet. "Okay then," I said pleasantly. "Mole, call or track me down when your time's up." I left without making a scene. See? It could be done.

I joined Quinn and Doof outside. We piled into the Geländewagen and swung past Quinn's house. Mole had made calls to the same cleanup crew he'd used before to see to Quinn's place. There were no signs that anything had taken place there just hours prior. Quinn ducked inside for a quick shower and a change of clothes.

"We need another set of wheels," I said when he emerged from the bathroom with a towel wrapped around his waist. His torso was beginning to color from the beating he had taken. It bothered me that I noticed how loosely he wore his towel. I hated that I willed it to slip. Would it have actually killed him to get dressed before coming out of the bathroom? I cleared my throat when my first attempt to speak failed. "Hungry?"

He shot me a coy look. "Going to need context with that inquiry." Quinn had to know that I wasn't being sexual. Not really. Okay, maybe there was a hint of unintended innuendo in there, but considering the present circumstances, sex was the last thing on my mind. Close to the last thing.

"Food, Quinn. Sustenance. This time I'm talking about a meal."

"Sure," he said in such a way, it wasn't clear if he was doubting my intention or agreeing that he, too, could use something to eat. "What did you have in mind?"

"I know a place. And bring an overnight bag."

Quinn raised his brows at my instruction but disappeared back down the hall. I found a cold one in his refrigerator and helped myself to it. It wasn't a porter, but it was a locally brewed amber ale. I gave a satisfied grin.

Quinn called ahead and made a deal with McBride to borrow his weekend-warrior Jeep Gladiator for a couple of days. I had no idea what excuse he'd used for the arrangement. The Jeep had four doors and a lift kit. When we picked it up, I could tell by McBride's expression that he had questions, but he didn't have the balls to voice them. Or maybe he just didn't want to know the answer. I get it.

Ninety minutes later, Quinn and I were sitting at the bar inside the Riverside Gastropub which conveniently overlooked the datacenter's main parking lot. Doof stayed in the Jeep. The center itself was over 100,000 square feet, but it employed few people. Fewer than forty cars almost filled the small lot. Outside of the handful of system admins and techs, the place was a nerd fest. Mole's people. A guard shack was stationed at the mouth of the lot. The entire campus was surrounded by a high chain-link fence topped with spirals of razor wire.

I ordered a porter, which arrived bottled, and watched the lot. Of the thirty-four vehicles, twenty-six of them were boring conservative four-door sedans manufactured within the decade. There were four minivans—two of which appeared to double as full-time housing. There was a small, ratty Toyota pickup truck whose red paint had oxidized and faded to a sort of dusty-rose color highlighted by Rorschach tests of rust. A recently muddied 4x4 truck. A vintage and refurbished VW Beetle, and a Mercedes-Benz E-Class that was at least a couple of years old.

Of all those vehicles, only the Benz stood out because of sticker price. Everything else on the lot was reasonable in comparison. The Oregon plates said MENSA. As in, the smart club.

I reached for my cell to run the vanity plate past Mole to see who it belonged to before I remembered he was incommunicado for the next twelve hours.

"Penny for your thoughts," Quinn clichéd me back to the present moment.

"I was just pondering the Benz down there." I pointed down at the lot.

Quinn sipped his whisky sour and squinted. He used his phone to snap a picture of the plate then zoomed in to read it better. He gave a chuckle. "Wow" was his first comment regarding the owner's statement to the world on his vanity plate. "Sounds full of himself."

It was my turn to laugh out loud. "My thoughts exactly!" We guffawed together. "Can you pull a string and run the plates?"

Quinn was already tapping out a request on his cell phone. "Your mentals are turning," he observed, his attention split between me and the results on his phone.

"I'm looking for a way in, right?" I took a hefty pull from my bottle of porter and smacked my lips in satisfaction. "Maybe I stroke Mr. Benz's ego and see what I might get out of him." I ran that statement over again in my head. Quinn shot me a look like I'd insulted his modesty. "You know what I mean."

He didn't hit me with a comeback for that. "David Kodlin," Quinn read from his screen. "Lives in Hood River, along the river in those trendy, newer townhomes." Quinn gave a low whistle. "Leases are *not* cheap there." He went silent for a moment. "Oh—hey! Here's his dating profile." Quinn turned the screen to show me.

I took the phone from him and scrolled through the profile. I scoffed. Mr. Kodlin was as bald as a cue ball and read like a textbook narcissist. That explained the car and condo. His over-inflated sense of self-importance was staggering. No wonder he was single. "What an ass clown." I pointed at a line in his profile. "Look at this: He warns he'll only buy vegetarian meals. Not because he's one, but because 'meat is too expensive.'"

"I bet he's never been laid," Quinn assessed.

Personal estimations of Mr. Kodlin aside, I caught a glimpse of my way in, but I had to let it percolate.

"Just don't hurt the guy," Quinn said when I told him my plan. "Do you have a dating profile out there, online?" he asked, not meeting my eyes.

Seriously? He seriously just asked me that? It was as if he'd never met me before. Nothing about my personality lent itself to being open to sharing things about myself with strangers. Sure, I was all for no-strings hookups, but I'll find you.

I looked at Quinn squarely. "No."

His squint deepened. "So, you're willing to date this guy—and whatever that requires—to get what you need from him?"

"You don't have to make it sound so cheap," I said defensively. "Nobody said I was going to sleep with the guy." Geesh, Quinn almost sounded resentful.

"What if that's what it takes?" he pushed.

"I'm a big girl, Quinn. I can navigate my way through getting what I need from an egotistical tool without sacrificing my dignity."

Quinn scoffed, "So what, you just make yourself a fake profile and stalk this Kodlin guy, and make him an...offer he can't refuse?"

To be honest, I hadn't really thought through the approach until just now. "Maybe," I said with zero conviction in my voice. "Or maybe I get close to him and jack his security swipe card."

"That doesn't sound like a solid plan. This place has security up the wazoo," he said, with a nod toward the datacenter. He lowered his voice when his intensity caught the attention of the bartender.

"Then I have a gun. It can be pretty convincing," I stated and ordered another porter. Quinn ordered himself another whisky sour, and then we settled in over the food menus. I went for the filet mignon with all the trimmings. Quinn ordered an elk burger with a side salad. We drank and waited for our meal in silence.

My gaze was fixed on the parking lot. I watched men and women in business suits trickle in and out, some escaping to their vehicles (never driving away but lighting up or pulling on their vape pen, others to power nap). Kodlin came out and walked to his car. He was thin but not fit. I could tell his clothes were tailored and fitted. Even from my vantage point, I could tell he wasn't a particularly good-looking man.

I sighed and signaled to the bartender for the bill. She produced it from a pile beside the register and laid it on the bar between Quinn and me, not sure who was picking it up. I slapped my business Amex on it and slid it toward her. The buxom redhead eyed Quinn as she plucked it from the bar like he was some sort of deadbeat date.

We were just rising from our barstools when a dark SUV, the likes of which I'd become increasingly familiar with, approached the parking lot's front gate. The armed guard seemed familiar with the driver and allowed him to pass. It circled around the back of the building, out of our line of sight.

"SUVs in general are popular in these rural parts," Quinn pointed out. "Could just be an employee."

"Then why didn't they park in employee parking?" I asked. "Could also be Bauer's team. Do you think they know I'm here?"

"How could they," Quinn asked, "unless they put a tracker on your person? More likely they know how you operate." That I'd become predictable didn't make me feel any better than the thought of wearing a tracker did.

"For shits and giggles," I mused, "let's say that SUV is part of Bauer's team. That validates the idea that there's something here worth securing." I sipped my beer and pondered. "Stay here. I'll be right back," I announced as I slid from the barstool. Quinn didn't offer to accompany me as I headed for the door. I made my way downstairs and toward the datacenter's parking lot. I didn't get far.

The moment I entered the lot, I was met by a uniformed security guard who occupied the shack. He was a big guy, just entering into middle age, with a momma's Iowa farm-boy softness about him. His stomach created a soft bulge that ringed the bottom of his shirt where he'd tucked it into his slacks and overlapped his belt. A thin moustache sat above his red lips. It wasn't overly warm, yet his cheeks and forehead glistened with a fine sheen. Unable to be buttoned, the tan blazer of his uniform hung open over his belly. He kept his hand firmly on the butt of his sidearm, a Walther P22. *P* for peashooter, if you asked me—barely threatening. That wasn't to say that a .22 round wouldn't penetrate my flesh and make life suck for a minute or two.

"Ma'am, if you don't have business inside, I'm going to have to ask you to please remove yourself from the vicinity," he said as if reading from his official handbook.

"Define *vicinity*," I said, challenging his script.

Officer Cornfed cleared his throat and began to recite what the handbook said: "Within ten feet of the entrance, within eighteen inches of the perimeter fence. I will use force to make you comply."

Bring it, was what I wanted to say. But instead I put my hands up in a peace gesture and stepped back two strides to satisfy his definition of *vicinity*. He couldn't say anything if I wanted to walk around the outside perimeter of the border fence. I didn't look back at him. I didn't stick my tongue out. I didn't flip him off. I didn't kneecap him. I just followed the boundary fence around to the back side of the building, staying aware of the eighteen-inch zone. I found the SUV backed into a space along the fence.

The land behind the center dropped down a slope to the lower floodplain behind the center. The hillside was protected against erosion by large ballast rocks. Nobody noticed when I picked my way down the boulders and out of eyesight of the center. The floodplain was an overgrown tangle of big-caned blackberries and the garbage remains from several homeless camps. I stayed to the rocks as I paralleled the fence then scrambled back up, right behind the SUV. I spied cameras at each corner of the building and over each doorway. I stayed low and out of the cameras' line of sight as I crept up directly behind the rig.

After several long moments of no movement, it was determined the SUV was empty. I eyed the surrounding lot. No sign of foot guards. Cornfed wouldn't leave his post, but would he call in for a perimeter check? Did he even have the authority to make that call? I grew bolder and tried to see through the windshield but couldn't make out anything besides the leather interior.

I backtracked, avoiding interacting with Officer Cornfed again, to the Jeep we'd borrowed from McBride. A pack of gum was sitting on the console, and I shoved a piece in my mouth. In the trunk was the duffle bag that I'd transferred from my Geländewagen. Inside were a few things I kept onboard at all times: a taser; a box of cuff-style zip ties; a couple of unregistered burner phones; extra ammo for my HK, Walther, and Glock; a box cutter; spool of lightweight wire; and a magnetic tracker about the size of a postage stamp for times I couldn't be in two places at once.

I rummaged through my bag to come out with the small metal box. It was an inexpensive global GPS tracker I'd gotten online. The device had a two-month rechargeable lithium battery. It also had pinpoint accuracy and sent real-time information to my phone. It worked anywhere on the continent. I only needed it to work short-range.

A row of maple trees separated the restaurant's lot from the sidewalk. Nobody noticed—or at least nobody came after me—when I used my knife to saw a branch stout enough for my purpose and stripped it of leaves. I circled back to the rear of the center, down the ballast rock, along the garbage, to the SUV, and still nobody was in sight. The gum in my mouth was worked to a pliable wad, and I used it to affix the tracker onto the denuded maple branch. The tracker was small enough to fit through the diamond-shaped opening of the chain-link as I carefully threaded it through. The magnetic side of the tracker stuck to the SUV's undercarriage, just under the back end. I used the app on the phone to access the device and waited for it to blink live on the screen before I returned to Quinn.

CHAPTER **FIFTEEN**

WE DECIDED NOT TO RETURN TO THE CITY THAT NIGHT. INSTEAD, we opted to stay in the area and wait for Mole to reach out. Quinn and I found lodging at an Airbnb on the outskirts of town. The tiny log cabin was located at the end of a long, graveled drive. We had optimal visibility of the rural road in both directions. The cabin was set against a vertical rock bluff. I was satisfied with both the visibility out front and inaccessibility from the rear. We'd call the place home for the night.

A sign on the front door requested visitors remove their shoes at the threshold. Quinn input the digital code on the lockbox containing the door key. Inside the front door was an antique dynamite box to hold said visitors' shoes. I slipped mine off and donned a complimentary pair of warm, skid-resistant slipper socks that would keep my feet toasty against the cold wood floors.

The cabin was tiny but cozy with only the single great room, which served as living room, kitchen, and bedroom. Only the one bed. We'd work out the sleeping arrangements later. A large picture window overlooking the town and Columbia River beyond took up most of one wall. Quinn had packed an overnight bag, and I had my bug out kit. He dropped both onto the bed while I looked around. Clean towels were piled on a chair beside a squat clawfoot tub in the tiny bathroom. The room was so cramped, one could use the toilet while washing their hands in the pedestal sink. Once the door closed, it was the only privacy in the cabin.

The kitchen area wasn't much larger and was mostly counter space. Fresh-ground coffee filled a canister on the counter. A glass percolator sat on the stove with printed instructions for brewing taped to the lid. Add water, scoop grounds, put on fire. Straightforward enough. Single-serving flavored creamers filled a small ceramic bowl beside a shaker of raw sugar on the counter. Our host had left a fresh loaf of bread and a dozen brown eggs in the refrigerator with a note on the carton proudly telling guests that these were from their own chickens. The last guest had left a fifth of Jack Daniels behind in the cupboard under the sink. I pulled a swig from the bottle and grimaced. There was a reason my tastes ran along a liquor store's top shelf. I took another pull from the bottle anyway, fought the gag, and screwed the lid back on for the next sucker who found it.

A worn leather loveseat with a soft red-and-black plaid throw folded over the arm sat against the wall opposite a cast-iron woodstove. A rocking chair that had seen a few decades sat invitingly beside the hearth. A leather sling cradled a stack of seasoned firewood, and a large kraut crock was filled with small dry twigs of kindling. Wooden matches sat in a box on the windowsill.

The cabin itself sat in the shadow of the surrounding bluffs, and the sun was beginning to fade from the western sky. Doof pricked his ears when a lone coyote called a mournful howl. Then he settled beside the tub as I began to fill it. I thought better when submerged, so I shut the door with a slippered foot, stripped off my clothes, and sank gratefully into the almost too hot water. The tub was short but deep. My knees were drawn up and jutting from the water. The singular coyote had been joined by its pack, and they raised their ruckus in earnest. Doof sat up and rested his chin on the edge of the tub. His big dark eyes were wide and darting.

"Just coyotes, bud." He whined and licked my shoulder. "I'll protect you, bestest boy." I gave the big guy a scratch beneath the chin.

Quinn cracked the bathroom door open then stepped inside without invitation. I slid deeper into the tub until only my head and knees were exposed. Quinn gave Doof a scratch on the head, then moved him over so that he could sit where the dog had been, with his knees drawn up almost to his chin.

"Scrub your back?" he offered.

I heard what he'd said but made no effort to move. The water was crystal clear, and every inch of me was exposed but mostly submerged. I inclined my head toward the sink edge, where the burner phone, through which I was tracking the SUV, was balanced. Quinn plucked the device from the porcelain and handed it to me, purposefully not gazing down at my starkness. I was almost offended. I looked down at the screen. The red dot that represented the SUV hadn't moved. I needed Mole and the access to pertinent information only he could provide. I'd grown complacent and dependent on our arrangement.

"How many laws do you destroy in a day?" Quinn asked. "On average?"

"Depends on what I'm after," I replied, not trying to sound snarky or flippant, but honest. I didn't have to be empathic to feel how torn Quinn was between supporting my effort to take down Bauer and the Fraternity, and honoring the oaths he'd taken as an officer of the law. The last thing I needed was a sudden case of ethics from him. "Are we going to have issues over the way I do my job?" I asked blatantly.

Quinn didn't answer, but the way he stared me down told me I needed to be careful. To watch my step. Not to get too cocky. I got it—when you joined the force, you made a moral commitment to an organization and your fellow officers. Each time Quinn observed me bending the edges of the law until it was no longer recognizable rubbed against his inner programming. On top of that, Quinn was former military. He understood laws, rules, and their inflexibility far better than I ever would. To me, all the above were pliable. Quinn and I may have shared the same goal—to arrest those responsible for the Lannisters' deaths, to see justice served—but our approaches to those conclusions couldn't have been more contrasted. I had a strong feeling that if I pushed it too far, I could end up in a cell. That was probably why he hadn't asked too many questions about how I got him out of the bad situation at his house. Or how the bodies were disposed of. If anybody understood plausible deniability, I did.

"You treat the streets as your own lawless playground in pursuit of an arrest. You *do* get the irony there, right?" When I didn't answer or otherwise rise to his words, he added, "Don't mistakenly believe that I wouldn't arrest you, that I wouldn't take you to a holding cell. In cuffs. You're inside the law, Harris, just like everyone else."

I didn't have time for a crisis of morals. I half-heartedly promised to keep my actions more to regulation. Was I convincing in my lip service? Who knew? "I can conform. But understand that will be reflected by killers remaining on the streets for longer." I played an offhand shrug like I was refusing a dare. As if wrangling and rerouting my personality was an easy task, something effortlessly tackled. I could do it. Did I expect special privileges because I let him share my bed? Of course not. Was I entitled to a wider margin just because Quinn had exclusive access to my pink bits from time to time? A little tit for tat? Well, sure. That was sort of how the world worked.

Quinn didn't find my frivolous attitude amusing. His face was set in a stern glower. "What's going on between us, Harris? One minute I think there's something amazing building here—the next minute you're slashing my tires and ditching me in the middle of nowhere. There's playing hard to get; then there's unaddressed psychological issues. Which one are you?"

I stared at the faucet at the other end of the tub. I felt myself shrink away from the upcoming discussion. "Don't take anything personal."

"What the hell does that mean?" Quinn snarled. "I like you and the way we are together in bed. I thought you liked me right back, Samantha." My name dropped awkwardly from his mouth. He'd never addressed me by my proper first name before. "I like you way more than I should."

"That's the problem," I heard myself say.

"Why is that a problem?" Quinn countered.

How could I ever explain what I meant, how I felt, without it coming out hurtful? When someone got too close, expectations were set. Emotions were invested, and someone eventually got hurt. "Because that's when things get chaotic."

"It doesn't have to be that way." Quinn sounded more frustrated than dejected.

"Why do we have to be more?" I asked frankly. "Why can't we just be...friends with benefits?"

"That's never worked for me in the past," he answered, rising from the floor.

"Why the hell not?" I sat up and turned to face him.

"Because someone gets hurt in the end." He exited the room and pulled the door gently closed behind him.

He'd used my same reasoning against me. So the bottom line was, we were damned if we did, damned if we didn't. Either way, someone was going to get hurt. *What does he really want from you, other than your time?* my inner voice challenged. More, that's what. Human nature always wanted to make more out of something. Feelings weren't my forte. I didn't know how to process them, and it made me uncomfortable when I tried.

Doof remained curled up on the floor beside the tub. I let the water out and refilled with more that was a touch warmer than was really comfortable. I cracked open the window above me and hung a leg over the tub's edge. The cool breeze teased gooseflesh along my thigh. I put both feet on the lip of the tub, my knees like dorsal fins rising up out of the water, and slid down until only my legs were above the water line, my head fully submerged. The world was instantly muted by warm bathwater. I closed my eyes and felt the heat ripple across my submerged body, the way it felt on my face, how it moved through my hair. An image of Lannister's bloated, discolored corpse surfaced to chase away all thoughts of comfort. I had a job to do. I'd work out the logistics of Quinn after that.

The ping from the tracking app filtered through the water. The SUV was on the move. I sat up exuberantly, creating a wave that sloshed water front to back and slopped a little onto the floor. I toweled off with one of the thick terry bath sheets and quickly redressed in the same jeans I'd just taken off, then pulled on a fresh shirt from my bug out kit, a white tee on which was printed I Wouldn't Have to Be Such a Smartass if You Weren't Such a Dumbass in bold letters.

Quinn had built a fire in the woodstove and was sitting in the rocker beside it, scrolling through his phone. He looked up when I exited the bathroom. He couldn't suppress a reluctant smile when he read my shirt.

"SUV's on the move," I announced and began pulling on my shoes.

"What's the rush?" Quinn asked. "Let your tracker do its job. You'll have a record of exactly where it went, and where it eventually lands." He indicated toward the leather loveseat. "Let's finish our conversation."

I eyed the loveseat like it was a coiled snake. "I'm not good with feelings," I warned, "and worse with words about them."

Quinn's brows were knit. He sat with one leg crossed over the other, his fingers steepled beneath his chin. "I'm not willing to just walk away from you, Sam."

"Then try running." Again, my tone belied what I really meant; I was attempting to be lighthearted. Maybe that was the problem.

Quinn shook his head slowly. "I don't want to do that either. I want to throw you on that bed and..."

I waited the span of a heartbeat before I asked, "And what?"

And then he showed me. In a tangle of soft, cool sheets, beside the blazing fire, Quinn showed me exactly, exquisitely, what he wanted. And in that moment, I gave in. I didn't try to control the past, didn't care if I was losing myself in another human being. Neither of us said another word until morning. It was in the depths of that silence that I knew Quinn and I had found our equilibrium.

CHAPTER SIXTEEN

THE SUN HADN'T YET COLORED THE EASTERN SKY WHEN THE BURNER phone began jangling. The sound yanked me from the comfortable depths of slumber. I was snugged up against Quinn's muscular shoulder, the length of my body warm against his. I could have gotten lost in the moment. The burner rang again.

"Yeah...hello," I mumbled semi coherently into the phone. The inside of my mouth was fuzzy and tasted like baby dragons had pooped in it while I slept.

"Sammy, I've hit pay dirt!" Mole's words had the slurred quality of sleep deprivation because he'd pulled a second all-nighter in as many days. "But I can't give you this over the phone. We need to meet up."

I checked the time on the clock radio beside the bed. It wasn't even six in the morning yet. "I can be to you by seven thirty," I offered.

"Don't come here! You might be followed, and these guys are professionals. You wouldn't even know you were being tailed until there was a gun in your face. It's not safe for you to come into the city to me. I'll come to you. Where are you?"

I shared our general location, that we were east of the city. Mole told me to meet him at Cousins, a homestyle eatery in town he said was just off the highway. He'd be there by eight, which meant I wouldn't see him until eight fifteen. He'd take that extra fifteen to scope the place, look for anything suspicious or SUVs. I knew that because that's what I'd do. I didn't ask Mole how he was going to get mobile, and he didn't volunteer the information.

Mole wasn't a shut-in per se, but I'd been doing his errands for as long as I'd known him. If he said he'd meet me, he'd be there.

I hung up the phone and rolled back over toward Quinn, who hadn't moved a muscle. *What are you going to do about this, Sammy?* I pondered. *Why not just let him in? Tell your guard to standdown and give it some well-deserved time off? Or are you too chickenshit to take a chance?* Ouch. That one stung. Truth has a way of doing that. The sheets had ridden down to Quinn's waist, and he had his arms drawn up behind his head. It wouldn't suck waking up to that every morning—I could at least admit that much to myself. But what happened when things weren't blissful, when tensions and the accompanying words would inevitably arise? Isn't it better to avoid the entanglement from the get-go than try to gracefully extricate oneself down the road? God, I hated emotional predicaments.

"You're doing it again, Harris." Quinn didn't even open his eyes to speak.

"What—I have an appreciation for visually stimulating objects," I claimed as my defense. "Sue me."

Quinn opened his eyes and rolled over, propping himself up on an elbow. "I stimulate you?"

"You frighten me." The words were out of my mouth before I realized. I was as shocked by their utterance as Quinn was to hear them.

"The most dangerous thing in the room is afraid? Of *me*?" He clearly had no clue.

I suddenly felt like a doe aware of the oncoming truck barreling at her. Could I blink my eyes and rewind twenty seconds? Teleport myself to another location? My heart was racing around for somewhere to hide. "I like you, Quinn," I said, going for broke. "I'm attracted to you, but too much so. You make me question myself and break my own personal rules." I had, after all, broken the main one—thou shalt not sleep with cops—without putting up much of a fight.

"Love makes people challenge themselves, gives them the opportunity to do something different than they've done before," he said coolly.

I felt my face betray my silent cringing. Love was a wild card that nobody could predict, let alone control. Historically, love was responsible for as many battles as politics were. Love was used as leverage. Affairs of the heart were the perfect weapon.

My silence was my rebuttal.

"Even animals who've known nothing but cruelty at the hands of man learn to accept affection." Quinn wasn't trying to be spiteful. He was trying to make a point.

"Let's just get through this case"—I complied the best I could—"and see where we are. That's the best I can offer you, Quinn." I put my palm flat against his chest. He was warm to the touch. Solid. I leaned in. Our lingering kiss was a silent communication, an agreement that he wouldn't push and I wouldn't pull away. A pact—for now.

We had time before we had to meet Mole. Quinn stoked the fire in the woodstove and made a pot of coffee. I stood at the window and silently watched the moody sky play out its drama over the craggy mountaintops. I envied those rocky points their ability to stoically weather any storm and remain standing. We drank coffee by the fire and discussed the case. It was a blissful couple of hours until the app for the tracker pinged and broke our bubble.

"The SUV's on the move, heading westbound," I observed, "back toward Portland."

"Good, we can relax." Quinn sighed and gestured me back to the loveseat. "Wait—what are you doing?"

I was pulling on my shoes. "We don't relax until the end of this," I said. *Maybe not even then.* "I have to go meet Mole."

"I'm going with you." Quinn went for his shoes.

"That's fine." I slid the HK into my jeans. "I'm going to need someone to watch the lot for me while I'm inside." Mole had been more than his usual level of paranoid when we'd spoken.

Quinn didn't reply to that, but by the displeasure that flashed across his features, I could tell he wasn't thrilled about being left out of the conversation. I fed Doof, then turned him outside to take his morning constitutional. He disappeared around a grouping of boulders, some of them the size of houses, for some time, and I was beginning to get concerned until he came bounding out with a coat full of dried, prickly seeds shed by some plant. Quinn and I took five minutes to pick them out of his fur, taking extra care to examine between the pads of his paws.

The Dalles was pretty quiet that time of morning. The bulk of the highway traffic was truckers, with a smattering of commuters coming off the eastbound interstate to refuel or grab a quick bite to eat. I had Quinn park across the street from the restaurant, where we had the best vantage point of the restaurant's lot, front and back. We observed for twenty minutes before I determined none of Bauer's men were lying in wait and I felt it was all clear. I had Quinn drop me at the diner's front door, which mooed like a cow when opened. Annoying.

With Quinn and Doof remaining in the car, I stepped into the restaurant's lobby. The interior was done in 1990s farm chic. As one who'd never visited an actual working farm before, I wasn't sure how much of the decor was authentic and how much might be cheesy interpretation of farm life. Black-and-white cow print was the dominant pattern.

I rounded the corner into the dining room. Large livestock replicas were scattered around an oversize brick fireplace. Bowls of peanuts sat in the center of each table. Shells purposefully littered the floor. The waitresses were dressed in jeans and flannel. I wasn't sure if the casual attire was the restaurant's official uniform or just what country folk wore. Honky-tonk filtered from tinny speakers mounted along the ceiling. Four tables were occupied with multiple diners, and a table in the far corner was occupied by a single person, someone hunched in their seat, hands stuffed into the front pocket of their hoodie, which was pulled low over their face to obscure their identity. Mole. From where he sat, he could see both the doorway into the kitchen and the front entrance. He pushed the chair opposite him out from under the table with a bright-purple Chuck Taylor.

I pulled the proffered chair further out and took a seat. Mole was visibly shaken. His eyes ping-ponged around the room like he was a caged animal looking for escape, or in Mole's case, attack. The other diners were too engaged with their meals or chitchatting amongst themselves between bites to pay any notice to the weirdo in the corner. Nobody seemed overtly interested in my arrival or Mole's existence. But something clearly had him agitated. That had me spooked.

"Everything all right?" I ventured, not expecting him to break out into the nervous chuckle that he did.

Mole took his hands from his pockets to lean forward on his elbows, which were planted on the table in front of him. He meant his words to be for my ears only. "You've got to let this one go, Samantha. I can't be a part of this."

The fact that Mole had addressed me as Samantha rather than his customary Sammy deepened my alarm. "What's going on, Mole? You're freaking me out."

Mole looked around the room one more time and leaned in further still. "The CIA," he hissed.

For a moment, he had me at a loss. We'd already discovered the CIA's involvement in certain aspects of Lannister Sr.'s life. I think my shrug may have shortened Mole's life because his face blanched an unhealthy shade of pale, and he seemed to forget how to speak. Then, his words suddenly came back to him in a rush. "I found a former IT tech who used to work in that datacenter. It cost me, but I got him to come clean on some details about said center." Another nervous look around. "There's an area of the second floor that nobody is allowed to enter. Your first day on the job, you receive a lengthy warning regarding penalties should you break this singular, hallowed rule. But..." Mole had always been a fan of well-placed, dramatic pauses. "One day there was a glitch in that area. One of the drives overheated. This guy I talked to was escorted into that part of the building, not by guards employed by the center, but by private security. These guys were armed with more than just stun batons. He didn't know what was being stored on those servers, Sammy, but whatever it was, they're protecting it with automatic rifles."

"That doesn't scream CIA," I pointed out. It may have hinted, but it didn't yet scream. I'd seen cartels with the same protection plan, though a drug cartel having control of the second floor of a datacenter was pretty far-fetched. I had to get inside to know for sure. "Did he give you any ideas on how to get inside uninvited?"

Mole grew agitated and clenched his hands into fists. He kept his voice on the downlow, a hushed whisper. "Sammy, have you not heard a word? *C-I-A!* You know, those sons of bitches who have zero sense of humor and a penchant for deep, dark holes where they put people who've displeased them?" He sat back with his arms crossed resolutely over his chest. "I'm officially tapping out of this discussion, Sammy." He literally tapped the tabletop three times then made the motion of closing a zipper over his mouth and tossing the invisible key over his shoulder.

"That's all right," I said with purposeful bravado. "I'm sure if I sit and stare at the center long enough, I'll come up with a solution." I knew acting flippantly confident would immediately bring Mole back on board in a bid to mitigate my danger. I was fully aware of the mental game I was playing with another human being. I was also aware of the karmic pang it caused. Someday I was going to have to go deep with personal introspection and unpack my habits. In layman's terms, I manipulated people's thoughts and emotions to get what I needed from them. I knew if I led Mole to believe I planned on crashing the center, he'd immediately take it upon himself to find me a way in, even at the detriment of his own security. What was worse, I was going to let him do it.

"I hate you," he growled. I knew he didn't mean it. He may not have been my biggest fan in that moment, but he didn't hate me.

"No, you don't," I rebutted, "but you do hate the predicaments we find ourselves in." I added a flash of a genuine smile at the end that softened Mole's entire demeanor.

Mole caved. "Okay, I don't hate you, but I *really dislike* when you think you can take on big bad guys, like the mob, or the Agency, with the actual expectation to walk away from the experience unharmed or uncaged. I love you, Sammy. But sometimes, I really loathe you."

That was the biggest kick in the feels to date and made me feel like a complete dick. "I love you too, Mole." The words were awkward in my mouth, regardless of the fact that the sentiment was true. I could say it because there were no heartstrings playing background music. It was a you-have-my-back, I-have-yours sort of working relationship, not the kind filled with hearts, flowers, or orgasms.

Quinn buzzed the burner in my pocket with a text. We had company—the kind we didn't want. An SUV identical to the one I'd tagged the day before had just pulled into the lot, but my phone hadn't pinged. Hastily I checked the app. The dot had stopped at a truck stop just outside of Sandy and hadn't moved in over an hour. "We've got incoming," I explained to Mole as I scraped my chair back. He stood up, his eyes wildly searching for a way out other than the front exit.

"With me." I instructed Mole to follow me through the double doors leading into the steaming confines of the kitchen. He didn't hesitate.

"Health inspectors," I said from the doorway as I reached into my jacket and pulled out my leather wallet. I dropped it open then flipped it closed again in one swift motion, too fast for anyone to register it was my old Washington, DC, driver's license. "Everyone put down your utensils and step away from your workstations."

"I didn't get any report of an inspection today," piped a thickset woman with graying hair escaping her hair net and a lunch-lady scowl.

"That's because this is a surprise visit," explained Mole, "a pop quiz, if you will." He ran his finger along the top of the stove's vent and came away with black grime. "Oh, look at this...Agent Hall...black grime."

I appreciated Mole's getting into character. "Oh, that's serious," I stammered, "violation of code 8675309. I'm going to have to report this to the Salem office. Good find, trainee..." I searched for a cover name and said the first one that came to mind, "Oates. Let me go get form 26D89C from the car. Come with me. I'll show you where I keep them."

Mole and I made a fast exit out the kitchen's back door and down the stairs to the dumpster-lined back alley. The door at the top of the stairs banged open, and the thickset cook emerged looking disgruntled, a cordless phone screwed to her ear. She likely had the health department on the line, checking my story. By the way she was animatedly hollering into the phone, Mole's and my cover had been blown and she was reporting us for the impostors we were.

The cook's rant was cut off when she was shoved aside by a tactical-clad man with a balaclava snug over his face concealing everything but his cold eyes. He brought up a suppressed handgun and squeezed off two rounds. They both ricocheted off the blue dumpster behind us. The cook yelped when he shoved her back through the door. The missed shots had to be intentional. Warnings. *Freeze or the next ones won't miss.*

My HK was in my hand and returning fire when the Jeep's revved engine roared around the corner of the restaurant. Quinn skidded to a sideways halt that threw road dirt and pebbles up in our direction. The passenger-side door opened.

"Get in!" Quinn screamed as more bullets zinged the air.

I looked over to Mole. His eyes were the size of saucers. An anxious sweat bathed his face. He quaked from fear and nerves. Mole had never been shot at before. His world was in sudden chaos. It was more than he could process. His legs could no longer hear his brain's command to run. They'd become paralyzed by terror. Quinn's instructions and my urging did nothing to break his fear trance.

I slipped the HK into the front of my waistband in order to take Mole by the shoulders with both hands. His eyes were glassy and red-rimmed from lack of sleep. He had no way of accessing any part of his fight-or-flight system.

"Mole," I said serenely amid the gunfire. "Mole, look at me. Mole." I raised my tone a notch. I needed him to snap out of his fugue. It was useless. "Mole!" I shouted and gave his cheek a sharp slap.

That did it. Mole snapped his shocked eyes to mine and raised his hand to his cheek. "Ouch."

"I'm going to lay down cover fire. You run like hell to that open car door. Got it?" A bullet zinged off the dumpster. Sirens were closing in. Faces of brave and curious kitchen staff peered cautiously around the corner of the transom. The shooter had already reached the bottom of the stairs and was out of the spectators' line of sight. It was a dangerous situation. Too many civilians at risk of being caught in crossfire. I shoved Mole hard toward the awaiting Jeep then stood up and began a spray of automatic cover. Mole didn't wait for further invitation. He took off for the open car door, diving in, all but planting his face in Quinn's lap.

The shooter had taken cover behind a brown metal bin marked with the logo of a local pig farm. The overwhelming scent of organic table scraps emanated from its ajar lid. I waited, poised, for the shooter to look out, and I shot over his head when he did. The bullet was close enough for him to feel the wash of its passing, and he ducked back behind cover. I took advantage of the moment and made a run for it. I knew I'd only have a split second.

Mole clambered into the back seat beside a barking Doof. He clutched Doof's collar to keep the loyal animal from coming to my rescue while crouching on the floorboard. I heard a shot ping as it hit McBride's Jeep. I made a dive much as Mole had, landing on my belly partially on the seat, my feet dangling out of the door behind me.

"Drive!" I shouted.

Quinn hesitated, afraid the force of his acceleration might pull me from the Jeep.

"Drive!" I screamed again as I reached down and depressed the accelerator with my hand. The Jeep's tires responded to the punch and spun in place, throwing up rocks and debris until they gained purchase and catapulted us forward. I was able to pull my torso up into the seat enough to brace with a knee and foot against the doorframe to keep from spilling out onto the pavement. Doof covered me with wet, sloppy kisses.

Quinn regained the accelerator and stomped the Jeep into a half circle. He righted us out of a fishtail, jumped the curb, and raced down a side street just as two The Dalles police squad cars bumped into the restaurant's parking lot. I righted myself and pulled the Jeep's half door closed. Mole was hyperventilating in the back seat. Doof whined low in his throat in reaction to the intensity inside the vehicle. He leaned heavily over the back of my seat to lick my cheek. Finally, and without ceremony, he worked his way over the center console, into the front of the cab, to lay himself across my lap. He used his bulk as if to hold me down and shield me from harm.

Nobody spoke. Quinn drove in no particular direction other than away from where we had just been. Both of us kept an eye on the road behind us for police pursuit.

"That was unexpected," I said to break the silence. Quinn scoffed, and Mole punched me in the shoulder from the back seat and shot me a death glare.

"We need to regroup," Quinn pointed out. "Figure out the next move."

"2338 Morrel Drive," Mole spouted. "I already took the liberty of securing a place."

I had my phone out and was looking at the Maps app. "Morrel Drive," I reported, "is in the center of a residential area."

"Seems a bold choice," Quinn threw in his perspective.

Mole scowled at Quinn. "Self-preservation is strong in me, Deputy Quinnlan. If I made a reservation to stay in the center of the residential district, surrounded by houses with computers and laptops within range, maybe trust that I have a plan."

"Quinn," Quinn amended, "and when do we get read-in on these plans of yours before you make them?"

Mole was visibly rankled. He wasn't used to someone other than me second-guessing him, and I got a free pass because I was, well, me. To Mole, Quinn wasn't necessarily the enemy, but he was certainly someone to keep at arm's length until he proved himself worthy otherwise. One didn't rest comfortably at the top of the FBI's Most Wanted for as long as Mole had by slap dashing their next move.

"Furthermore"—Quinn was going into full law mode—"is it a good idea for a known hacker to have access to civilians' computers? Your plan is to hack into them, isn't it? Why else would you choose to expose yourself—"

"Here's the thing, officer." Mole turned his glare my direction. "I never chose to expose myself." He was speaking directly to me at that point. "I was outed. Thrown under the bus. By no choice of my own." He turned his attention back to Quinn. "So if I choose to move forward without sharing, either follow my lead or jump out of the boat before you sink it." He sat back, eyes forward on the road, and didn't say another word.

I was in the front seat managing my shock. I'd never been on the receiving end of Mole's outburst before, so witnessing my first was startling. Good on him!

Mole directed Quinn down a series of narrow, shrub-lined streets laid out in the typical squared lots. Car-length driveways. Attached garages. 2338 Morrel was a tan, single-story ranch from the mid-'80s with a Spanish-style tiled roof. A quintessential white picket fence enclosed the rental's front yard, which had white decorative gravel bordered by beds of drought-resistant plants. A squat cactus with fluorescent-orange button flowers sat in a wide terracotta pot beside the front door, which was paneled with stained glass depicting mountain scenes and tulips. Inside, the house was done up in Southwestern colors—turquoise, adobe, and sage green, coupled with green Irish knotwork stitched into pillows to match the Celtic-knotted throw clinging to the wall by three tacks. It was difficult to pinpoint the designer's theme or the owner's tastes.

"I'm dizzy," Mole mumbled his reaction.

"That's visual jet lag." Quinn attempted to make a funny.

I coaxed Doof into the strange house. He entered with his hackles on alert, his nose working the air.

"You damage anything, dog, and it's coming out of your owner's pocket. I had to pay a hefty fee just to allow you to be here."

"Aww." I was touched that Mole had thought of Doof. I just hoped housekeeping had a vacuum good enough to capture his downy undercoat, which got onto everything. Mole was already setting up his workstation on the dining room table. He connected to the internal Wi-Fi, configured his VPN, and set to work. Within minutes he'd gained access into the neighboring systems. It wasn't long before we heard him exclaim victory.

"What's happened?" Quinn innocently asked. I put my hand on his arm and gave him a silent head shake. *You don't want to know.* If anybody needed to distance himself by remaining ignorant, it was Quinn. I suspected Mole had just located precisely what it was he'd been hoping for: the nearby system of someone who worked from home for an outside company. Better still, he was able to gain access to that business's computer. By the size of his feces-eating grin, it was a large enough network in which to bury his activity. A hacker's favorite scenario.

"What I need you to do," I suggested to Mole, "is get your friend on the line, the one you talked to about security at the datacenter. I want to know about shift-change schedules, how many security guards are on site at any given time, and the system's weakest points. Do you think he'll give that to us?"

"I can try," Mole answered. He slid his headphones over his ears and set to work answering my questions.

Just then I was struck with brilliance. *Of course,* I thought. *It's worth a try and it's the best angle yet.* I had the answer to our dilemma: how to get a look inside the datacenter. "Watch Doof for me until I get back, will you?" I asked Quinn when I was halfway to the front door. "I'm going to go do a little intel on my own. On foot. Alone," I added when he got up to follow.

It was a bit of an urban hike, but I made my way along the residential side streets, down through a lumber mill lot, to the bar overlooking the datacenter's parking lot. It was the same random smattering of vehicles as before. I watched what must have been a shift change. A handful of employees exited the building with bags and lunchboxes to be replaced by a handful of fresh employees carrying the same. Nobody in any of the in-and-out flow struck me as potentials. They all wore the same bored expression.

I took another walk around the perimeter of the building, approaching again from the north, over the boulder field. I wondered what the response time might be to a disturbance. A rock the size of my fist helped determine that when I forcefully hucked it over the fence to crash against a side door. *One one thousand, two one thousand, three one—* The side door flew open and two uniformed guards stepped out, one with his sidearm drawn, the other with a stun baton that he slapped menacingly against his open palm.

Both impressed and put off by the quick and serious response to my disruption, I made my way back to the rental. Doof was passed out in the middle of the floor. Quinn was sitting on the couch flipping through an ancient copy of *Field & Stream* but not paying any attention to the pages. Mole had his headphones on and didn't immediately react to my return. I kicked my shoes off and dropped cross-legged onto the floor beside Doof, burying my hands and face into his thick, lush fur. "Who's my bestest boy?" I muffled against his neck. He didn't even twitch.

Mole took notice of my return. "Any luck with your endeavor?" He dropped his headphones around his neck but continued working on whatever it was he was invested in.

"If I find my way in," I curveballed him a hypothetical, "then what?"

Mole spun in his seat to face me. "Then you stick this bad boy"—he plucked a thumb drive from tabletop—"into any USB port."

"Any?" I needed clarification. "So, like, the guard's station? Any workstation? Or do I need to actually access an IT workstation?"

"Any," he reiterated. "Just as all datacenters are connected to one another, every computer inside those centers is networked together."

"That seems like iffy security," I pointed out.

"That's because it's impossible to get inside," Mole rebutted.

"Maybe." I gave a shrug and left it at that.

Quinn put down the magazine. I had his full attention. "Did you find a way in?"

"No," I admitted, "not yet." What I didn't admit to was having a plan.

"Then I'd say it's still pretty good security." Mole dragged his headphones back over his ears.

I took the thumb drive from Mole and turned it over in my hand. "What's on here?" I asked.

"I could take the next several minutes to explain, Sammy, but would you even understand if I did?"

Okay, yeah, I was a little slow when it came to technology and nerd-speak, but he didn't have to be a butthead about it. Mole did have a point, though. He and I had both racked up hours on explanations that I still couldn't comprehend. That was a lot of time neither of us was ever getting back.

"I was able to get ahold of my confidential informant from the datacenter." Because he didn't have a printer, Mole gave me a handwritten copy of the guards' shift-change schedule and everything else I'd requested.

I perused the schedule while mentally working out my strategy. Much of my plan would require getting precise reactions to my actions. That wasn't something I could predict, but it was possible I might be able to control the narrative on my end. My whole approach was sketchy at best, but it was a move nobody would be expecting.

Not even Mole or Quinn.

CHAPTER SEVENTEEN

Just find a way to get me back out.

I hadn't said it was the safest, best idea. Hell, I didn't have any way of knowing if any of my foolhardy plan would play out as I wanted it to or if I'd end up in federal custody. Odds were, it would backfire, and the mess could get everywhere. No, I wasn't having second thoughts. I was thinking about others, something I'd been told I don't do enough of. Whatever. Look at me now.

I chose early morning the next day, when David Kodlin wasn't in the office, to make my move. I figured that would give Mole and Quinn more daylight hours to do their part and get me back out. They'd both been terse when I'd explained my plan. Quinn immediately went on the defensive, which prompted me to point out that his reaction was precisely why I typically didn't share plans with the rest of the room. Quinn was insistent I was setting myself up for disaster. I pointed out to him that this was what I was entrusting him and Mole to prevent. I gave Doof a pat and told him to behave. With a loving last look at my HK, promising the cold steel we'd be reunited soon, I'd left the two humans and the dog standing in the doorway. I felt more attachment to my weapons than I did human beings. I'm sure that alone would make me a psychotherapist's wet dream.

I was armed only with a clean burner phone, compliments of Mole, and the thumb drive he gave me, which was inside my bra, along the underside of my left breast. I stuck a paperclip under my other breast to even out the detectable metal. The procedure, once I got inside, was a thorough pat-down and a pass-over with a metal-detecting wand. Most pat-downs weren't as methodical as they should be. It's difficult to detect something that's barely there when using the back of your hand in sensitive areas. The wand would pick up the hard drive for sure, but it would be perceived as an underwire in my bra.

Mole had taken measures a step further when he stuck an American flag lapel pin to my jacket. I wasn't the pin-wearing sort, and if you knew that about me, you'd recognize the pin was, in fact, a bug. Mole and Quinn would be able to hear every word by me and those in proximity. A tiny molded transmitter inside my ear would allow me to hear Mole.

I made my way down to the datacenter's perimeter fence. I recognized several of the cars in the lot from my earlier recon.

Before I'd left, I had Mole confirm that the same guard wouldn't be on duty. Officer Cornfed would be a game changer. Mole's intel had been spot-on. An older gent with kindly eyes manned the security station. He'd perched himself on a three-legged stool before a flat computer screen. Probably playing solitaire or online poker; nothing about him fit the perverted-old-man stereotype. He didn't seem creepy. Didn't strike me as the kiddie-porn sort.

When I stepped onto the datacenter's property, I made an effort to look pointedly into the lens of the security camera stationed at the gate. The guard looked up from his screen, smiled, and nodded when he caught my eye. I was now officially trespassing.

Up to that moment, I'd spent so much of my effort navigating around anything that brought tears as its by-product that I couldn't even muster a single one when I needed it. I tried thinking of something sad. Nothing. I thought of my own failure. Blank. My plan's first step was already failing. Nope, still not a drop. Dammit. With the heels of my palms, I rubbed my eyes until they were puffy and red. Dry, but with a few well-placed sniffles, should be convincing.

As I had rehearsed in my head on the way over, I let my shoulders quiver just a bit (don't overdo it) and bit my bottom lip. I sniffed exaggeratedly and dabbed at my dry eyes with my sleeve. I was even able to manage a convincing emotional whimper that had the guard rising from his stool, his face full of concern. If my current security gig didn't pay out in the end, I could go to Hollywood. My performance was ideal. Award worthy.

"My goodness, miss," the guard said gently, a huge contrast from Officer Cornfed's attitude. He was careful not to lay the comforting hand on my shoulder that would normally have been his nature. "Can I be of any assistance?" he politely asked.

The guard's uniform was neatly pressed. He smelled of fabric softener and Ivory soap. By the nameplate fastened to the front of his tan uniform, he went by Fionn. That was a strong Irish name. As in Fionn MacCool, a central character in Irish folklore and myth. Fionn gave off a compassionate, grandfatherly vibe. Maybe it was owing to the white crown of hair that ringed his tanned head. Or the length of his carefully trimmed beard, long since gone white. His complexion was that of someone who'd spent a lifetime toiling in nature. A farmer, or a rancher, or a park ranger. A once-virile body gone soft with age and the absence of manual labor.

"I need to speak with David Kodlin," I said in a shaky, hiccupping voice. "Please?"

"I'm sorry, ma'am," Fionn began to beg off, "but I'm not authorized—"

I buried my face in my hands and let loose a howling sob. "Please," I pleaded, "the deadbeat son of a bitch refuses to return my calls."

Fionn put his hands up to deflect my outburst. "Please, ma'am, there's no need for language."

Fionn's passiveness wasn't going to get me anywhere. It might take me time I didn't have to wear him down. I took a long, shuddering breath, scrunched my face up the way it naturally would if I were trying to fend off tears, hid behind my hands, and let my shoulders quiver and quake as if I were having an actual emotional breakdown.

"Ach, don't cry, ma'am," Fionn tried to placate. "Everything is going to be all right." His words were genuinely meant to take the sting out of the moment. There were no doubts that Fionn had experience with kids and grandchildren. "Maybe I can fetch you a bottle of water." He indicated toward the dorm fridge under the counter inside his guard shack. "And offer a supportive ear, if you want to talk about it?"

I caught a quick glance inside the guard shack when he reached for the fridge. A still-steaming coffee mug with World's Greatest Grandpa printed on the side sat on the edge of the standing-height desk and validated my profile. A wall calendar featuring the Shamrock Rovers Football Club hung by the window. A serene poster of the Irish countryside, with a romantic ode to Old Eire hung on the back wall. A laminated photograph of the Pope was taped to the bottom edge of the computer monitor. Fionn was a football fan (*soccer* in American vernacular) and a family man who deeply identified with both his heritage and his religion. Every detail was a possible point to exploit.

I snuffled and dragged my sleeve across my nose and gave a hiccupping thank-you. Fionn brought out his stool and set it in the shade of the guard shack. Ever the kind man he was, Fionn loosened the cap before passing me the bottle of water.

"Th-thank you," I stammered and gave a heavy sigh as I leaned back wearily against the guard shack's exterior wall.

Fionn checked the screens of the security monitors before joining me in the shade. He didn't say anything for a long moment, just held still, silent space with me. God, he was a good man, and I felt more than a little shitty for what I was about to pull on him.

I let him be the one to break the silence when he said, "If you don't mind me asking, miss, and I certainly don't mean to be nosy, but something's got you terribly worked up." He clasped his hands behind his back and leaned a shoulder against the shady wall. "I'm told I'm really good at hearing things out."

Mole was suddenly in my ear. "Pace yourself." I'd almost forgotten he was there. "Don't rush it, and don't overexplain."

I took a deep breath and let it out slow like I was trying to compose my jumbled emotions. Truth was, I was working the best angle for my short con. "David and I went on a date, and I got pregnant." I sniffled and hiccupped for effect. "As you might know, David is...frugal. When he found out I was going to have a baby, he freaked. He said he couldn't afford a child and his stuff. He said he wouldn't pay, but he told me I had to get an...an..." More sobs until Mole cued me back on track.

"That's good," I heard Mole in my ear.

"I couldn't do *that*," I cried. "David told me he wanted nothing to do with either of us." I stammered my way through the sob story I was creating on the spot about a toddler child in need of the essentials to thrive—food, clothing, shelter—of a deadbeat and loathsome father, and the pitiful single mother trying to get by. My stuttering soliloquy surged and fell in emotional waves. More snuffling and wiping at invisible tears.

Mole was in my ear again. "That was some acting, Sammy. Cue the little gold statue."

"Oh," Fionn fussed, trying to defuse my moment, "I'm sure Mr. Kodlin's heart will eventually find its way to the right place." Fionn fretted, wringing his hands. "It's not easy being a young father. Why, when my eldest, Aengus, was born, I had a devil of a time settling myself into my new role and responsibilities. Mr. Kodlin, he'll come around. You'll see."

Wait—what? Was Fionn actually trying to stand up for David the Deadbeat? Had I misread the room? Jumped to stereotypical conclusions? I'd expected Fionn, the dutiful Irish father and man of faith, to jump to the defense of me, the alleged single mother who was only trying to do right by her child. In short, I'd wanted Fionn to play into my con. Getting into the front door didn't depend on getting Fionn into my corner. He was only stage dressing. I was just incensed he was standing up for deadbeat man-whore David.

"Get mad at David. Get mad at the guard for defending him," Mole said in my ear. "Make a scene."

I abruptly changed tactics. "How dare you come to David's defense," I seethed and threw the bottle of water he'd given me back at him. The uncapped bottle caught him in the chest. The drenched look of shock on his face was instantaneous. Like a slap of betrayal. I wasn't standing there to make friends. I had an objective, regardless of whose feelings got slaughtered. I called Fionn a wretched human and tried to push past him.

"Now hold on a minute, miss." Fionn tried his best to resolve the situation, but I heard doubt, or maybe it was his Catholic conscience, in his voice. He recovered when he added, "I cannot allow you access to the property. I'm deeply sorry for your situation. I wish you the best of luck."

I needed to push a little harder, apply a little more pressure on his personal ethics. "If the baby hadn't been born so weak, he'd have a fighting chance against David's abandonment. The pediatrician says he's so..." The word suddenly vanished from my vocabulary.

"Emaciated?" Mole suggested. "Sickly? And mention allergies. Sickly kids always have an ass ton of allergies."

"If he weren't so sickly and allergic to the world, he might have a chance at a normal childhood." Another attempt to squeeze tears out. "But that's all right. I understand your company's policy," I added with another sleeve-dragging sniffle. "You're just doing your job." By using the passive-aggressive method my mother had often wielded like a ninja, I hoped Fionn would give me what I needed. And that he would cave soon—I was running out of tricks. I put my face into my hands and went for broke, wailing, shoulders shuddering, and snuffling as if to run snot back up into my nose. "Can someone please just get David Kodlin for me so we can talk? *Please?*" I squeaked out my final plea.

Then, like a certifiable crazy woman, my mood shifted 180 degrees. I raised my voice and worked my mouth into a snarl. "Go get that son of a bitch!" I screamed and pointed at the front doors of the datacenter. "Get David Kodlin out here right now!" My demand was filled with the venom.

Fionn's surprised and rattled reaction to my intensity was promising. His mouth worked like a fish gulping for air as his ability to make words failed him.

"Never mind," I said abruptly. "I'll go in and bring him out myself." I spun on my heel and marched toward the datacenter's front doors.

By the time the entrance doors slid open and I strode inside, another uniformed security guard was there to meet me. This guy was younger than Fionn by a good three decades. He was fit and wearing the same company uniform Fionn had. His nametag said Jeff. Jeff didn't seem to be the same compassionate type like his elder coworker. The wall behind Jeff was filled with monitors, screens from the many security cameras sprinkled around the property. I marched toward the counter with my hands balled into fists and a sneer set on my face.

Jeff lifted both of his hands in a halt-there motion. "Ma'am, I'm going to have to ask you to remain calm."

"I don't want to remain calm, asshat," I hissed.

"Whoa!" Mole was in my ear again.

"Ma'am, there's no need for violence and name-calling," Jeff stated matter-of-factly.

"Then get David Kodlin out here, *now!*" I screamed. A clip-board for visitors to sign in and out sat on the counter that separated the lobby from the door leading into the rest of the building. I hucked the clipboard at him.

"Careful, Sammy," Mole said in my ear. "Don't oversell your anger."

Jeff reacted the only way he could, the way his training had taught him in situations such as this: he fingered a switch that lay just out of sight under the edge of the kiosk's hip-high counter. Now we were getting somewhere! Within seconds a door in the middle of that wall of screens opened, and backup stepped out.

This guy was young enough to be Fionn's grandson. A grand-son who clearly had a gym membership and a penchant for pumping iron. His uniform was different from both Fionn's and Jeff's. This guy's dark-blue trousers had a matching blazer with a gold-and-red Touchstone Security logo embroidered on the breast pocket and obviously had to be tailored to accommodate his bulk. He didn't wear a nametag. Both a holstered Glock, not Cornfed's peashooter, and a taser wand hung from his belt. His mouth was set in a hard sneer like he was bored and itching for a fight. I may have overstated my request. But I was precisely where I wanted to be.

This big guy had no qualms about rounding the counter and taking me by the elbow. He moved awkwardly in his uniform, like he was afraid of hulking out of it if he made the wrong sud-den move.

"Steroids," I said in my best commercial voice. "Side effects may include ill-fitting clothes and a painfully tiny penis. Ask your doct—" He took offense at my snarkiness, and the grip on my elbow tightened painfully.

"This is how you treat visitors to your facility?" I asked Jeff, pointing up at the big guy's square jaw and whiskerless face as

I was none-too-gently escorted through the door in the wall of monitors. His rough handling was going to leave a mark—but I was officially inside the datacenter.

I didn't make it easy for my escort and purposefully lagged in my steps. My uncooperativeness forced him to pull me along. I was half-dragged, half-led through a series of heavy industrial doors leading deeper into the datacenter. I suspected I was close to that inner sanctum Mole's snitch had spoken of. I'd like to get inside, but I doubted that was going to happen.

We went past glass-walled offices, some of them empty, some with glassy-eyed occupants starring at computer screens. Nobody paid attention to our passing. I noticed the moment we entered the secured area. The barely noticeable buzz of Mole's comfortable presence in my ear disappeared behind the heavy steel door.

"Where are you taking me?" I asked the Big Guy as we passed a series of office doors protected by both an electronic keypad and an ocular scan. "Is this the way to David Kodlin's office?" He didn't offer up an answer. In fact, he didn't even acknowledge I'd spoken.

The thumb drive was rubbing against my skin under my boob. I wanted to retrieve it, but not before I might be patted down. I wondered if all visitors, invited or not, were ushered down the same long hallway? Another set of security doors and we entered into an additional long, windowless hall that ended in a final security door. There were no signs on the door denoting what might lie beyond.

"Where are you taking me?" I repeated without raising my voice, snarling, or threatening in any other way as the Big Guy thumbed in a numerical sequence then leaned forward with his forehead to the wall while a red laser scanned his retina. He grunted his answer and pushed me in through the door.

"Is this how you treat all visitors?" I incensed.

"My boss phoned Mr. Kodlin," the Big Guy sneered. "He's never heard of you, has never fathered a child. So, we will find out who you are and deliver you to the appropriate authorities."

Appropriate authorities? That was vague. Why not just say the police or the Feds? I began to get a sick little pit in my stomach. Maybe my plan to infiltrate the datacenter had worked too well. I still had no idea who was behind the Lannister hits. Could have been a zealous collector of Cold War intel, could have been an enemy of the state. "Appropriate authorities" was purely subjective.

The Big Guy swung open the door into a windowless room. There was none of the usual furniture to denote an office. Heavy steel shelves I'd seen before in automotive shops lined the walls, but nothing was on them. A copy machine sat behind the door. He pushed me inside and used nonverbal commands to order me down, shoving me forcefully to the floor beside the copy machine. His sharp scowl stapled me to the floor, telling me to stay put, or else.

The Big Guy turned away to make a call on his radio, glancing back at me twice in the duration of his conversation. I didn't think it was to ensure I was following his instructions and stayed put. He was discussing me with someone. I got a bad feeling in my gut. A bad, bad feeling.

The copy machine was half the size of a chest freezer. It looked like any other copy machine I'd ever seen, with a hinged lid with an auto-feed tray, and drawers below to hold different sizes of paper. Most copy machines in an office or facility like this were networked and tethered to the workstations. They were programmable manually through the onboard computer screen.

The Big Guy was conversing with someone in a hushed tone. His back was turned to me, so I couldn't hear what was being said. As silently as I could, I got my feet under me and balanced in a low crouch. I retrieved the thumb drive from inside my bra. Mole had said any USB port in any computer would work. He could access the datacenter's internal system from any USB port within the building. This wasn't a workstation, but like I said, it was networked to every computer at every workstation in the building.

I had to trust this would work. I brought my hand up slowly, creeping it up the side of the machine, out of the Big Guy's line of sight. I thought he'd caught my movement in his peripherals when he shifted his weight from one foot to the other and turned so that he was facing the wall at my back. His eyes slid sideways and pinned me down. I froze, balanced in that low crouch, my quads burning. Note to self: do more squats.

The corner of the copy machine obscured my lower half from full view. My quadriceps burned. I ignored the cramping and focused on my breath. I couldn't reach the port without shifting my position. I couldn't do that unless the Big Guy himself moved, turned around, or walked away. I expected him to do none of those things. I willed him to do something. Anything.

My mental effort was rewarded. For whatever blessed reason, in the middle of his hushed conversation, he turned his back to me. I moved quick and silent. The thumb drive was on a direct trajectory for the port. The Big Guy had his back to me. It was the perfect opportunity.

Then it all went sideways.

The thumb drive slipped from my fingers, fell to the floor, and skittered beneath the copy machine. I froze. The Big Guy spun on his heel at the sound. He caught me where I'd frozen—crouched and reaching.

"I'm going to need to call you right back," I clearly heard him growl into his radio.

I stood up fully and squared my shoulders. A smile spread across the lower half of my face. This was the fight I'd been expecting. The brawl I'd been itching for.

Unimpressed by my show of bravado, the Big Guy shoved a pointed finger at the floor. "Down. I won't ask you again."

"No." I let that mocking grin of mine deepen. "You didn't say please."

The Big Guy's eyes narrowed dangerously, the way I imagine a predator's might when it was about to make its lethal pounce. "Down." His order was barely above a whisper. I recognized what was happening inside his head. The mechanisms that kept him from being on a murderous rage were silently stepping aside, disengaging. He was no longer safety-on. But would he be able to pull back in time? Retract the claws? Reengage before ripping my head off? We were about to find out.

"Make me," I challenged.

The Big Guy met my challenge head-on. He brought his radio up to his mouth and said the worst thing possible for my situation. "I may need backup."

I wasn't sure who was going to show up. If backup were Fionn or Jeff, I could end the conversation really quick. However, it would be a complete game changer if a couple of guys built like the Big Guy arrived. We'd have to wait and see who answered the summons.

I stood my ground against the Big Guy's threatening silence. He rounded his shoulders and puffed his chest. Pure posturing. Then he took an intimidating step forward, his meaty hands in fists.

I didn't flinch. Didn't budge. Instead, I egged him on with a tittering of laughter. Soft at first, like I was working to contain my mirth, until it burst out in a loud cackle. I put my hand up apologetically. "Sorry," I managed between spasms of laughter, my lips tight between my teeth in an effort to rein it in.

"On. The. Floor!" he roared, punctuating his demand with a fist punched hard into the opposite palm. It brought to mind a professional wrestler's over exaggerations. The Big Guy's effort had the opposite effect and made me burst out in a genuine guffaw. His face turned a deep, unhealthy shade of red.

I raised my middle finger. That got a reaction. His balled, angry fists curled even tighter. His lips quivered into a sneer. He was ready to punish me for my insolence. We closed the gap between us with two steps apiece. He reared back to throw a knockout punch. I raised my bent elbow when he released, set my shoulder and core, leaned into it, and met the full brunt of the punch, elbow first.

There are twenty-seven bones in the human hand. I felt most of those collapse under the force of the collision. The power of the impact travelled up my arm and was absorbed by my counter stance, but I'd feel it for sure in the morning. The Big Guy cradled his broken hand against his chest, but he was already adjusting for another go at it. Before he could get ahold of me, I climbed his torso like a tree, wrapping my legs around his head and neck and twisting so that we both went crashing to the ground. He punched against my legs with his good hand. There was nobody around to hear our scuffle. I reached a well-placed punch to the groin to keep him down.

Every individual has their snapping point. Under certain conditions, the human psyche can be extremely fragile. Instances like extreme stress or uncontrollable rage have the ability to break a person. Had the Big Guy gotten ahold of me, he would certainly have ended me right then and there. I wriggled like a fish out of his grasp. While he was incapacitated by his groin injury, I easily got him into a choke hold. The Big Guy bucked and kicked, but I was able to hang on for the full eight seconds. Not my first rodeo. I checked his vitals when he went limp.

Don't judge me. I knew it was poor sportsmanship to kick a guy in his junk and worse to choke hold him while he was penialy debilitated. But someone somewhere said that all was fair in love and war. Or something like that. It didn't matter the direct quote; it was the sentiment that mattered. There was nowhere to stash the Big Guy's inert body, so I propped him up against the copy machine. He'd rally soon enough. I didn't want to be anywhere near when this bull woke up.

Now I needed to finish what I'd started. Accomplish what I'd come here to do.

On my belly, I peered under the machine for the runaway thumb drive. I saw it, just out of my reach. I slid my arm as far as I could until I was up to my shoulder under the machine. I swept my hand back and forth, careful not to push any object I encountered there further away. My fingers brushed against something small and hard. There it was! There was no way to grasp it with the very tips of my fingers. Each time I tried, I inadvertently moved it farther away. I needed a tool of some sort.

A quick search of the Big Guy yielded nothing useful aside from his keycard and radio, both of which I relieved him of. I eyed his belt. Maybe I could snake it under the machine and bring the thumb drive within reach. Ack—that meant handling the Big Guy's trousers and risking jostling him awake. I didn't see any other option.

"Don't take this personal," I muttered as I undid his buckle and gently unthreaded the hole end of the stiff leather back through the loops of his uniform, one at a time, until I could effectively pull the belt free. He didn't move.

Back on my belly, I worked the buckle end of the belt under the machine. I caught an edge of the thumb drive and slowly, gently began to coax it toward me. It took a dozen attempts and me nearly losing my shit in frustration before I was able to retrieve the tiny drive. I slid it home into the face of the copy machine and prayed something was happening on Mole's end of things.

I used the lifted keycard on the door at the end of the hall and followed the stairwell up. I swiped the card again to gain access to the corridor and stepped into a stark hallway. White linoleum floors and overhead fluorescents gave the hallway a cold,

lonely air. Only two doors led off the corridor. One at the opposite end, the other on the left midway down. Security cameras
were mounted above each. There was no way to avoid them and
probably no reason to try to. If the Big Guy hadn't yet rallied, it
was only a matter of time before his previously requested backup
would materialize. I had to keep moving and eyed the two doors
with indecision.

My deliberation was short. I opted for the one nearest me,
mid-corridor. The same keycard let me in. At that point I was
flying completely blind, and for a brief moment, it was as if I'd
stepped into the inner workings of an actual computer. Server
racks eight feet high stood in multiple parallel rows separated
by a narrow access path. The all-pervasive, mechanical drone
of the servers overrode all other sounds. The air was kept cool.
The space was dimly illuminated by caged bulbs affixed above
the ends of each row.

I made a fast once-around in the server room when I heard
shouting outside the door. Security had arrived. A team, judging by the number of raised voices. Red fire extinguishers were
mounted to each vertical support beam. I worked one free and
used it to smash the keycard panel beside the door, banking on
the fact that each panel was hardwired together and what happened to one would affect the others, triggering a lockdown. The
pad obliterated, I hoped I'd bought myself at least a few extra
minutes to find a way of escape.

Mole was still absent from my ear, the building still blocking
his transmission. Things suddenly got plenty more stimulating
when the caged lights dimmed to red and a deep, rhythmic blaring began. The intruder alarm had been sounded. Lockdown
engaged. I was sealed inside hostile territory. *Think, Sam!* I
looked up, as if the answer to my predicament were going to
miraculously appear. And then it did: if going out through the
in door wasn't an option, perhaps going *up* was.

I examined the nearest server rack. The frame was bolted to the ground. It seemed secure enough to climb. Not as easy a task as it sounded in my head. There were no footholds or anything to grasp on to. I ended up having to move to the end row nearest the far wall to leverage my back against it. I inched myself up vertically until I was able to grab the top edge and pull myself up. The towers were bolted to each other and to the floor, but I felt like it wouldn't take much to topple them if I wanted to, domino style.

The ceiling was just overhead, easily within reach. I stretched both arms up and moved the insulative fiberboard panel aside with flat palms. Beneath me the rack's casing popped as it caved slightly under my weight. An enclosed channel of thin aluminum ran the length of the ceiling space affixed to the upper roof by vertical metal support rods. Inside the channel I knew would be bundles of fiber optic and networking cables. I hauled both legs up and pivoted to sit on my butt. I didn't bother with replacing the panel I'd moved.

On all fours and balancing on the narrow channel was the only way I was able to navigate through the electronic vascular system and not be too concerned with electrocuting myself. I'd gleaned a few things about basic low-voltage wiring from Mole. I understood datacenters generated high temperatures and required outside arrangements—usually in the form of water—to keep them from overheating. That's why they were typically built along waterways or submerged in the ocean. Natural resources utilized as coolant.

So, hypothetically, if I could cut my way in through the air conditioning ductwork and find a way to stop the circulating fan, there was a slim chance of escape through the exterior unit mounted to the roof. Getting to the roof was one thing. Attaining freedom from there was a detail I had yet to figure out. I'd figure it out on the fly. One crisis at a time.

The way was slow in the dark. I needed both hands to fumble my way along the conduit deeper into the datacenter's vascular system. Following the whirring sound emanating from the ceiling, I worked my way to the base of the nearest A/C unit housed in the roof, high overhead. The unit itself was large, about the size of a compact electric car. The ducting dropped to the ceiling floor and snaked the length of the ceiling under the conduit channel. Industrial air-conditioning units required wide ducts to distribute large quantities of air. This duct was wide enough for me to crawl through on my hands and knees. It took some effort to work a hole low in the side of the shiny foil insulation with the sharp end of the lapel pin. When I could grope my fingers into the hole, I began tearing and ripping through the yellow insulation until it was wide enough to slip through.

It was a little more work crawling inside. The thick-gauge wire that spiraled through the ducting tube, structurally meant to hold the ductwork's shape, created stiff metal ribs. My first attempt to use those ribs as ladder rungs failed when I could find nothing to hold on to. I used the lapel pin again to slice handholds that became toeholds as I climbed. It was painstakingly slow going, but I eventually made my way up the sagging duct to the base of the unit.

I listened for signs of both approaching security or the duct tube ripping away from the base of the unit under my bulk. It was never meant to carry the weight of a human. There was nothing detectable but the cold rush of airflow. Wide fan blades moved in deceptively slow, seemingly lazy circles that still had the force to embed themselves in me. I needed to get them stopped. But how? I wasn't a fan (pardon the pun) of the answer when it came to mind. I knew what I had to do and that I'd only get one opportunity, one chance to get it right.

First, I had to open another hole in the insulation. Time consuming but simple enough. Once that was done, I pulled my head and shoulders through. There was no light to see by as I felt around with my hands for anything I could grab ahold of. I found nothing. The thin rim that formed the base of the unit was just wide enough to grasp with my fingers but not my whole hand. I intended to get myself away from the duct tube when I activated my plan, but that meant suspending myself by the fingertips of one hand above the processors, separated by twelve feet of empty air. *Piece of cake*, I reassured myself. *I've been in more precarious situations than this.* None actually came to mind just then, but I didn't pay attention to that.

For my plan to work, I needed something rigid enough to stop a spinning fan blade. I stooped back into the ducting tube. With my bare hands, I began to skin and pull away the insulative casing to expose the reinforcing wire. The wire was thin but much too strong to be flexible. I gathered the loops of stripped wire and held them like a handful of lassos that fought to spring free. Though the wire was long and continuous, I was able to gather enough in my hand that it would forcefully release and entangle in the spinning blades (if all went according to plan).

I felt time that I didn't have ticking away. I took a deep breath and assessed the validity of my plan. It wasn't perfect. Hell, it was just that side of sketchy. Truth be told, I'd be surprised if I didn't wind up dead or maimed by twisted metal.

With the lariat of wire loops in my right hand, I positioned myself outside of the duct tube. I took a deep breath as I transferred the whole of my weight onto the fingertips of my left, less dominant hand. Instantly my digits cramped and grew slick with the effort it took to dangle my entire body off them. I forced the discomfort aside and readied to release the tension of coiled wire into the slow spin of the fan blades.

The sound of a door crashing open somewhere beneath me made my heart jump. I froze, still precariously dangling from the thin rim of the cooling unit's base. When voices erupted beneath me, I knew I'd run out of time. I held the taut loops of wound wire as close to the rotating blades as I could and opened my hand.

The taut wire sprang directly into the circulating fan. Everything went explosively fast from there. The rotating blades grabbed hold of the wire, and the slow-turning mechanism pulled it in with force. The loud mangling sound of twisting metal and the screech of a burning motor were cringe inducing. The spinning fan blade came to a stuttering halt.

The concussion of the bits crashing together was almost enough to shake me loose. I couldn't hang there by my fingertips for much longer. My right leg swung up onto the twisted mess of metal, and I prayed to Anyone who'd listen that I didn't get myself wrapped up in that twisted metal mess. I nudged it with my foot—the motor, with some life still left in it, gave a sickening lurch. The material I was balanced on gave a powerful heave, knocking me off balance in the dark. I didn't know what to grab hold of. I scrabbled for a grip on anything stationary. My hands found the sharp edge of the unit, and I gouged the pad of my palm on the corner. When I rearranged my hold, the back of my hand hit something hard, but not sharp. I grappled for it—the edge of the steel support I-beam of the roof. I grabbed the edge and walked my hands out, away from the dangerous position I'd put myself in.

When the fan blades settled into another grinding halt, I held my breath and counted to twenty. *One Mississippi, two Mississippi...* At *fifteen Mississippi*, voices erupted directly below me. When I hit *twenty Mississippi*, the fan blade hadn't stirred again, and there were no longer screeching complaints coming from the motor. A voice was on the radio calling for assistance. I figured my odds weren't going to improve, and opportunity's knock, in this case, was loud. *Don't think. Just do!*

I was no gymnast, but in that moment, I became one. Still suspended by my hands on the steel support beam, I began swinging my legs back and forth, like a kid on the monkey bars. I gathered enough reach with my outstretched legs to be able to jam them, feet first, through the negative space between the stilled blades. I had no idea what I was going to do next. *Don't think. Just do!* my survival instinct urged again. It had a point. Don't pause, keep moving, and hope for the best.

The bottom edge of my butt cheeks rested painfully on the upturned ridge of the fan blade. I scooted forward until all my weight was on the jamb of twisted metal. When I did, the fan motor gave a nauseating last heave and came to momentary life. My pantleg caught in the lurch of metal that began eating the denim. I ripped my leg out in a panic and scuttled the rest of the way through.

Once safely through to the inside of the unit's housing, I began hearing the crackle and pop of static in my earpiece. Then: "Sammy? Sammy, you there? Come in! I don't know, Quinnlan. I can't just make her magically appear on the other end—"

"Awww, that's sweet," I crooned. "You guys all worried and shit about little ol' me?"

In their collective relief, Mole and Quinn began talking over each other—Mole directly in my ear, Quinn as an echoey voice in the background contributing his perspective and correcting his name.

"Guys!" I shouted to get their attention. "A little help would be nice."

Quinn took the mouthpiece from Mole. "How can we help, Harris? What do you need?"

What did I need? Aside from a really stiff drink (make that two), a tropical vacation, and a handle on affairs of the heart, what I really needed was to get out of the tin box I was squatting in. I caught the two of them up on my escapades and shared that I was currently crouched inside the air-conditioning unit, having made it through the turning blades.

"Sammy, it's me again." Mole had the mouthpiece this time. "All that's standing between you and freedom is the protective mesh that should be just over your head."

Daylight was pouring through the diamond pattern overhead. The mesh's purpose was to keep birds and debris from finding their way into the mechanism, but it wasn't closed enough to keep rain or snow out. Point being, it shouldn't be strong enough to keep me *in*. I raised this observation with Mole.

"It's a cooling system, like the radiator of your rig," he explained. "It's designed to be exposed to the elements, the open air. That's how they work."

"Are they steel or aluminum?" I asked.

"I think the latter. It won't be spot-welded into place, just stamped and slotted together. Most likely held in place by hand-tightened screws."

I stood up and put my hands against my thighs, my back against the mesh. "So if I push up, like this—" My effort was in my voice. "Nothing happens."

"Try again, Sammy. I think it's more a matter of lifting and twisting."

"Which direction?"

"The one that works," I heard Quinn throw in from the background.

"Not helping." I gritted my teeth and tried again. This time I was on my knees, reaching up, my fingers threaded through the mesh as best they could. I lifted and twisted to the left. Again, nothing happened. I repeated the motion, this time to the right—and I felt a slight give. It worked! I doubled my effort, but nothing more happened.

"Try moving your grip closer to the edges instead of the center," Mole offered.

I tried as he suggested, and the grate moved an infinitesimal amount. It was enough to keep me trying until I was able to push the grate up and slide it off to one side, where it fell noisily to the roof. That was the first time I noticed the sound of alarms filling the air around the building. I pulled myself up and out, free of the unit's housing. My feet crunched on the graveled roof.

"Okay, I'm out. Now to get off the roof."

"That's easy," Mole scoffed. "See those tall towers alongside the building?"

"Yeah..."

"You're athletic. You should be able to jump from the roof to the tower then take the ladder down to the ground."

"Without being seen?"

"Sounds like you need a diversion." I could actually hear the maniacal tone of his thoughts. "Find a spot to hide for a few. When it's time, run like hell for the perimeter fence. Quinby will be there to pick you up." Mole made it sound so simple. He even anticipated my next question. "Trust me, you'll know when it's go time."

A cacophony of banging and yelling came up from below, in the server room I'd just escaped.

"You better hurry, guys. They're almost on me."

I needed a weapon. *Jesus Christ—throw me a bone already!* That's when I discovered maybe there *was* Someone listening to frantic requests. A length of aluminum pipe had been abandoned by the edge of the roof where they'd been doing some drainage work. With a yelp of glee, I grabbed the pipe and crouched in the most obvious spot—behind the roof access door, poised as if I were ready to hit a home run. If someone came crashing through the door, they'd get a face full of pipe. Timing seemed to be the key factor in this move. I just hoped it worked out in my favor. I was already beginning to picture the orange of a federal lockup jumper and the way it messed with my skin tone. I heard the scuffling of shoed feet against the concrete floor on the other side of the access door. I changed plans and wedged the pipe under the door knob. When the knob turned, I put my shoulder into the exertion of keeping it closed.

Time crawled, and I was slowly losing the battle. The push from the other side was gradually inching the door open despite the leveraged pipe. I fought against that door with everything I had. The other side redoubled their labors. My feet began to slide out from under me. "*Aaarrgghhh!*" I screamed in frustration. I was working out in my head how to take down the guards should they crash through the door when the loud blaring of alarms filled the air from the opposite side of the building.

The furor on the other side of the door died away as aid was called to the site of the new drama. I didn't waste any time getting myself to the edge of the roof. The tower Mole spoke of was lower than the ledge I stood on and about ten feet out from the building. I'd need a running start. I backed up and took several deep breaths, filling my lungs with oxygen that would power my muscles. Mole believed I was athletic. My trigger finger was likely the most fit part of my entire body.

I took off at a run...but my courage failed me at the last second. I chickened out and couldn't do it. I also couldn't do incarceration. I counted the steps back to my starting point to try again. The problem was, I couldn't see my target, where I wanted to land, until I was ready to jump. Leaps of faith and all, I had to swallow my qualms. *Don't think. Just do.* I told my feet to run, and that's what they did, my arms pumping, my shoes kicking up gravel. I counted the steps to the edge—*five, four, three, two...jump!*

It was sheer grit and determination that had my feet leaving the solid surface of the roof. My legs bicycled in the air as I tried to close that ten-foot gap while dropping the same distance. I remembered to keep my ankles together when I stuck the landing. It wasn't graceful by any stretch. I tucked and rolled out of it, skinning my palms in the process.

"There!" sounded a shout from the rooftop above me. A persistent throng of three guards had abandoned the alarm and broken through the door.

I wasn't going to wait around to see if any of them were set on following in my footsteps. I'd only seen what I was about to do done in the movies, but how hard could it be? I stepped down several ladder rungs, wrapped my arms around the handrail so that the hollow of my elbows trapped the vertical rails, turned the insoles of my shoes against the outside of the rails, and let gravity slide my body down, my arms and feet controlling the speed of my descent.

My knees bent to absorb the impact when I reached the ground with a grunt. Mole was in my ear again: "Your path should be clear, Sammy." A quick look to my right and left, and I took off at a dead run for the perimeter fence. Fionn saw me coming. He stood in the doorway of his guard shack, mouth agape, eyes wide. He made no move to stop me. He made no move at all, only stood there in shock.

Nobody came running at me from the building. Nobody chased me as I ran up the sidewalk toward the highway. No one was in pursuit when I ducked evasively between houses that gave me a rear approach to the rental. Quinn, Mole, and Doof were all standing in the middle of the living room when I rounded the house and pushed through the front door.

"We have to get out of here," Mole said. "Like, right now. I had to make a call to get you out of there, so I jammed the datacenter's alarms. I didn't have time to cover my tracks, so I expect someone from the center's security team to knock on that door"—he pointed to the front door behind me—"at any minute. We really need to go."

Quinn was already out starting the Jeep. Doof and I followed while Mole took a few minutes to wipe down surfaces like knobs, tabletops, handles. All of it self-preservation motor skills. By the time he met us in the Jeep, sirens were close.

I hadn't even gotten my door closed, and we were backing out of the drive. Quinn jammed the Jeep into gear, and the rig jack-rabbited forward. It struck me in that moment how far outside of his professional comfort zone Quinn had come. He'd laid his career on the line to follow my lead. Did I have a right to expect that of him? What was I putting on the line on his behalf?

Blessedly, Quinn kept me from pondering inequities when he asked, "Which way am I going?"

"Highway!" Mole hollered.

"Hills!" I screamed over the top of him.

"Hills it is." Quinn ignored the stop sign and fishtailed around the corner. We began winding south, up into the rocky hills near where Quinn and I had spent the first night.

"Forest road!" I pointed out a thin strip of numbered road sign on the left shoulder. Quinn slowed just enough to make the turn. It was a dirt two-track that, judging by the growth of the sagebrush down the center of the lane that tickled the Jeep's undercarriage, hadn't been driven on in some time. The Jeep's height cleared the small rocks that had broken free from the surrounding rocky cliffs. Its four-wheel suspension made it possible to crawl over the ones too large to straddle. Doof, it turned out, was not a fan of the jolting, bumpy going of off-roading. He whined and climbed into Mole's lap in the back seat, insisting he bury his head in the crook of Mole's armpit. Mole was a good sport about it, but his discomfort was written in the furrow of his brows. He wasn't yet a dog guy, but Doof would eventually change that.

Our passage along the powdery dirt track sent up thick clouds of dust. "This dirt cloud is going to be how they locate us," Quinn noted. The road led up a steep hill, then leveled off as we entered a boulder field. The Jeep was able to skirt around several of the house-size rocks. We parked behind a rocky outcropping, and Quinn cut the engine.

"So now we wait," he said.

"There is zero reception in these hills," Mole said miserably. "If you'd taken the highway, like I *suggested*, I would have made sure we weren't being tailed or tracked. I could get us out of here sixteen different ways from Sunday, but no. Boy toy had to listen to you, not the voice of reason, not the guy who can control the airways, jam frequencies—"

"Are you done?" I asked, cutting him off from his tantrum before it really got going.

Mole sat back and scowled at me, but I knew he was just having a moment. Mole didn't do adrenaline-fed situations. He didn't like danger, and he had a very healthy (too healthy?) sense of self-preservation. Who could fault him for that? But he wasn't going to be any good to me, or himself, if he lost his shit sitting in the middle of a boulder field.

A niggling in the center of my chest had been bothering me for a while, a couple of days at least. Was it guilt over what I perceived I was doing to Quinn's career? It had been his choice to be as involved as he was. And Mole—I'd dragged him out of his comfort zone, exposed him in a way he hadn't been since we'd known each other. The common factor in all that was me. I'd never been good with other people's sensitivities. It wasn't my job to babysit anyone's feelings. I understood that. And everyone I associated with understood they were doing so at their own risk. So why did I feel so culpable?

"We wait for nightfall," I said, taking charge of the situation. "Once the sun goes down, we stick to backroads and make our way back into Portland. We'll figure out what to do from there, and at least we'll be out of the woods." Pun intended.

By the collective silence, I gathered my idea wasn't a hit. But I didn't hear any other offers hitting the floor, so there we were. I took Doof out for a small hike around the area. We climbed to the highest point that would afford us a view down into the valley. Dusk came quickly when the sun dipped behind the rocky bluffs and cast us in shadow. With the dropping sun, so fell the outside temperature. Quinn ran the Jeep's heater. With all his fur, Doof was his own radiator. I traded places with Mole: he sat shotgun up front beside Quinn, and I crawled into the back seat with Doof, who was panting.

When there was nothing left of the day but moonlight, we made our way back out to the main road. Mole was able to scan the local police radio. There didn't seem to be any chatter about a break-in at the datacenter. He was able to secure us a circuitous route back to the city, one that would bypass as many traffic cameras as possible. The road dropped us considerably south, down near the rafting town of Maupin, then swung us back up through the national forest. We had to join Highway 22 north for a short portion. We approached Portland from the west. The entire excursion took us five hours. We arrived back in the city in the wee hours of the morning, just as the eastern horizon was beginning to color. Mole kept track of police chatter the entire time.

We keyed into our building from a never-used alley entrance that had been a carriage dock back in the day when the building was a textile mill. Somewhere in its timeline someone had replaced the original heavy-timbered, padlocked door with an equally stout steel one and had installed a digital keypad lock on the wall beside it. I knew it was Mole. I suspected he owned the building. How else could he get away with wiring the place for audio and visual security? That essentially made him my landlord. Why had we never had *that* conversation? Because curiosity aside, we didn't really need to. What we had going worked. Why would I mess that up?

Mole caught me by the crook of my arm and pulled me aside before I followed Quinn and Doof through my front door. I popped my head inside and told Quinn I'd be right back then followed Mole to his place. I didn't ask Quinn to join us simply because Mole hadn't included him in the bypass. "They didn't find the thumb drive you planted straight away, so I was able to grab big chunks of data. I focused my efforts on what was behind the biggest firewalls and grabbed everything that fit the parameters of my search. I used one of my custom algorithms to scrutinize for intel relevant to the metatags Bauer, Coppice, and Lannister Sr. What did I find, you ask?" Mole gave a low whistle. "This changes everything, Sammy."

My interest was piqued by his dramatic delivery, but I knew he wouldn't continue until I asked, "And...what did you discover?"

"Where to start?" Mole gave another of what would be a series of low whistles. "First off, the fire that took out Lannister's ancestral home back east was arson, pure and simple. I downloaded an internal government memo that ordered the 'neutralization' of the family farm. Granted, it was after the family-directed probate sale, but it was ordered destroyed nonetheless."

"To what end?" I pondered aloud.

Mole screwed his face up, like he was disappointed by my denseness. "To destroy any hidden secrets Lannister Sr. had stashed and forgotten about, on purpose or otherwise, seems like a plausible scenario. The Feds can be the ultimate asshats. They don't want anyone having something they don't. Or can't. *They're* the enemy of the people—"

"What else did you discover?" I knew when to risk being rude and cut Mole off before his tirade against the establishment really gained traction.

"Okay..." He searched his memory bank. "Aside from dastardly orders and plans, I uncovered a list of off-the-book operations and projects—all of them funded by the CIA's black-ops budget, and highly classified. Hidden even from congressional oversight." Mole paused. "Are you sure you want to open this can of worms, Sammy? What do you plan to do with the information?"

That gave *me* pause. My first goal was, of course, to get Wickowski back. I needed to figure out who killed the Lannisters.

I wanted to shut down Bauer. That was all—wasn't it? Or did I subconsciously (or not so) also want to throw some light into the darkness of the federal government's dirty little secrets and make the roaches scurry? I realized my thoughts reflected the sentiments I'd heard Mole voice so often. God—was he rubbing off on me?

"I'm going to do my job," I heard myself say, "and protect the American people while upholding the Constitution of the United States." I quoted the oath I once took. Of course, I'd practiced my own loose translation of that oath, but I always got my target.

"Yeah, but you don't work for the bureau anymore," Mole countered. Touché. "Ask me about the Fraternity."

"What about them?"

"You want to protect the American people? Protect them from these jerk wads. I mean, I suppose you could say they're simply a group of like-minded folks sharing a common interest, if your interests lie in acquiring technology, intelligence, weapons, and military secrets by any means necessary."

"Was Lannister Sr. involved with the Fraternity?" I posed. "Was he aware they even existed?"

"Oh, I'm confident he was aware of them." Mole riffled through a stack of printouts and came out with a letter written on Coppice's letterhead. The correspondence stated he wished to seek an audience with Lannister Sr. regarding his relationship with Dr. Wolff. "These guys were already circling, hinting at their intent to obtain any notes or ideas left behind."

"So, the Fraternity, or someone connected to them, torched the Lannister estate to destroy anything Lannister's grandfather may have stashed in secrecy for his friend, Dr. Wolff? An 'if we can't have them, nobody can' move?"

"That doesn't seem plausible to you?"

Of course it did.

"Sammy, what I'm trying to tell you is, old tech was not all the Fraternity was about. Not even close. We were way off base with our assumptions." He fell silent. Mole had an irritating habit of drawing out explanations. Was it for dramatic effect? I had no idea. The best way to deal with it was to just wait patiently and listen. He'd get to the point soon enough. "What do you know of extraterrestrials?"

"Come again?" Had I actually heard him correctly? Aliens?

"Extraterrestrials. Quantum technology. Reverse engineering." Mole rattled off nerdy terms that I'd heard before but that weren't often used in my circle.

"How about we start over, Mole. Explain in a way you know I'll understand." Essentially, I was asking him to dumb down his approach for the sake of the technologically challenged laywoman. Me. Duh.

"Fine. Try these three on for size: The Fraternity isn't just procuring unrealized technology—they're also involved in cover-ups, assassinations, and coups. They're not only associated with the Agency—they *are* the Agency, and they operate without oversight. They answer to no one. Not even the commander in chief holds sway over them. These guys are the big bad I've always warned about." Mole grew solemn. "And you just crawled into bed with them."

I wouldn't put it that way. Not exactly. It was more like I crashed their party. If the Fraternity believed Lannister Sr. had secrets whose whereabouts went to the grave with him, would they have destroyed the opportunity of discovery by torching the place to the ground? Were they so brazen that they believed any alleged secrets belonged to them or they belonged to no one?

"So essentially the Fraternity is a group of egomaniacal elites who collect technology, intelligence, military secrets. But they're also CIA?"

Mole paused to put his explanation in order. "They don't have badges or offices, or get W-2s at the end of the year, but they're part of the Agency, yes. Think of them as the CIA's personal acquisitions team whose procurements are funded by the Agency's black fund and whose movements are safeguarded by their off-book spending. We've all heard of the $100,000 toilet seats in the Pentagon. If there's one thing the federal government appreciates, it's a paper trail, regardless of whether it's purely fictional or not."

It wasn't that I was having a hard time wrapping my brain around the level of douchery that existed inside the federal government and was tolerated, but it was also the fact that these were the guys dictating how we lived our lives. *Don't let your ego make decisions for you,* I heard my inner guidance say. What I was asking myself was, did I really want to take on the Fraternity? Sometimes, maybe, you just let things like that slide—for self-preservation's sake.

But could I do that? Let whomever was responsible for the Lannisters' murders just slip away into the night? Bauer may not have been personally responsible, but I knew he was connected to whomever was. Theirs was a small, close-knit world. Was I living in a noir reality? The good guys needed to win. The bad guys had to be punished. If we didn't have that as a society, then what the hell was the point of democracy and the pursuit of happiness in the first place?

"I don't like the wheels turning on your face, Sammy." Mole observed my dilemma. "You furrow your brows, squint your eyes, and purse your lips just like that"—he circled the air in front of my face with a flat hand—"only when you're morally constipated."

"I have to go after them, Mole," I declared with determination I wasn't wholly feeling. Yet.

"And you'll either end up in CIA custody, which translates to a dark hole somewhere, never to be heard from again, or dead," Mole rebutted. "Which is pretty much the same thing."

Mole's vote of confidence was overwhelming. He wasn't wrong in his perspective. I was well aware my ego was trying to make my decisions. The CIA wasn't a couple of rednecks in a bar needing to be schooled in manners. Their reputation was synonymous with black ops, torture, and unfair gameplay. In my book, they were federally sanctioned tormentors, and we all knew how well I got on with bullies. I could literally feel myself being torn in two: self-preservation versus the drive to not let them get away with murder, to kick them down a few rungs.

"So...what's your plan?" Mole asked with wide-eyed anxiety.

Excellent question. An inkling told me not to rush into making a decision just yet. This was the Agency after all. And Wickowski's life hung in the balance. Whatever I chose to do, it was a one-way decision. There'd be no turning back. No do-overs. I needed to take my time in making my next move. Not days, but I could sleep on it. I had to afford myself at least a night's slumber to decide what to do with what had the potential to be the rest of my life. I needed space around the situation.

"I'm going to go to bed, pull the blinds, and sleep on it."

"No way," Mole argued. "That can't be your answer. You're going to just go to bed while your world hangs in the balance?" he asked incredulously. "I've known you to be risky, but do you think lackadaisical is the best approach?"

I didn't give his query a response. I couldn't. There were times in one's life when the best approach was not to think, just to do what the moment dictated. I supposed the key to that method was knowing the right action at the right time. I was fresh out of answers and solutions at that moment. I needed the clarity that a few hours' rest might provide. With clarity came confidence. The danger would be in second-guessing myself. I said I was going to sleep on it. That was exactly what I was going to do. I turned for the door.

"I'm gonna keep working at this for a few more hours. Where can I find you if I find something else pertinent?" Mole asked my back.

I turned and looked at him, facetiously, my hand on the doorknob. "Um, my bed?"

"Oh!" Mole exclaimed. "You were serious? I figured you'd go hole up somewhere off grid."

"When have you ever known me to run from anything? Ever?" I couldn't believe Mole and I were having this conversation.

"What about the others who dwell in this building?"

"What others?" I rounded impatiently. "We both know there are no other tenants living in this building, Mole. You own this building. My monthly lease payment circles back around to you, doesn't it?" He didn't respond, but he also didn't meet my eye. "I expect a few upgrades to my unit."

He let me slip out the door without any further discussion. I returned to my loft where an anxious dog and deputy both paced the floor outside the kitchen.

"Hungry?" I asked the deputy. The dog was always famished. I opened my cupboards, rummaged through their emptiness, and came out with two cans of soup, one vegetable beef, the other broccoli cheddar, and half a box of cheesy fish crackers. I offered a can of his choice to Quinn and microwaved the other for myself.

"These expired six months ago," Quinn said, reading the box and chewing a mouthful of stale crackers.

"Yeah." I shrugged. "But they're better than your other crackers."

Quinn looked at me weird. "I don't have any other crackers."

"Precisely." I nodded my response.

We ate our heated soup and stale crackers without conversation. Doof lapped up the remains from our bowls then settled on his bed for a nap. I grabbed a quick shower—alone—and retired to my bed. Doof got up and followed, claiming space at the foot of my comforter. I offered Quinn the option of the couch or...the couch. I trusted Mole to keep us secure while I fell into a light slumber listening to the rhythmic snoring of Doof on my bed and Quinn on the couch in the other room.

CHAPTER EIGHTEEN

At some point, Doof jumped off the bed and Quinn slid in beside me.

I was dreaming of paradise—white beaches and sunshine. The heat of Quinn's body pressed against the length of mine translated in dream-world as radiant heat reflecting off the sand. His slow, rhythmic breathing, the calm in-out, was the ocean's gentle tide. I could taste the salty air on the back of my tongue. It tasted like metal and chemicals. *That's not right*, a lucid part of my brain pointed out. It wasn't. I'd lain on the beaches of Saint Thomas, Jamaica, Maui. They all smelled like the warm breeze off the ocean, a combination of water, sunscreen, coconut oil, and fruity rum drinks. This stung my sinuses.

This isn't right—something's wrong! That still-articulate portion of my unconsciousness insisted. I felt hands on me, jostling my body, the sensation of being lifted—and none too gently. My head grew light, like I was suspended. Were my arms hanging down by my ears, or were they straight up in surrender? It was impossible for me to tell the difference. Was I falling? There was a lightness about the way I moved. I was moving, right? I tried to lower my arms, but they wouldn't respond. No, I was pretty sure I was moving—I could feel the breeze of movement on my face, on my arms.

Things began to clear when the air through my nose changed. I recognized the flow wheezing through my nostrils. It smelled like cold bricks, the pine-scented cleaner a janitor would use, and the unmistakable musk of age. It smelled just like the lobby of my building. I heard the creak of the front door. The front door of my building. I was no longer in my bed; I was downstairs. Where were Quinn and Doof—were they okay? What about Mole?

Then the air changed again—this time it was rain, wet pavement, and exhaust. And it was cold, a humid kind of cold that gets into your clothes. I had no control over my limbs. I felt like a marionette whose strings had been clipped. There was the burble of an idling motor as I was slid into a seat. Hands righted me and a shoulder belt clicked to keep me upright. The long muscles of my lower neck strained as my head slumped forward, my chin almost to my chest. My sinuses were no longer stinging. Multiple car doors closing. The same cologne and brute force I'd smelled days ago, when I'd been snatched. Seemed I was once again travelling with Bauer and his wicked band of mercenaries.

Well, shit.

The adrenaline that dumped into my system was enough to rouse me from my induced incapacitation. The safety of my friends we'd left behind became a sobering concern. Bauer must have gassed the entire building through the ventilation system. I'd love to hear Mole's defense on that one.

I righted my posture by sitting up and raising my chin and was rewarded with a knife of migraine-size pain through the back of my eyes. I could feel my quickening pulse in the tension of the muscles responsible for supporting my head. My vision was blurry when I first blinked my eyes open. I was surrounded by men, but there were no hoods. No dim lights to obscure identities. I immediately picked out Bauer. He was evident by the expensive cut of his cream-colored linen suit, a bold choice for neurotic Portland weather. A thin scarf meant for accessory, not warmth, was wrapped fashionably around his neck.

Bauer crossed a knee over the other and clasped both hands together on his lap. His smile was a semblance of friendliness, like he was settling in for a conversation about the weather over coffee. "If you recall, Ms. Harris, the last time we met, I made you a promise. Do you recall?"

Oh, I remembered. I recalled perfectly how Bauer had threatened the lives of those closest to me. The threats I'd thought I was bigger than. I believed I could push back. The Lannisters lost their lives just because Mr. Lannister was someone's grandson. That didn't seem right. Neither of the Lannisters were party to his grandfather's activities. They were innocent collateral damage. Someone needed to stand up to that. For better or for worse, that's what I did.

"If anything happens to Wickowski," I stated matter-of-factly, "I vow to put a bullet in the center of your face. It'll be quick." I shrugged. "Probably painless. But you'll be dead nonetheless. Your loved ones will have to pay their last respects to a closed casket." There was no frivolity to my tone. My words didn't hold any of their usual sarcasm or salt. I made the man seated across from me a solemn, deadly promise that only death itself—my own—would break. Maybe Bauer doubted my threat. Maybe he didn't. His game face gave away nothing.

Then Bauer's position changed. He sat up and dropped his leg from his knee. He leaned forward, resting both elbows atop his thighs. The hardness of his face softened. "I have a different proposition for you, Ms. Harris, one that might get us out of what my grandmother would have called a sticky wicket. An undesirable situation."

Bauer's change of character was a ploy. One of the more sinister mind-fuckeries that government agencies employed to get what they wanted when threats didn't work. I knew that. Still, my interest was tickled. "Go on."

Bauer's serpentine smile made my skin crawl. "Ms. Harris, I want you to disregard our previous exchange. I no longer wish you to cease and desist in your search into my and my associates' affairs. I would be a fool to believe you're not aware of the particulars my associates and I seek. I now want you to go forth and locate the journals belonging to Dr. Wolff. Do this for us, and in exchange, I will deliver you Detective Wickowski." He handed me a sleek new phone. I knew without looking that only one number would be programmed into it, and it would be his. "This is how we will communicate moving forward. No more hit squads breathing down your neck." He smiled like the Cheshire Cat. "We can work together."

I heard what Bauer said. Still, something deep inside my psyche cracked. I suspected that fracturing was rational thought, the last bit that kept me human, and with it had gone fear, guilt, doubt, and regret. I felt nothing but stone-cold rage, the kind of fury that lent itself to murder. I had shut down all processes other than those that dealt with revenge and killing. The only thoughts that flitted through my mind were deadly and gore splashed. Fantasy images of a 9mm bullet obliterating the fine bone structure of Bauer's face. My breath came slow and shallow. I mulled over Bauer's offer. It was acceptable.

But first: "I need proof of life."

Expecting this, Bauer produced a phone from an inner pocket of his suit jacket and thumbed a number. He gave the other end of the line instruction when they picked up, then turned the phone to face me. What I saw on the screen gave my heart a lurch. Wickowski was bound. His head hung at an odd angle, and I couldn't tell if he was dead or just battered.

"Wick!" I hollered at the phone's screen. His head lolled to one side. Then he picked it up and gazed into the phone's lens. He was bloodied and bruised, his eyes swollen and his nose mashed. He held himself like that for only a moment before his head slouched forward again and the feed cut off.

Bauer slid the phone back into his pocket and grinned smugly. "You retrieve what I seek, and I will hand the detective over to you with no further harm done to his person."

Oh, I was going to find what Bauer sought. I'd even turn the journals and notebooks over to him in exchange for Wickowski—and then fulfill my promise of a bullet. "Deal," I said flatly.

Bauer gave a barely perceivable nod of instruction to the man beside me, who raised his arm and encircled the top of my shoulders. With the back of his hand against the side of my cheek, he forced my head aside, exposing my neck. There was a sharp prick, followed by a flood of immobilizing warmth as the sedative entered my veins. Gravity seemed to amplify and my body slumped forward, and again, everything went black.

CHAPTER NINETEEN

I HAD NO IDEA HOW LONG I'D BEEN OUT. THERE WAS A KINK IN MY neck. A sharp tang at the back of my throat raised nausea. What the hell had they given me? The CIA was prone to using a broad span of nasty substances to incapacitate. Bauer could have used any number of them. The bitter taste on the back of my tongue suggested it had been quinuclidinyl benzilate, something both the US and Soviet militaries used as a debilitating agent.

I was back in my bed. Quinn was snoozing gently beside me, Doof on the floor next to my side of the bed. I was aware of the usual sounds of my loft. My sinuses burned as they had earlier. I nudged Quinn beside me. He responded with a groggy groan.

I fought against the pain in my head and the nausea pushing against the back of my throat to sit up. My head was in a fog. I stumbled my way to the window and opened it wide. Fresh air rushed in, and with it the sounds of the city. Midmorning was in full swing. Sun streamed through my half-drawn blinds. I leaned down to pat Doof, who didn't immediately respond.

"No, Doof!" The emotion of loss slammed into my feels. I buried my fingers into the thick scruff around his neck and gave a gentle shake. "Doof, come on...wake up, Doof..."

A light thump struck the floor as Doof's tail came to life. Whatever compound had been pumped into the building's ventilation system had had an effect on the canine as well as the humans.

Quinn was sitting up when I turned away from Doof, who'd raised himself up on his dog elbows and was panting. "What the hell happened?" he asked holding his head with both hands.

"Why do I feel like I went drinking with you, then you beat the shit out of me?"

Well, that wasn't a fair assessment and comparison. If I'd beat the crap out of Quinn, he wouldn't be sitting up, wouldn't be speaking. "We were paid a visit—"

Quinn was cut off when Mole came crashing through my front door using the key he'd had since...forever. "Sammy!" he screamed my name. I'd never heard him sound so terrified and anxious. "Sammy!" He skidded through my bedroom doorway in socked feet. "Oh, thank God!" he exclaimed, a hand planted on his chest, his breath coming in panicky gasps when he saw me sitting on the edge of the bed beside Quinn. "I thought for sure you were gone."

"I was. They deemed it necessary to return me." I shared the harrowing tale of my night.

Mole instantly blanched at the news that his fortress wasn't, after all, incursion proof. I watched the acknowledgment play out over his face as he worked to wrap his mind around the fact that Bauer had found an effective way in that he hadn't thought of. Then his raised brows of shock crumpled menacingly and a sadistic snarl curled his lip. I wasn't sure if he was working out how to remedy the problem and weighing it against the option of relocation, or working out retribution. I'd support any decision. Especially the one that involved vengeance.

"What's in these notebooks and diaries that this Bauer goon wants so desperately that now he wants you to find what he previously scared you away from?" Quinn asked.

"*Tried* to scare me away from," I amended. Nobody has ever frightened me away from anything. That probably wasn't something I should be boastful about. It's a sign of a fragile ego, one afraid of being broken. "Besides, I don't care at this point. I just want to do the job and get Wick back." And put a bullet in the middle of Bauer's face.

"Give me a direction," Mole instructed with a deadly determination set to his face. Part of me wondered how far down the retaliation rabbit hole he'd already descended. The other part of me wanted to remain ignorant but hoped he would destroy them digitally, leaving no survivors.

"I vote you and I go search the Lannister home one more time," Quinn suggested. "Maybe you missed something?"

Under normal circumstances, I'd be offended by Quinn's questioning my ability to search a crime scene. I didn't know what I was looking for before. Journals, but Lannister wouldn't have kept them at his home, not after visiting the police and their suggesting he lock them away.

"I think you're looking for a hidden safe. I can search and see if Lannister had a safe in his office," Mole offered.

"If he did, Bauer's men would have already hit it," Quinn pointed out. "I'm leaning more toward a safety deposit box."

I listened to them both. I'd go give the residence another search, but I didn't believe there was a hidden safe that Bauer's men and I would have both overlooked. Hiding a safe was a covert action. To make it an effective act, concrete would have been used. Hiding a concrete pour was harder than it sounded. That we might be searching for a hidden key to a safety deposit box—now that was wholly plausible. None the easier, but reasonable.

I followed Quinn in the Geländewagen while he returned the Jeep, and then I sped from the curb once he hopped into the passenger's front seat.

"It's a forty-five zone through here." He pointed at a black-and-white sign as I cruised past, my speedometer pegging near sixty.

"Doesn't count if I'm rolling with a deputy, does it?" I tried.

Quinn slid me a sideways glance. "You're kidding, right?" When I didn't answer, he pushed on, "You don't have lights, you don't have a siren to alert other drivers—"

"So stick your head out the window and go '*whoo-whoo-whoo*,'" I suggested as I tabbed the emergency four-way flashers on the dash.

I was beginning to realize Quinn didn't appreciate my brand of sarcasm nearly as much as Wick did. Or at least Wick was a better sport about it. Quinn didn't rebut my suggestion, only fumed wordlessly from his seat. He'd need to thicken his skin if we were going to hang out together.

We pulled into the Lannisters' driveway without further exchange. I cut the engine, and the cab was instantly silent. We sat that way for the span of a breath or two. I wasn't sure if Quinn was keying up for a lecture on the merits of following the law or if he was waiting for me to exit the vehicle first. I jumped out before he could open his mouth.

I'd already picked my way through the front door when Quinn joined me. He didn't mention the police tape that was now wadded in a ball just inside the door. He walked through the home, turning on lights as he wandered from room to room.

"Where do you want to begin?" Quinn asked, attitude still tingeing his voice.

I let out a heavy sigh and turned in a circle where I stood. "The kitchen," I stated and began moving that direction through the wreckage left by Bauer's men.

"It'll be more thorough if we double-team it," Quinn said as he joined me. "If it were me wanting to hide something small"—he began pulling open drawers and cupboards—"I'd go with a diversion safe. Are you familiar with those?"

I was. Diversion safes were easily obtained and just as simply hidden in plain sight. Quinn began examining the canned foods in the Lannister pantry, turning each can over, testing its weight, and attempting to twist it apart. Diversion safes were often disguised as normal household items, like canned food or cleaning supplies. There were no covert cans, but I did come across a jelly jar half-filled with loose change in the very back of the top pantry shelf above the stove. I moved the coins around in their glass containment. Nothing hidden among the coinage.

It took Quinn and me a solid hour to search the kitchen. Every jar, can, or box in every cupboard and on every shelf was scrutinized. Quinn pried at the floor trim and removed the faceplates from electrical sockets and light switches, another popular diversionary hiding spot. Still nothing.

We picked our way through the debris left by Bauer's men to the master bedroom. I looked through the rubble on the floor inside the closet. Bauer's men had shredded through the clothes hanging in the closet and cut their way through the Lannisters' mattress and pillows. Every book that had graced the tall wall shelf had been opened, their pages fluttered through and unceremoniously discarded on the floor. Quinn examined the architecture for false panels, hidden nooks, covert crannies in which to hide something small. Nothing, but my spidey senses told me we were close to something.

When Quinn moved his search to the garage, I turned my attention to the panels covering vents and the ductwork throughout the home. I came up empty-handed, having discovered nothing more than a couple of scurrying dust spiders, until I got to the air duct in the living room, just above the coat closet door. I had to pull a chair over from the dining room and stand on it so I could plunge my arm inside, up to the pit, in order for my fingers to feel around the turn in the duct. Lannister may have been frightened, but he hadn't been stupid. He'd been rather clever, in fact, when sealing the key inside a thick manila envelope and affixing it to the thin aluminum duct wall by way of Velcro, out of sight, around the bend in the tube.

I ripped the envelope open and spilled its contents into my palm. A tarnished brass key stamped only with the identifying mark of 42. It was devoid of any other descriptors. It could fit into a safety deposit box, a bus locker, an old hotel room. There was no way of knowing. If it was a safety deposit box, the next question was, where was it located?

I climbed back down, not bothering to replace the grate cover, and found Quinn in the garage where he'd been clamoring around up inside the attic crawlspace. Bits of pink insulation dotted his clothing when he emerged.

I had the key trapped between my index finger and thumb when I lifted my hand to show him what I'd found. He immediately started down the attic's folding stairs and plucked the key from my fingers to turn over in his own hand.

"What do you think it goes to?"

"I don't know, but I know someone who can help us." I set the key on Lannister's workbench, snapped photos of it from different angles, and sent them to Mole. I didn't know how he'd be able to identify it, but Mole worked a certain kind of magic that I didn't question too deeply. I explained this verbatim to Quinn, who watched me with a questioning look.

I turned to head back toward my rig when Quinn stopped me with a hand on my forearm. "You know Bauer's men are aware that we're here, and they're going to assume we've discovered what they couldn't. They're going to be watching our every move extremely closely. It's too dangerous to return to the loft. You need to warn your friend there." He pulled me a little closer and leaned in as if sharing a secret. "Things are going to get extremely dangerous from here. Bauer's going to send his army after you."

I looked up into his soft, soulful eyes and saw concern in there. I gave him a reassuring smile. "God, I hope so."

I was itching for a fight.

CHAPTER TWENTY

"TAKE THIS NEXT EXIT," QUINN INSTRUCTED AND POINTED AT THE road ahead.

"That takes us into downtown," I pointed out questioningly.

"Yes," Quinn said simply. "I think we should get to the precinct and turn the key over to Wickowski's people. It's evidence."

"Yes," I agreed. "It's evidence, but why Wickowski's division? Why not turn it over to your guys at county?" I was genuinely perplexed.

It took a long time for Quinn to answer. When he did, he admitted, "Our division is small at the county level. Their security and manpower would be no match for Bauer and his men should they storm the building."

"You think the skeleton crew Burnell is forced to run on would fare any better?" Budget cuts had been citywide and ongoing. None of it mattered though. We weren't going to have the debate because I wasn't passing the key off to anyone.

There was a long stretch over many miles where neither of us spoke. I knew Quinn was wondering where we were going to land, and it was a valid question. My only objective was to get away from the place I'd known to be Bauer's last location. I needed to get out of the city. Get some space around myself so I could think. Lannister had been very intelligent in how he'd handled the situation—up to the point of his death, that was. He'd made an official paper trail by going to the police. He'd worked out how and where to stash the key, which for the most part had been successful. So, keeping with Lannister's mode of process, I knew we were looking for a secured box at a secure location, not conveniently located near his home.

Quinn didn't ask questions until we'd taken the exit off the interstate that took us south. I'd seen a cute little bed-and-breakfast in the rural town of Sawtell while working another case several months ago. It hadn't looked overly popular, and it was in a depressed town that most people had never heard of. It would be as good a hideout as anywhere else that had running water, a soft bed, and a coffee shop downstairs.

We checked in with the owner, who had the handshake and smile of a politician. She wasn't a fan of dogs, but it turned out she was a big fan of a folded Franklin. Doof, Quinn, and I climbed to our room at the top of the narrow stairs where I dropped my go bag on the bed. The small L-shaped room was cozy. A radiator beneath a paned window overlooking Main Street kept the room warm. I could have done without the vomitous pink tones of the walls and bedspread, but it was better than sleeping on the street.

A clawfoot tub occupied the side nook of the L-shaped room, hidden from view behind an accordioned wooden screen. An opaque plastic shower curtain ringed the tub from a metal rod suspended from the ceiling. The only lighting available was in the form of lamps. Tall ones took up the corners of the room, shorter ones sat on the bedside tables, and there was another on a three-drawered bureau with scrolled woodwork running down its legs. A loveseat that pulled out into a twin-size hide-a-bed sat beside the door like it was an afterthought. The worn wooden floors had seen a century of foot traffic.

Quinn caught my eye and raised his brows. "So we're out of the city. Now what's the plan?"

That was an excellent question. One thing at a time. We'd gotten ourselves shelter for the night. I needed time to think. I eyed the clawfoot. "Are you pro pineapple with your ham on pizza, or are you a weirdo?" I asked from left field.

"Pro?" he answered cautiously, suspicious of my angle.

"Perfect! Me too. I bet there's someone who delivers in town." I pulled some cash from my jeans pocket and handed it to Quinn before beginning to fill the clawfoot with comfortably hot water. I felt his eyes on my back for several seconds while he processed if I was being serious or not. Then I heard him dial using the room's vintage rotary phone.

When I stepped into the near-scalding water, I didn't invite Quinn to join, and thankfully he didn't ask. Besides, someone had to fetch the pie from downstairs when it arrived. I closed my eyes and focused on the problem at hand: Where were the journals? If anything could be garnered from the photos I'd taken of the safety deposit key, Mole would discover it. I exhaled all my breath and let myself sink to the bottom of the tub.

My head was resting on the bottom of the porcelain tub. What little air remained in my lungs escaped through my nose as little bubbles when Quinn's shadow cast over me. I opened my eyes. He was standing over the tub with a pizza box balanced on his open palm. I sat up with such gusto that the displacement of bathwater sloshed onto the floor. I squeegeed the water from my eyes with my knuckles and deeply inhaled the scent of Hawaiian pizza. My stomach growled in anticipation. Quinn peeled off a slice and handed it to me, and I ate with wet hands. Doof watched longingly from the edge of the screen, too suspect of it to walk around to the edge of the tub.

"It's not like I can go door to door, bank to bank, and start trying the key on any boxes labeled 42," I thought out loud around a mouthful of pizza. I finished the slice save for the last bite, which I lobbed to Doof. No matter how I tacked at the problem, I kept arriving at the same blank conclusion. I was stumped. I had no next move to try. I was helpless to get Wickowski back until I located those journals, and I had literally zero starting points. Just a key with no home.

I slipped beneath the water's surface again, my head settling once more to the bottom. Another flurry of tiny bubbles escaped my nose as I emptied my lungs completely. I didn't resurface for another breath. Sometimes I operated best under pressure. Water wanted to flow into my nostrils. *Come on, Lannister, talk to me.* My lungs began to burn. I'd need to surface soon. *Where did you hide those journals? My friend's life depends on locating them!* I heard no inspirations. No inner dialogue of direction bubbled from the ether. There was only the sound of the water that filled my ears. I sat up again, this time not sloshing water. I lay submerged to my neck until the water went cold. I begged, I pleaded, I coerced the Universe to give me something, *anything* to go on. A detail from the Lannister home that hadn't registered at the time that might suddenly click. A missed snippet from Mole's research. It seemed Nobody upstairs was listening.

Mole hadn't yet rung to tell me he'd made a discovery. At that point, I was banking on him working his nerd magic. I had no other avenues to take, no leads to follow. My impatience and frustration could wait no longer. I dialed Mole's number. My call rolled over to voice mail, where I politely requested an update.

Several moments after I'd left my message, he called me back. "I've got nothing yet, Sammy." Mole sounded both dejected and frustrated. He wasn't used to failure. It was certainly by no fault of his. I wasn't used to it either.

"Did you check his cell phone records? GPS history?" I asked, knowing those were the first tasks he would have performed. "Credit card statements going back to just after Lannister went to the police?" There had to be something we were overlooking. "Maybe outbound traffic cams?"

"Sammy," he jeered, "you act like you've never met me. Of course I've accessed all of the above. And found nothing. As for this key itself—it's a common nickel-brass alloy. Your gym locker key is made of the same stuff. Point being, there's no way to narrow down what facility uses this specific key."

"And it's not like I can start asking around for a box 42." I was aware I was getting a little grumpy, but I was running out of time. Wickowski was running out of time.

I felt the first hiccup of emotion trying to bubble up inside of me. That wasn't going to happen. It couldn't happen. My parents once took me to a therapist when the middle school counselor raised her concerns that I didn't have friends and didn't form any sort of relationship with others. I'd tried to explain how I feared the emotions that relationships with others created, and I didn't want feelings coming to play at my house for fear they may never leave.

"Why don't you just bluff those assholes?" Quinn suggested from where he stood at the edge of the screen. "They don't know what those journals look like or what's in them." He shrugged. "So make it up."

A low, thoughtful whistle filtered through the phone line. "Well done, Quincy," Mole scoffed, slaughtering Quinn's name on purpose. "Gold star to you for coming up with the best plan to get Wick killed."

"Hold up, Mole," I intervened. "Think about it for a second. Bauer has never alluded to anything precise that they're seeking. He's never even made mention of anything specific." I went silent for a second as I rolled the scenario around in my head. "It could work. If you can't dazzle them with brilliance, baffle them with bullshit. What do you know of physics?"

"It doesn't matter," Mole stated, full of doubt. "It'll never work. Bauer and his men are killing for this shit. We should assume they have, if not a good idea of what they're looking for, then at least a ballpark. I can't just spin a bunch of sci-fi malarkey and trust they buy it. What if they don't?"

"What if they do?" Quinn pushed back. "Slap some theoretical quantum equations on some paper of a high-linen content, age it with a light tea wash, set it overnight among mothballs, and voilà. A passable replica." I wasn't sure if Quinn was genuinely suggesting we weigh Wick's life against the success of an art project or if he was strategically goading Mole.

"Your thoughts, Mole?" I asked.

There was a long silence from his end of the line that I didn't know how to interpret. When he finally spoke, his tone had changed to confident and authoritative. "Leave this to me. Give me twenty-eight hours." His time frame was oddly specific. "Trust me, Sammy," he said, which wasn't something I did easily with anyone. However, if I was going to lay my faith at someone's feet, it would be Mole's.

"I can't guarantee the loft is safe," I told him. "We can come get you and bring you somewhere secure where you can still work."

"Pshaw," Mole said. "It's for instances like these that I had my safe room constructed. It's stocked with food, water, internet access—the whole nine yards. I even had air tanks delivered should someone try to gas the place again." He'd clearly learned he had some weaknesses from our recent experience.

I tried thanking Mole before hanging up, but he told me not to. Not until Wickowski was home. My bathwater had cooled more than I wanted by then. Instead of emptying the tub and refilling it with hot water as I'd been doing most of the evening, I got out and toweled dry before stepping out from around the screen in nothing more than my scars.

Doof was ecstatic to see me, like I'd left and suddenly returned. He had no shits to give about journals or mercenaries. All he knew was he had a human he adored. *Back at ya, doggo*. When I died, I wanted to come back as a dog. Dogs harbor no regrets about the past, no worries about the future; they're always living in the present moment. Humans could learn a few things there.

I crawled beneath the bedcovers and leaned back against the plush headboard, knees drawn up, quilt pulled to my knees.

I patted the bed beside me in invitation. It wasn't extended to either of them in particular, but Doof was the first to take up the proffered space. He nuzzled his nose under my elbow and buried his head in my armpit with a heavy sigh like he'd claimed his sleep spot for the night. Quinn glowered down at the canine hogging the space and my attention. He tried to coax the dog off the bed, but it turned out Doof suffered from the same selective hearing syndrome that had plagued me my entire life. Ask anyone who's ever known me. Quinn looked to me for support in relocating Doof to the floor.

"You want him to move, you're going to have to make him," I suggested.

"*Down*, Doof," Quinn commanded. Doof just shifted his eyes sideways to look at him without lifting his head. I wasn't fluent in dog-speak, but I was fairly certain Quinn had just been told to go...love himself.

"Okay, Doof, get down, please," I asked nicely and pointed to the floor. Doof slid his eyes up to meet mine. There was nothing but respect in his gaze. "I know, buddy." I scratched his favorite spot behind his ears. "I love you too." Doof slid from the bed to the floor, shooting Quinn a glare as he passed.

"I don't think your dog likes me," Quinn commented as he stripped his shirt off over his head and dropped trou before climbing on the bed beside me.

"Maybe he's just slow to warm," I said. "I get it."

There wasn't a whole lot of talking after that. Not that Quinn and I weren't communicating. We had a slow, deep, intimate conversation that was dangerously close to meaningful.

A wet tongue across my cheek, accompanied by a needful whine, woke me the next morning. "Okay, Doof, okay," I mumbled. Noticing success in his efforts, Doof grew more excited, animated. He was back to his leap/spin/happy bark. I pulled on some jeans and grabbed Doof's leash. I armed myself with my

HK in my waistband under my shirt, which appropriately read I Fucking Dare You in neon italics, and hoped the weather didn't warrant a sweatshirt.

I let Quinn's inert body know I was taking Doof out for his official business. Before he could answer, I'd slipped into the hall and down the stairs. The coffee shop on the main floor, off the lobby, had a short line. Heads turned when Doof and I entered. My shirt got a few glares and one snicker.

It was a beautiful and almost warm country morning. I saw no SUVs like the ones that had haunted us in the city, but I was still on high alert as we navigated the quiet neighborhood to an old, defunct lumberyard where Doof was able to go off-leash and do his dookie in an empty field.

Quinn was outside pacing the sidewalk when we returned to the inn. "This thing has been going off." He waggled the phone Bauer had given me in the air.

I snagged the device just as it came alive again in his hand. "Harris!" I barked into it.

"Ms. Harris," Bauer's genteel voice purred, "I'd like a status report. Have you located my property?"

His property? That sounded terribly presumptuous. "You only just changed direction on me yesterday. I appreciate the confidence in my abilities, but I'm going to need another minute or two."

"Do you honestly believe the detective has that kind of time?" Bauer jeered. "I would have imagined he'd become your top priority."

"What makes you think he's not?" I was picturing that bullet in the middle of Bauer's face again.

"I need results, Ms. Harris. There are things that are...time sensitive within those journals."

"Time sensitive?" What could possibly be time sensitive in decades-old material?

"Perhaps one day I will get the opportunity to explain myself and my actions to you, Ms. Harris." Bauer's genteelness disappeared completely, replaced by a rougher, more deadly tone. I had a sense I was getting the authentic him. "Save your friend, or be the reason he no longer exists in this world." The line went dead in my ear.

I turned back to Quinn, who'd been silently observing the exchange. "What's so time sensitive?" he asked, repeating what he'd overheard.

"I don't know," I growled. "The prick never got to that." A rage-filled exhale escaped through my nose. "I hate him." I looked Quinn dead in the eyes. "I'm going to kill him."

"Sam, don't." He clasped his hands over his ears. "To do so now would be premeditative. I wouldn't be able to ignore that."

I narrowed my eyes at him. "You'd arrest me for removing that asshole from the population? For real?"

Quinn grunted and diverted his eyes. "You can't just execute your enemies, Harris. They have to stand trial. That's how the system works."

"But I can save the taxpayers money, free up a prison cell, send a message to others." Yes, I was purposefully yanking Quinn's chain. Mostly. The part about the taxpayers was true. As was the freeing up of space. The last bit could be argued to be true as well.

Quinn cocked a brow and shook his head but moved on. "Senseless. Why didn't Lannister just hand over what these guys wanted and go on with his life?"

It was senseless. All of it. According to the office of the medical examiner, Mrs. Lannister's cause of death was drowning, but it was tap water in her lungs, not river water. And she was the first to die. It read like a classic interrogation setup. Mrs. Lannister was simply collateral damage. Influence. Witnessing his wife's execution, Lannister had a choice at that point. Was he going to give them what they wanted, or was he going to die too? Imagine the pressure, the personal dilemma. But then something happened that nobody involved anticipated. Lannister's battle with anxiety and high blood pressure came around full circle with inevitable consequences. His heart gave out. The stress and anxiety he'd tried to medicate against killed him anyway. Lannister's ultimate cause of death had been his own body's betrayal.

I shrugged. "Maybe he'd read the journals. What if there was something so volatile in them that he felt it was his moral duty, and familial obligation to his grandfather, to keep them suppressed for as long as he could? Maybe he made an ultimate sacrifice for the continued freedom of his country."

"I don't even know many front-line soldiers that selfless. Are laypeople really that self-sacrificing when their own death is on the line?" Quinn pondered, more to himself than out loud.

"We'll never know for sure what drove him."

I phoned Mole and let him know Doof, Quinn, and I were staying out of town for a second night, and filled him in on Bauer's change of heart.

There were still unspoken threats hanging in the air from Quinn regarding my actions, so Doof and I escaped the tension the next morning by finding a green space we could walk to that had a meandering path through a grassy meadow. The asphalt trail culminated at the decorative gates of a rural elk farm. Doof nearly lost his mind when the herd of broad-antlered animals startled and stampeded across the field. He whined; he danced; ears perked, he gave several exited barks. I told him no, that the elk lived there and he was being rude by barking at them. He shot me a look of utter disappointment.

Though he resisted, I was able to pull Doof away from his wishful thinking, and we backtracked toward the inn. We paused at a fishing pond beneath an inviting canopy of cottonwoods. The bench beneath the tree's leafy sprawl was a good spot to watch a pair of ducks paddle lazily across the murky green water. Their movement rippled the surface of the pool, creating a mesmerizing wake that quietly lapped at the grassy shore. The sun dappled through the tree's high cover, and for a moment, I almost felt peaceful. I was quickly reminded it was a quietude I didn't deserve. Wickowski was being held by hostiles, Quinn was on the verge of cuffing me (not in the fun way), and I was questioning if I'd done the right thing by trusting in Mole's success, and that in and of itself had me feeling like a unsupportive cad. For one who didn't entertain feelings, I found myself drowning in them.

CHAPTER TWENTY-ONE

"HELLO, SAMMY, QUINCEMEAT," MOLE SAID AS HE LET QUINN, DOOF, and me in his front door later that same day. He'd phoned me earlier that afternoon, beckoning us back to the city for a "face-to-face," as he termed it. He'd insisted his security measures hadn't picked up any sign of Bauer or his men lurking. I asked him how far his new security perimeters extended, and he answered with "no comment," which I knew meant I didn't want to know because it was either highly illegal or possibly unethical, but most likely both.

A thick book bound in smooth, tanned leather sat in the center of his desk. A rawhide thong was wrapped around the bundle to keep its contents contained. "Pièce de résistance, Sammy," Mole stated, motioning toward the book.

I sat in his desk chair and pulled the book onto my lap. The covering was soft, brown, and worn. I unwound the leather cord and let it gently come open. The dry, dusty pages were raw edged and eaten lacey by silverfish. I thumbed through the pages filled with scientific formulas, mathematical equations, a bunch of stuff that made no sense to me. There was no way this was an art project he threw together. This looked real.

"Sammy, I cannot begin to explain to you how much you owe me for this one. I all but signed away my firstborn, and it's both my balls should anything happen to this in particular." He patted the journal.

"What is this?" I asked as I continued turning pages.

"When you called me back yesterday morning and mentioned the time-sensitive aspect of your conversation with Bauer, that got me to thinking. I have a friend who...dabbles...in quantum cryptography. Primarily the hacking thereof," Mole explained.

"Dabbles?" I asked, one brow cocked.

"He's made an illicit career of it. The government in his home country wants him imprisoned. Our own government wants him under their control. It's a bunch of suppression bullshit he inherited from his great-grandfather. But all of that is neither here nor there. When you said Bauer was searching for something that was time sensitive, I couldn't figure out what that could be. Nothing in anything I've uncovered about Lannister Sr., or the projects he was involved with, has hinted at time sensitivity as it relates to contemporary sociopolitical climates. I mean, if they were looking for a leg up in modern warfare, we're engaged in nothing currently that's pushing a timeline." Mole paused for suspenseful effect. I sometimes disliked it when he did that.

"And..." I tried not to sigh the word out.

"And that got me to thinking outside of the box. What if what Bauer's looking for didn't stem from American intel but from someone Lannister Sr. could have been associated with professionally, but from a distance?" Insert another annoying pause.

"And..." I repeated.

"And so I went back to the beginning. I scoured through every transcribed syllable I'd accessed in my earlier investigation into Lannister Sr., and a name surfaced—Alan Turing."

"Who was Alan Turing?" I immediately cued instead of waiting through another pause.

"Alan Turing is well established as the father of theoretical computer science and artificial intelligence," Mole explained in a posh British accent before returning to his own voice. "He was an English bloke, a wicked-smart mathematician, logician, philosopher, and—this is the important part—cryptanalyst. During World War II, Turing developed the Turing machine, which helped break the Germans' Enigma code. It ultimately shortened the war in Europe by a couple of years."

Mole stood and began pacing as he spoke. "Turing's legacy continues. You see, the problem in today's level of computing and security is that there's no way to claim anything to be a hundred percent secure. Nothing—and I say this as one with experience—is wholly inaccessible. That can only happen at the quantum level, and as of yet, quantum cryptography is only a theory, one that lies just inside the mystery of quantum computing." Mole beamed like he knew something I didn't. "Whoever reaches computing at a quantum level first rules life as we know it. Scientists right now are mining mathematics for hard problems from which to concoct new algorithms. They're searching for the key to breaking the code of encryption at a quantum level." He stopped pacing and turned to Quinn and me. "Is any of this making sense?"

I shook my head at the same time as Quinn nodded.

"So back to my aforementioned dabbling friend, Paul Turing. This was his great-great-uncle's notebook. Authentic. He overnighted it to me from London, heavily insured—a tab I picked up and you're totally paying me back for. What's in here"—he carefully fingered the leather binding in my lap—"is the real deal. This is as close to real intel as we get, Sammy. It'll work."

That was all well and good, but there was still a caveat hanging in the air. "I have to give this book to Bauer."

Mole nodded. "That's why I scanned the contents onto a thumb drive. Of course, I've taken the liberty of excluding important bits of some calculations, rendering them completely inactive, but that won't be discovered until someone attempts to put them into practical use, which won't be while you're standing there." He pressed the small drive into my palm then closed my finger around it. "Put that in your pocket," he instructed, hands on my shoulders. "Don't take it out until you make the exchange.

And don't leave it laying anywhere." His hands gave my shoulders a final squeeze that felt awkwardly intimate.

"Okay," I said, standing up from his grip.

"Leave the book here as insurance. Tell Bauer that every bit of that intelligence goes on the market to his competitors should anything happen to you."

"Competitors?"

"If the Fraternity wants this stuff, any number of foreign governments or terrorist groups are going to be interested in it as well."

I took a deep breath and let it out slowly through my nose. "I guess it's now or never," I said with as much levity as I could muster, though the moment warranted none. "Time to reach out to Bauer and get this over with. Get Wickowski home."

And put a bullet in the middle of Bauer's face.

CHAPTER TWENTY-TWO

I'd insisted on making the exchange with Bauer in a public place and suggested a restaurant in the city. Bauer countered my proposal with one of his own: the downtown Park Blocks. The blocks were a popular gathering place on a warm spring evening. It would be populated by a multitude of people: Decompressing students feeling the crunch of looming finals from nearby Portland State University. Couples on benches with after-dinner espressos from the coffee cart parked in front of the art museum. Casual people watchers. Buskers. Homeless people. The blocks were open and public, but they also offered potential civilian casualties should shit go sideways. Quinn, with Portland PB support, would already be in place by the time I arrived. They'd be scattered around, plain-clothed and incognito. The mayor was prepared to lock down the entire park if things came to that. I was confident in everyone's ability to watch my back. This scene seemed oddly familiar.

Mole had been adamant in his instructions that I keep the thumb drive in my pocket and not remove it until the handoff. He didn't say as much, but I suspected he was afraid I'd lose or misplace his hard work. Or maybe he was concerned about what kind of hell would rain down on the city if anything happened to Wickowski. But who knew with Mole? I patted the tiny drive in the chest pocket of my denim jacket to assure it was still there. *Dammit, Mole.*

Midtown traffic was normal for that time of day. The work-force commuters had made the mass exodus from the confines of their nine-to-five hours prior. The plan was simple: park near the blocks, get a coffee, find a bench. Bauer or someone from his camp would find me. I'd also insisted on proof of life in person, meaning Wickowski needed to be within eyesight of my position before the exchange. Once everyone was in sight, SWAT would take it from there. I'd give Bauer the drive, Wickowski would at that point be set free, and the two of us would walk out. Meanwhile, Quinn and his men would descend. Wickowski and I would go home.

The last thing I remembered was driving into the intersection on the green light at SW Morrison. Headlights that hadn't been there a breath before came from out of nowhere on my left. The collision slammed my head into the side window, spiderwebbing the glass at the point of impact. The force of the crash sent the Geländewagen sideways. Lights whizzed past my vision as the world spun out of control. My rig came to an abrupt stop when the front end struck a parked car. Inertia bounced my face off the steering wheel and whiplashed my head against the headrest. Stars swam against the black backdrop of my wavering consciousness. Blood flowed down my face and filled my mouth.

Move, I instructed my limbs. Nothing responded. Even before I heard booted feet scuffling to get my door open, I knew I wanted to get out. Get away from what was coming. Arms, legs, both—I didn't care which or in what combination it happened, I just needed them to *move!*

I became faintly aware of voices, deep and male, shouting instructions. Then the protest of twisting metal as my door was pried open. I knew I wasn't being rescued. Rough hands with no bedside manner dragged me from behind the wheel. I fell to the ground with a heavy thud. Hands unceremoniously rummaged through my clothes until they found the thumb drive. "Got it," I heard someone announce, followed by a genteel voice instructing, "Get her up. We're taking her with us."

I felt my body being dumped into the back of a vehicle. My nose and eyes were becoming one swollen mass. Air could no longer flow through its usual sinus routes. I swallowed copious amounts of blood as it flowed freely down the back of my throat. I wasn't yet aware of my dislocated shoulder. That painful realization would hit when the adrenaline pumping through my system subsided. Yay, me.

I rode in the back of the vehicle for what seemed like hours but was likely only several blocks. I tried to track each turn and red light on the map of my mind, but the throbbing crescendo of what was becoming a substantial migraine was a formidable barrier. Somewhere in that, I blessedly lost consciousness and escaped into the velvety darkness.

Consciousness was slow to return. The first thing I became aware of when I came to was the searing pain in my upper body. It all seemed to radiate from my shoulder. I tried to adjust my position, but something rough and fibrous was wound around my wrists, keeping my hands bound behind by back. I could tell by the hard, conformed surface beneath my butt that I was on a folding metal chair, the sort my father used to pull from the garage at Thanksgiving when relatives visited for dinner. An odd memory for my situation.

Blood, cold and coagulated, sat in an unrealized drip off the end of my nose, which was a swollen ruin. My breath stuttered ragged and shallow through my mouth. I could make out the hum of traffic punctuated by the occasional diesel rumble of a passing big rig. The air felt cool and humid, like I was surrounded by concrete. Concrete held a certain unsympathetic dampness to it. Cold and unforgiving. They were holding me in either an abandoned building, of which there are very few in the city, or one that was under construction. Or they'd taken me out of the city completely. I had no way of knowing. For some reason not knowing where I was set my pulse to spin into double time.

I had to keep it together. It would do my survival no good to panic. I imagined a single point of light, a candle flame, and focused my mind's eye on it. As long as I stayed focused on that solitary illuminated point, I knew I could control my mind. Panic wanted me to believe I was going to die, and if I spent too much time with that thought, I could see how it might be a foregone conclusion. And how much pain would be involved.

I did my best to slow my pulse by breathing as deeply as I could through my mouth. The beatboxing in my chest slowed in tempo, but that proved to be short-lived when the telltale ding of an elevator's arrival echoed in the empty space. Unable to crack my puffy eyelids even a fraction caused a rush of panic.

The elevator door slid open, and I detected feet—one pair light-soled, like loafers, the other heavily booted—accompanied by an odd squeaking and metal-on-metal bumping as it came closer. My panicky mind wanted to envision Bauer and one of his goons with something being rolled in on a handcart. I'd seen plenty of espionage films where the protagonist is tortured by the bad guys. I fought against imagining what that something on a cart might be.

There was the rustle of fabric. Bauer removing his suit jacket. Rolling up the sleeves of his shirt like he was preparing to exert himself. The directional wave of a hand. The squeak and bump of compliance accompanied by a new sound—or had that been there the whole time? My blood ran instantly cold, and for the first time in my life, I wished I had the ability to stop my heart at will, to take myself out of the experience. To quit.

I heard the cart come to a heavy stop in front of me, followed by the same sound, the heavy slosh of a quantity of water as it waved back and forth to a stop. My heart stuttered when comprehension soaked in. I heard a whimpering, frantic and terrified, and realized it was coming from me.

"I'm glad to see you're with us again," said Bauer in his damned genteel voice. "That was a nasty collision. You would benefit from some medical attention. I can assure you, you and the detective will both be tended to when we're done here."

I struggled to lift my head and let it loll unevenly atop my shoulders for a moment while I fought against the sick rising in the back of my throat. Once I swallowed it down, I mumbled, "Remember the promise I made you." Bauer's only reply was a condescending chuckle.

I fought against the swollen tissue and crusted blood impeding my vision until I could peel my right lid open, just barely, and peer through crusted lashes. It took several seconds for my eye to adjust to the lighting and to running solo. I ping-ponged my limited vision around the space. Wickowski was nowhere in sight.

Bauer shook out a square of handkerchief from the pocket of his slacks and began to dab at the crusted blood that clogged my eyes as he softly spoke. "We have a few things we need to discuss, you and I." My right lashes free, he began on my left, wiping gently at the delicate skin around my eyes. It was almost nurturing. "Here we go," he cooed as he gingerly helped pry my lids apart. "How's that?"

I gave a slight nod of appreciation. Images were blurred. Through the swollen pressure on my eyeballs, I was unable to make out fine detail, only faint shape and color, shadow and light. I still didn't see Wickowski.

Bauer's gentle tone altered, becoming threateningly serious. "I'm going to ask you a question, and I'm going to need you to be completely transparent with your answer." He crouched beside my chair, a hand on my knee. "I appreciate the effort you've put into getting your friend back, but what you've delivered me is only a mere copy. Where is the original journal, Ms. Harris?"

"Where's Wickowski?" I managed to mumble, though even to my ears it was barely audible.

"He's waiting for you to save him. Now, where is the original?"

Tell him it's stashed for your insurance should anything become of you! reminded my inner voice. *Tell him!* I mumbled a reply and couldn't help the painful guffaw that followed.

Unable to hear or understand me, or perhaps incredulous at my answer, Bauer leaned closer. "Come again?"

I lifted my head to capture Bauer's gaze and held it unsteadily, my words hardly perceptible. "I said, if it was up your ass, you'd know." With a calculated effort and precise aim, I lurched forward with a headbutt.

My action was quicker than Bauer's reaction, and I caught him in the bridge of the nose with the arch of my forehead. My skull bones were anatomically stronger than his nose, which made a sickening sound when it mashed. Crimson erupted down his chin, staining his shirt. The force of the blow reverberated down my neck to jar my fractured collarbone. Raw, jagged edges of bone slid back and forth against each other. The wave of agony that shot through me nearly rendered me unconscious. I squeezed my eyes together and willed myself to breathe through the nauseating pain, focusing on the air as it flowed in and out against my teeth.

Holding his anger in check, Bauer straightened and stoically dabbed at his ruined nose with a knuckle. I expected him to lash out at me in retaliation. Instead, "I was giving you an opportunity, Ms. Harris," he said, eerily calm. "I have an obligation to the continued safety and superiority of this country. To do so requires I make several...unsavory choices. Look at the world around you." Bauer spread his arms and turned in a slow circle. "Civilization is crumbling. Civil war is brewing." He stopped and dropped his arms, his features darkening. "The future isn't being threatened by novel viruses or dictator regimes. Climate change isn't our enemy." Bauer nodded to someone outside of my peripherals. "The greatest threat to our continued freedom and way of life is the internet." Somewhere behind me, an elevator door slid open and shut, then began moving.

Bauer pinched the bridge of his nose and slightly tilted his head as he began to pace. He cleared his throat and spat the bloody glob onto the floor. "Extremism flourishes around the globe, Ms. Harris," he said, pulling my focus back to him. "Cyberterrorists and our foreign adversaries are becoming more sophisticated, bolder, and more nefarious by the day." He paused when the elevator began to move again. "The United States faces a danger bigger than any bomb, a threat that could change our freedom and way of life." He paused yet again when something happening behind me captured his attention. "Ahh, now we're all here," he exclaimed with a jovial clap of his hands.

There was a scuffle and some grunting, and Wickowski appeared—half dragged, half on his own volition. He'd been roughed up. Taken a serious beating since our last visual. One eye, red and purple, was swollen shut like a prizefighter's. His other eye darted around, unfocused. Blood crusted his face and was dried down the front of his suit jacket, which was ruined. One shoe was missing from a socked foot. I wasn't sure how aware he was.

Hands suddenly grabbed my shoulders from behind and lifted me from the chair. I was deposited unceremoniously onto the concrete floor, my hands still painfully bound behind me, and secured around a concrete post. The metal folding chair was dragged across the floor to where Wickowski stood, wavering in place with the help of the two tactical-clad brutes who flanked him. They dropped him into the seat and bound his hands behind his back and his ankles to the chair legs.

Wick! I sent my thought out to him, wanting to get his attention. My psychic effort was interrupted by the squeak, bump, and slosh of the cart being wheeled beside Wickowski's chair. An inverted five-gallon carboy filled with water was fastened to the makeshift device so that the neck extended through a hole cut in the bottom of the cart. A hose gravity-feeding from the mouth of the carboy was affixed with a valve to adjust the flow of water. At the other end of the hose was a full-faced scuba mask.

My heart skipped a beat when I realized Bauer's intention. "No!" I muttered. "No!" My voice grew stronger. "Wick, no!"

Bauer seemed amused by my sudden alertness and picked up where he'd left off. "Thus far, our current cryptography has kept our nation and its secrets secure from our enemies, both foreign and domestic. The internet is secure. For now." Bauer began pacing. "Technology is growing exponentially, so rapidly in fact that our adversaries are creating new ways and avenues to infiltrate, to destroy us." Bauer's tone ramped up and, with it, his body language. His hands were balled into tight fists. Points of perspiration had begun to prickle his upper lip.

"You're power drunk," I slurred my accusation. "Fucking insane."

Bauer snapped around, his movement a blur when he squatted on the balls of his feet in front of me. "Never call me insane," he said in a voice somewhere between a hiss and a growl. Someone had a sore spot. "I'm going to be gracious here." Bauer softened, but his eyes remained serpentine cold. He placed a warm arm around my good shoulder and gave a gentle squeeze. My skin crawled. "Where is the original?"

I cleared my throat and improvised the truth. "It's somewhere safe. Insurance, should something happen to me. To us. If I don't return with Wickowski." I nodded toward my friend. "Within the hour, the contents of the journal go live and for sale. You want to protect this nation, set us free."

That got Bauer's attention. His countenance flashed a micro expression of fear—brows raised and lips flattened. It was there then gone just as quickly when his brows furrowed in anger. He stood and looked down at me, his hands planted on his hips. He dismissed me with a shrug, then turned toward Wickowski. "Let's see how tight-lipped you remain on the detective's behalf."

Bauer nodded to the two flanking Wickowski. One of them roughly lifted Wickowski's head by his short hair while the other, the one nearest the cart, lifted the scuba mask and straightened the hose before struggling it over Wickowski's head. Wickowski, suddenly aware of the mortal danger he was in, began to writhe and buck against his restraints. It took one thug to hold him down while the other adjusted the valve. Water began to flow. I watched helplessly as water filled the mask. Wickowski's eyes were wide and terrified.

Someone screamed, begging them to stop, and I realized the wails were coming from my own mouth. Wickowski's single-eyed, panicked stare latched on to my own. I struggled against my own restraints to no avail, but in doing so I created some play, a little bit of wiggle room. I worked my wrists back and forth. The coarse fibers of the rope rubbed my skin raw, lubricating the friction with blood. My flesh was wearing away under the abrasion of the bindings; my hands were sticky with coppery blood. I was able to work the bindings down enough so that only the knuckle of my thumb hung up escape. With force and a scream, I dislocated my opposable appendage and slid my wrists free.

My escape was interrupted when the stairwell door burst open and a sudden eruption of chaos ensued. It took a split second for my mind to register what was happening. Quinn came through the door, gun first. SWAT flowed in behind him, taking up their positions in formation.

I crawled my way to Wickowski, ignoring my shoulder, disregarding the jagged edges of my collarbone. The only thing I saw was Wickowski's face swimming behind that mask. A SWAT team member had already ripped the tube from the base of the mask, starting the water to drain as they worked at removing it. Quinn bent over Wickowski, who coughed and sputtered his first free breaths.

Wickowski safe, Quinn holstered his firearm and turned to address his team. I was operating on the heavy dose of adrenaline that had dumped into my system the moment Wickowski went under water. I didn't think what to do next. I just acted. Quinn's gun sat unclipped in its holster. Then it was suddenly in my hand. My arm swung around, the gun extended. I had a clear shot and I took it before Quinn or anyone else could react.

The shot was deafening. Time slowed. A crimson third eye exploded in the center of Bauer's forehead above the bridge of his nose. The force of the bullet knocked him back off his feet.

He was dead before his body hit the concrete floor.

I put a bullet in the center of Bauer's face.

As fantasized.

As promised.

A flurry of commotion followed. Benelli M1s swung around, trained on me. Quinn had his hands up, urging SWAT to stand down, lower their weapons. He was shouting. I recognized his words were aimed at me. Pleading with me to drop the gun. I was fixated on Bauer's body. Mesmerized by the way blood was flowing in a river down the side of his face to pool beneath his head. My arms dropped to my sides. Gravity slid Quinn's gun from my hand.

Quinn kicked the gun away like I was a criminal. I suppose in that moment I was. The captain of the SWAT team approached, nylon zip cuffs in his hand. Quinn stepped between us. Then he turned toward me, his back to SWAT. His expression softened as he held out his hand. I didn't understand the gesture. That's when he took mine in his and pulled me into an embrace. I was stiff at first, then melted into his chest.

EMTs appeared as if summoned by magic, and Wickowski was whisked away in a flurry of sirens. I was escorted by two uniforms outside to an awaiting ambulance. Bauer had been holding Wickowski in a vacant warehouse on the river that had recently become entangled in a legal dispute with the city half-way through construction. Ironically, he'd only been a handful of blocks away the whole time.

I stepped up inside and sat on the edge of the gurney. The two uniforms stayed outside on the asphalt, one on either side of the ambulance doors. Guarding. One kept his hand on his sidearm. Not resting it there, but poised. A middle-aged EMT, her hair swept back into a severe bun at the nape of her neck, took my vitals and pronounced me none the worse for wear, though she wanted to transport me to the hospital to have my collarbone set. When I reported cold and numbness in my fingertips, she wanted to keep me for observation lest the nerves and vessels had suffered damage from the jagged bone. With a kind smile, she offered me a towel wetted from the onboard sink. I looked down at myself for the first time since I'd sat on the gurney. Bits of matter and blood splatter that weren't mine marred the front of my shirt.

I heard a deep murmur, and the uniforms stepped away from the ambulance completely. The nurse followed suit. Quinn filled the doorway. He didn't look impressed but rather upset. Or was that disappointment I saw in the firm set of his mouth? It was only then that I noticed the zip cuffs in his hand.

"Is this the part where you cuff and stuff me and say, 'I warned you'?" If he was going to arrest me, I wanted him to get it over with.

Quinn climbed up and took a seat beside me on the gurney. He leaned forward with a sigh, forearms on knees and hands clasped wearily together. He didn't say anything for several moments. Then he cleared his throat, sat up, and began, "You know

I have to take you in. The whole squad was witness to you pulling my gun on Bauer. I'm gonna catch hell for letting it happen."

"I did what I had to do, Quinn. You of all people should understand that."

Quinn made an exasperated sound in his throat and stepped down from the ambulance. He motioned to one of the uniforms who'd stepped away. "Then I'm going to need you to step down and put your hands together in front of you."

I thought Quinn was joking. The grim look on his face said otherwise. He was serious. "Come on, Harris, just make this easy." He passed the zip cuffs to the uniform.

I dropped down from the ambulance. "Cuffs, Quinn? Are you for real right now?"

"Look, Harris, I don't like having to do this anymore than you do. But you shot a man in police custody in front of me and the entire SWAT team. With my gun. I have to play this by the book. Now please—" He gestured for the uniform to do his dirty work and slip the zip cuffs on. I held both hands together in front of me. The uniformed officer was gentle when he tightened the cuffs around my wrists.

"Samantha Harris," the uniformed officer began, "you have the right to remain silent—"

"How's Wickowski's condition?" I interrupted by directing my question at Quinn.

Quinn closed his eyes, as if he could find the right words on the other side of his lids. "I warned you, Harris." He raised his open eyes to mine. I was thrown by the emotion I saw in them. "Anything you say can and will be used against you in a court of law. You have the right to an attorney—" He picked up where the uniform had left off.

"You haven't answered me. About Wick's condition. Is he okay?"

Quinn took a long time to answer. So long, in fact, I feared he was working out how to tell me the worst. Wickowski didn't make it. Or wasn't expected to. "He's fine. EMTs expect him to make a full recovery."

I let out a deep breath of relief.

Quinn walked me to his own car, not a squad car, and let me into the back seat, guiding my head as I ducked inside. It was an odd thought: I'd ridden in a cop's car plenty of times, but always up front. Shotgun. Now I sat in back like a common perp, like the goon being loaded into a patrol car at the curb.

He led me into the sheriff's office through the deputies-only door off the parking lot. We didn't go to booking. He took the cuffs off in the elevator. We rode to the third floor where I followed him into an interview room. I was informed once more of my rights and that we were being recorded. A man I didn't recognize, in a pressed suit and way too sensible shoes to be anything other than federal, took over questioning me. We went over what had happened from the time the Lannisters were fished out of the Columbia River to the point I shot Bauer. There were details about what happened while I was in Bauer's custody that I either couldn't recall or chose not to share. By the end, Quinn was on the phone with the district attorney, pleading my case of self-defense, on Wickowski's behalf, after the fact. It was a muddled mess. I hired a top-notch attorney and let him deal with it. That didn't mean I didn't spend the next ninety-six hours in a federal holding cell.

CHAPTER TWENTY-THREE

I WAS EVENTUALLY RELEASED ON MY OWN RECOGNIZANCE. WHEN I got home, Mole gave me a long hug and Doof was full of leap/spin/happy barks. Mole couldn't wait for me to ask him how Quinn and SWAT had found Wickowski and me to rescue us. He went into a long dissertation that I admittedly zoned out of, but I did catch something about long-distance RFID tags and how he'd coated the thumb drive with them. His instructions to handle the drive then put it in my pocket until the exchange were strategic planning to expose myself to the tags for easier tracking. When I asked why he'd not informed me of his strategy, he only answered that he wasn't sure it would work, and he didn't want me expecting a rescue if one wasn't coming. That's Mole. Always keeping it real.

It took me several weeks to reclaim my equilibrium in the world. Distance had grown between Quinn and me. I'd meant to reach out to him when I was released from detention, after the Feds' storm of questions and threats, but I didn't. I hadn't planned on spending four days in their custody while I rehashed everything that had happened, shared everything I'd known in regard to Bauer and the Fraternity, sans everything quantum cryptography related. Mole was kept out of the conversation altogether. It had been an arduous debriefing. They eventually came to realize I wasn't a real threat to national security. Testimonies and reports digitally disappeared. I was eventually cut loose with the promise to appear if summoned. Whatever—at least I wasn't in anybody's cage.

As for the Lannisters' murderers, they were still in the wind. I had to trust karma would find its mark and see them punished. Maybe the dead had some control over that from their side. I wasn't sure I believed that, but I liked to hope. I told myself that putting Bauer into the ground was justice enough, for now, even if he wasn't guilty personally. He was culpable nonetheless. Some justice *had* been served.

Mole had forgiven me for all my trampling on our friendship. I was well aware his freedom was being held solely at Deputy Paul Quinn's discretion, but I trusted him to keep Mole a secret. If you asked me, point-blank, on what precisely did I base that perspective? I wasn't sure, exactly. I just knew Quinn wouldn't throw Mole—or me, for that matter—under the bus. He may not like me (he hadn't called me either), but I knew he respected me. For now.

Like I said, I'd planned on calling Quinn, but something stayed my hand in those first few days. Then two or three days became a week. Then two. Then…what was the point? It was for the best anyway—a clean break, no awkward final farewells. Portland was a big city. We didn't have to run into each other if I didn't want to. I didn't think I'd want to. At least, not any time soon.

So I was surprised when my downstairs bell rang weeks after my release. I hadn't been expecting anybody. Okay, maybe a part of me hoped it was Quinn. I peeked out my window at the street below. Double-parked with its flashers on was a dark sedan. Official looking. Not Quinn, but my curiosity was triggered.

I'd been lazing around my place in a pair of boy shorts and a t-shirt. I decided it best to throw on a pair of jeans, then added a hoodie to cover the HK stuffed in the front of my pants.

Mole must have heard my door open. I'd been incommunicado for a while, and he poked his head out into the hall. I thought he wanted to say hi, but he only issued a warning. "Don't go downstairs, Sammy," he said solemnly, slightly shaking his head.

He stepped out of his door and leaned his shoulder against the wall, his hands jammed deep into the front pockets of his chinos. "Due to recent events, I've rewritten the facial recognition program in the ringer." He pointed to the ground. "That's Agent James Dixon of the Central Intelligence Agency. A spook, Sammy. Down there at our door."

"No way," I mocked. "What would they want with me?" Okay, in hindsight that was an ignorant question. I did just sort of remove one of their players (by association or not) and absconded with the goods. From their viewpoint I was probably a little loose end that should be tidied. I turned on my heel for the elevator.

"Seriously, Sammy!" Mole started after me. "Did you not just hear me?"

I turned at the elevator as I awaited its arrival. "Calm down. I'm just going to see what he wants." The door slid shut on Mole's opinionated rebuttal.

I met Agent Dixon at the gate. The first thing I recognized when I glanced down was the validation of practical footwear, the kind stereotypically synonymous with alphabet agencies.

I looked at the wallet lanyard that flashed in my face: *Agent J. Dixon of the Central Intelligence Agency*. My not-too-friendly eyes slid up to meet his. I let my glare, rather than my words, speak for me.

Dixon cleared his throat. "Ms. Harris, my bosses would like to have a word with you."

"Why." I made the word a statement.

Dixon took a moment to put his answer together. "I am unauthorized to disclose."

"Then you better find authorization real quick." I knew I was antagonizing the situation with my attitude, but if Dixon wanted to play, he'd best know what he was getting himself into.

Apparently Agent Dixon wasn't familiar with opposition when addressing someone, specifically a civilian. Or maybe it was just me he had a hard time with. A shade of anger colored his features, and his mouth became a hard line. His eyes narrowed into fuming slits. "You've made...an impression. My bosses wish an audience with you."

"Yeah, that's not going to happen."

Still, he continued, "A car will arrive to pick you up. You will be taken to PDX, where you will be accompanied by myself or another agent. From there you will be flown to Washington. Make arrangements for your absence." Agent Dixon never let his expression falter. It didn't have to. The air between us crackled with tension. His stance was wide, and he clasped one wrist with the other hand down in front of him

"I get it, Dixon. You're just the messenger." I shrugged. "No harm, no foul." I stepped up and toed the gate. "But you can tell your bosses my answer is no. If they have a problem with that, you can also tell them to go fuck themselves."

Dixon seemed unaffected by my perspective on the subject. "Ms. Harris," he said with a lift of his chin, "they weren't asking."

ALSO BY DANI CLIFTON

DEATH BY ASSOCIATION

ISBN: 978-1-7343796-0-0
eISBN: 978-1-7343796-1-7

DEATH BY ASSOCIATION

Totally enjoyed it!

"I truthfully only got this because it is set in my neck of the woods. Then I ended up really liking it! She has a great way with words. The story was fast paced and believable. I will definitely read her again."—Kindle customer

Soo good, just WOW!

"I am beyond lucky to have gotten a signed copy of this book by the author herself! I have ADHD and have a hard time actually finishing a book, but I could not put this one down! Her attention to detail and description had this book playing like a movie in my head. Every time I put it down the story would stick in my mind urging me to pick it back up again. I cannot wait to read more Samantha Harris adventures!!—Ashley Hansen

Great Read

"I'm a die hard Michael Connelly and John Sandford fan particularly the Prey series. This book did not disappoint. I look forward to more of Samantha Harris. Author did a good job of developing her character making me want to read more of her adventures. Looking forward to the next in what I hope is a long series!—Amazon customer

A non-stop read!

"I couldn't set this book down! Samantha was relatable and focused. Each paragraph, each chapter kept me begging for more! Highly recommend for a edge of your seat read!"—A. Maldonado

Highly recommended!

"Loved all the characters, from the leading lady, to all her sidekicks. Kept me wanting to read more but all with some great humor as well!! Very enjoyable and entertaining!!!"—Teresa Caldwell

Five stars.

"Loved it!"—Kristin E. Parker

Thrilling page turner!

"Based on my affinity for true crime and thriller novels, Death by Association was recommended to me by a friend and it did not disappoint. Once I opened the book, I could not put it down! The book is written so that I felt like I was right there in Samantha's head, seeing what she was seeing and feeling what she was feeling. The story kept me on my toes until the very end when everything falls into place. Can't wait for the next installment to see where she goes next."—Kaitlyn R.

This novel has everything I love in a good read.

"Samantha Harris, a gritty but likable PI, pulls you into her seemingly normal life. Once there, you find things aren't so normal, and she is more than most people bargain for. Filled with distinctive characters and vibrant settings, "Death by Association" is witty, fun and a must read!"—Fire_and_Iron74

A new favorite!

"This book has everything I love in a good read. Distinct characters, vibrant settings, and a unique writing style that pulls you in and gives just enough to let you sink into the story. Witty and fun. I can't wait for the next Samantha Harris novel!"—Mama Bear

Feminist Noir

"Fun romp—I look for more adventures with Feminist Noir PI Samantha Harris!"—stan wisniewski

Made in the USA
Coppell, TX
11 April 2022

76351788R00177